CORPORATE LEASE ANALYSIS

CORPORATE LEASE ANALYSIS

A Guide to Concepts and Evaluation

Bennie H. Nunnally, Jr.
D. Anthony Plath
Helene W. Johns

Q

Quorum Books
New York • Westport, Connecticut • London

Library of Congress Cataloging-in-Publication Data

Nunnally, Bennie H.
    Corporate lease analysis : a guide to concepts and evaluation /
Bennie H. Nunnally, Jr., D. Anthony Plath, and Helene W. Johns.
        p. cm.
    Includes bibliographical references and index.
    ISBN 0-89930-513-X (alk. paper)
    1. Industrial equipment leases.   2. Industrial equipment leases –
Finance.   3. Industrial equipment leases – United States.
I. Plath, D. Anthony.   II. Johns, Helene W.   III. Title.
HD39.4.N86   1991
658.15′242 – dc20   90-45147

British Library Cataloguing in Publication Data is available.

Library of Congress Catalog Card Number: 90-45147
ISBN: 0-89930-513-X

First published in 1991

Quorum Books, 88 Post Road West, Westport, CT 06881
An imprint of Greenwood Publishing Group, Inc.

Printed in the United States of America

∞

The paper used in this book complies with the
Permanent Paper Standard issued by the National
Information Standards Organization (Z39.48-1984).

10 9 8 7 6 5 4 3 2 1

Exhibits 6-5 and 6-7 are copyright by Financial Accounting Standards Board,
401 Merritt 7, P.O. Box 5116, Norwalk, Connecticut, 06856-5116, U.S.A.
Reprinted with permission. Copies of the complete document are available
from the FASB.

Contents

V. The Role of Leasing in Modern Financial Management

Exhibits

I

Leasing Concepts

1

Introduction to Lease Financing

The practice of finance in the modern economy demands an alertness to improved decision-making techniques. Tools that assist the manager are not fad items that emerge and disappear on a seasonal basis, but the efficient use of those tools often requires new information. Academic research and innovation by practitioners are the two primary ways in which finance decision-making ideas and tools are made more useful.

This book is written for the purpose of presenting the latest developments in lease financing by businesses. In addition, the text discusses the leasing of automobiles by individuals for personal use. The book goes beyond an exposition of leasing theory and practice. The presentation emphasizes decision-making. To make leasing viable for the financial manager it must be presented with clarity. In addition, a particular method of assessing and then solving a problem using lease financing must be identified. That is especially important given the varied expositions of lease analysis seen in textbooks and other relevant literature.

As a result, the book's objectives are

1. a clear delineation of the various types of leases and their advantages, disadvantages, and appropriate usage
2. a thorough assessment of leasing decisions in view of the new tax laws
3. an expositional style useful to the practitioner

Those objectives are helped greatly by our willingness to take a position on a particular form of lease analysis and application from among the many combinations offered in the literature.

The book should be read by the practicing financial manager who is regularly involved in the financing decisions of the firm. Leasing, as the next chapter indicates, is well established as a financing alternative

for the acquisition of nearly all types of business assets. While leasing
was once a financial alternative for a specific type of asset, it now fills a
financing need across company classifications and sizes, and across
asset sizes and categories. It is for those reasons that the practitioner
needs a useful and general guide to leasing. If such a guide is to provide
a general approach to leasing in the myriad financial settings of the
modern firm, it must be comprehensive.

A BRIEF DEFINITION AND HISTORY OF LEASING

A lease is a contract that gives the right of use of an item to the lessee.
The right is given by the item's owner, the lessor. Before the time of
Christ, the governments of Greece and Rome used the lease arrangement. Generally, the government owned land, mines, and other valuable property, and leased such property to select members of the community. Such leases were often transferred from lessee to lessee and in
some cases were used as collateral by the lessee.

As the internationalization of trade and culture deepened, along with
the passage of time, the practice of leasing spread to England and to
America. A major consideration in early America concerning leasing
was with lease duration. There was a belief that monopolies and even-
tually, perhaps, monarchies would develop if valuable government-
controlled property was let for too long a period. The practice was to
try to limit the lease term in each instance.

The development of leasing activity in the United States spread from
the leasing of land to the leasing of housing, industrial equipment, and
railroad equipment. The leasing of railroad equipment, especially roll-
ing stock, became a major industry during the period between the end
of the Civil War and the beginning of World War I. That period of
extreme economic growth and territorial expansion gave rise to a constant demand for goods to which the lease contract was amenable.

In the period that followed World War II to the present, finance and
industrial output have become highly sophisticated. Leasing has found
its place as a flexible and widely used financing tool. It appears to be a
permanent part of the financing endeavors of businesses, municipalities and countries. A clear understanding of its characteristics and
uses is a necessity for the modern financial manager.

THE WIDESPREAD USE OF LEASING BY BUSINESSES

The macroeconomic reasons for concern about financial flexibility cannot be overstated. The ability to lease productive assets instead of
purchasing those assets allows firms to buttress themselves against

the shocks that may be created by the business cycle. The ability to transfer economic risk to someone else, the lessor in the case of leasing, was largely responsible for the leasing of over $100 billion of equipment in 1988 by U.S. firms. All types of firms participate in the leasing of assets, which include stock exchanges, airlines, and such municipal authorities as hospitals.

The American Association of Equipment Lessors (AAEL), in a September 1987 report entitled *Equipment Leasing Activity in the United States*, grouped equipment leasing activity into three sectors: transportation; computer/office and communication equipment; and residual activity including agriculture, industrial, and machinery and medical equipment.[1] Concerning the transportation sector (aircraft, autos, rail, trucks, and trailers), the AAEL reports $32 billion of equipment was added by that sector in 1986. Those assets were added via leasing. The growth of leasing in the transportation sector was forecast in the AAEL study as moderate, in the computer/office equipment sector as high, and in the residual categories, growth was forecast as higher than the growth for most of the industries included in that sector. These growth projections also illustrate the need for management familiarity with leasing as a financing alternative, especially important in the area of operating lease analysis wherein the academic literature has been sparse.

WHY FINANCIAL MANAGERS OF U.S. FIRMS NEED THIS BOOK

The competitive position of U.S. firms in the years ahead depends upon many factors. A partial list of those factors demonstrates why financial flexibility is important for U.S. firms, and leasing is a way in which financial flexibility may be increased.

1. In a recent *Business Week* cover story doubt was expressed as to whether the trade gap will ever be closed. Some of the reasons cited for the pessimistic outlook include a decrease in exports and an increase in imports. How does a discussion of international trade hold implications for the leasing of assets? The following quotation may shed some light on the connection between the two ideas: "The big, double-digit gains in U.S. exports are behind us, since the larger, more price-sensitive orders have already been placed."[2]

2. The price sensitivity of some goods made for export bears directly upon the demand for those goods. The financing of the assets that are used to make the products bears directly upon the production costs and hence the selling price of those goods. Admittedly, the cost-price-demand relationship is not perfectly coordinated in terms of timing but

its existence is undeniable. It is very important, therefore, for U.S. financial managers to have a thorough understanding of all relevant financing options.

The present move toward automation in the U.S. manufacturing sector will undoubtedly increase leasing volume. Factories will, from all accounts, move toward manufacturing that is integrated with the computer. As a result, only state-of-the-art equipment will be useful. The changes in technology of those assets will make rapid obsolescence much more of a factor than it is now. The importance of leasing's flexibility will be even more meaningful to the financial manager.

The implications for the financial manager of such a goal are enormous. In an environment where technology is constantly being advanced, one aspect of such advancement is obsolescence. In terms of leasing, obsolescence is one of the primary reasons to use that form of financing. In addition, the demand upon the financial manager to be creative in financing such turnover in equipment is quite strong. Knowledge of leasing and how and when it can be used is an essential part of the future competitive stance of U.S. firms.

LEASING INFORMATION SOURCES

The most convenient manner in which to gain insight into leasing analysis is to consult a business finance textbook. The lease analysis offerings in several recent texts are easy to follow and these are collected at the end of this book. Such textbooks, however, by their nature and purpose present only an overview of the topic. The practicing financial manager is in need of a comprehensive guide that is current. It is precisely these important needs that this book meets.

LEASING AND CORPORATE STRATEGY

As the sophistication of leasing continues to develop, firms will blend that specific financing tool into their strategic planning. The precedent has been set, as there is a body of literature, teaching materials (such as cases), and other research dealing with the relationship between financing and overall firm strategy. This text explores the likely relationship between leasing and corporate strategy in Chapter 3.

The way in which leasing and corporate strategy are linked is due, in one instance, to the type of assets necessary to maintain an operating unit. In its simplest terms an operating unit with leased assets will permit differing strategic considerations from a unit with assets not easily leased. From this situation comes the possible difference in funds allocation, which bears directly upon the unit's return on investment, which influences strategy. *Strategy* is defined as product and market considerations of a five-year duration or longer; that is, the competitive and survival aspects of the firm rely upon the corporate strategy for definition and implementation.

In terms of a strategic planning implication for leasing, there are other areas of the firm's long-term financing and functional activities to which leasing is applicable. These include the use of leasing in leveraged buyouts (LBOs), leasing swaps (analogous to interest rate swaps, or debt–equity swaps), and risk-sharing between lessor and lessee. The purpose of such a chapter is to demonstrate the flexibility and usefulness of leasing in all areas of financing for the firm. In addition, the preceding topics allow a fuller understanding of the relationship between strategic considerations and financing. It is necessary that a comprehensive guide to leasing by business include not only those aspects that are now in use or soon to be in use as dictated by the tax laws, but those relevant implications of leasing that hold importance for the future.

CONTENT

This book answers practical questions. It is a guide for the practicing manager. Its purpose is not to take a position, or to answer questions just for the sake of doing so. There is a very wide and well-developed body of literature on leasing by firms. That literature forms the basis for every illustration, example, and position taken in the book. Therefore, all questions answered are done so with a recognition of existing theory. Where practical use of leasing has moved analytical techniques forward, such efforts are considered equal to theoretical contributions and are recognized as such. What follows is a list of questions that form the basis for our task in this book.

1. What is a lease?
2. What are the various types of leases?
3. Do lease transactions represent an investment decision, a financing decision, or both?
4. How should lease transactions be evaluated?
5. What is the appropriate discount rate with which to evaluate lease transactions?
6. How should the net cash flows associated with the lease transaction be estimated?
7. How should different lease transactions be compared?
8. How should lease transactions be compared to borrowing transactions?
9. Is the popularity of leasing solely a function of the tax treatment of leases?
10. How does the current tax law treat leasing transactions?

11. How has the tax treatment of lease transactions changed in recent history?

12. How is the tax treatment of lease transactions likely to change in the near future?

13. How has the introduction of new financial instruments (financial engineering) and the trend toward securitization (of debt) affected lease financing?

14. How has structure and competition within the leasing industry changed in recent years?

15. How is the structure and competition in the leasing industry likely to change in coming years?

16. What are the functional mechanics involved in typical lease transactions?

17. What are the major types of lease contracts? How are these contracts similar, and how do they differ?

18. What are the major sources of lease funds available to the small firm?

19. When does leasing represent an alternate means of asset acquisition by small firms?

20. What are the major sources of lease funds available to larger firms?

21. When does leasing represent an alternate means of asset acquisition by larger firms?

22. What is the appropriate accounting treatment of lease transactions?

23. How does technological obsolescence affect the decision to lease?

24. How does inflation affect the decision to lease?

25. How does uncertainty in salvage value affect the decision to lease?

The questions that are answered in the book are not posed for the purpose of discussion only. The questions bear directly upon the latest developments, concerns, and problematic analytical areas of leasing. Such leasing questions are especially pertinent now that the 1986 Tax Reform Act (1986 TRA), as it affects leasing, is more discernible. The deepening of the financial manager's knowledge of and ability to use leasing centers in large part around the following issues:

Relationship between Lessor and Lessee. As the 1986 TRA begins to manifest itself in tangible ways in lease transactions, lessor and lessee may have to coordinate transactions better, for example, as a result of the loss of the investment tax credit (ITC). As a result of that loss lessors may be more aggressive in their assessment of the residual or terminal value of assets. In order to insure that such a value of the residual worth of an asset is realized, the lessor may have to play a more active role in maintaining the asset in a manner that ensures a pre–agreed-upon value at the end of the lease. When (not if) the lessor begins to assume this more active role, it will be incumbent on the lessee to manage those aspects of leasing under his or her control better. In most cases, the financing of the lease is most controllable by the lessee. As the demands for better maintenance and the resulting documentation become more pronounced, the net advantage to leasing, from the standpoint of the lessee, will shrink. Better cost control will be the reasonable reaction. Thus, the implicit costs of leasing, often ignored in the literature, are fully explored in this text. Financing choices are a part of cost control in the asset acquisition context.

International Finance and Trade. Overseas investors, that is, lenders domiciled in countries other than the United States, invest in leveraged leases of U.S. domiciled firms. The implications of such activity for the financial manager are clear. A currency exchange rate favorable to the U.S. financial manager will likely result in overall favorable lease terms. The financial manager, however, must be able to maintain such favorability. Will there be a sufficient flow of the foreign currency to assure adequate debt service? What is the nature of the reporting requirements for the currency translation gains and losses? These questions are addressed in this book.

Alternative Minimum Tax (AMT). The AMT is a complicated set of guidelines, as part of the 1986 TRA, apparently to insure that fewer firms pay no taxes in a given year. The lessor will invest in equipment for purposes of leasing for which the AMT consequences are least severe. It is incumbent upon the lessee also to consider the consequences of the AMT. The calculations, examples, and other issues that surround the AMT are addressed in this book.

ORGANIZATION

A leasing guide that is comprehensive must first highlight and thoroughly discuss the important issues in leasing. As the search for a correct leasing analysis has progressed, the important considerations, both theoretical and practical, have emerged. The book begins with a discussion of these considerations and an assessment of their importance to leasing analysis. Their appropriate place in the analysis of the lease decision is illustrated.

In those situations in the literature where alternative positions have been taken concerning a method of analysis, we take a position and defend it. In our explanation of why that position was taken, a clarification of the relevant issues, those critical to the analysis, results. Of course, such an approach includes the making of assumptions and the defense of those assumptions.

LEASING ACTIVITY IN THE FUTURE

American companies are steadily increasing their stock of productive assets. The acquisitions of such assets are, as some believe, of such a level to postpone a recession for several years. Approximately 25 to 30% of all original equipment in the United States is brought into use through a lease arrangement. The responsibility placed upon the financial manager as a result of a strong economy bears directly upon the

proper assessment of financing choices. Financing choices mean much
more attention has to be paid to the availability of money. As the
financial markets become more sophisticated, which usually means
increased specialization and segmentation, the financial manager who
evaluates the lease alternative must be aware of such sophistication. A
segmented-lessor environment will likely demand a segmented-lessee
environment. Lessors and lessees may "match up" according to funds
sources, asset maturity, and other areas of distinct commonality.

Leasing will likely figure more prominently into the overall strategic
plans of the firm. At present, leasing is a financial tool that is in wide
usage. Its flexibility, however, places leasing in nearly the same category of importance as the debt-versus-equity decision. That is, the long-
range plans of the firm, of which financing decisions are a part, will
more explicitly include lease-versus-buy considerations.

We certainly agree with the need to attend to financing matters with
complete consideration of the other functional and strategic aspects of
the firm. Financing activities must never be undertaken in a vacuum.
A financial plan is only relevant and useful if it flows from the firm's
strategic and/or tactical plan. The decision to lease or buy an asset, for
example, is a dependable choice only if the need for the asset is a part
of the firm's strategic/tactical plan. The link between those activities
should be clear to the manager who must make decisions in the complex business environment of the future.

This book attempts to present the positions taken in the context of a
planning-oriented environment, an environment wherein planning is an
integral part of the decision process. In such an environment, the decision process generally contains less risk. The measurement and control
of risk is the essential element of an environment wherein returns are
likely to be maximized. Maximization of return over a long period is the
goal of the financial manager.

NOTES

1. Robert R. Nathan Associates, Inc., "Equipment Leasing Activities in the
United States," American Association of Equipment Lessors, Washington,
DC, September 1987, pp. 1–41.
2. *Business Week*, February 27, 1989, p. 86.

2

Important Concepts in Lease Financing

The practice of leasing assets for business use instead of purchasing those assets is old and well established. The rapid increase in industrial activity in the United States over the last 50 years corresponds to the increase in the use of leased assets. In addition, that period of expansion has brought nearly every type of asset under the lease agreement.[1] "Fundamentally, the lease contract bestows on the lessee only a limited right, namely the right to *use* the asset for a fixed period of time, in exchange for the fixed payments."[2]

The leasing industry began to emerge as an identifiable entity in the 1950s. During that period, manufacturers began to organize their financing arrangements more firmly to accommodate sales of their products. The captive-finance subsidiary is a product of that phenomenon. Coinciding with manufacturers' efforts were favorable tax laws as manifested by the Investment Tax Credit (ITC). From 1963 to 1986, the ITC, while varying in its impact based upon the health of the overall economy, provided various tax advantages to lessees and lessors alike. Total commercial leasing volume at year-end 1989 was approximately $175 billion.

The advantages of leasing, seen generally as financial flexibility and as a hedge against obsolescence, attract companies of all sizes. Small companies as well as large firms have joined what has become a growth industry. "In 1986, leasing was the third largest source of funds for U.S. business."[3] The growth in leasing includes all types of assets for all types of business uses. The modern financial manager who does not consider leasing as a means of asset financing has overlooked a widely accepted financing option. While the payments made to the lessor are often found to be greater than those made in the case of a purchase,

leasing offers administrative and risk-related advantages that are highly desirable to decision-makers.

Some researchers and analysts have referred to leasing as having a
"dual nature."[1] That is, leasing relates to the financing decision and to
the investment decision. There is little argument today concerning
that idea. Leasing is a form of financing. The increase in the use of
leased assets by firms in the last several decades highlights the financial manager's desire for flexibility in both investing and financing the
firm's capital needs. As a result of leasing's dual effect upon the firm's
financial decisions, a great deal of attention has been paid, in recent
years especially, to the analytical techniques of the leasing decision.
The fact that leasing, by its very nature, includes many "theoretical
issues"[4] has received a considerable amount of treatment in the literature in the past few years (see, for example, Note 8). Such academic
interest has appropriately centered around the issues that concern valuation. Valuation includes specification of cash flows and the discount
rate or rates necessary to place the flows on a present-value basis. The
valuation emphasis is referred to in the current literature as *lease-
versus-buy analysis*, a categorization that includes many types of lease
arrangements.

RECENT HISTORY

Any discussion or analysis of leasing by businesses would not be valid
without close attention to the tax laws that seem alternately to encourage and retard leasing activity. The year 1981 saw passage of the Economic Recovery Tax Act (ERTA). The effect of ERTA upon leasing was
to shorten the economic or depreciable life for most equipment and to
increase the ITC. These results created more tax shelters, thus adding
further flexibility to leasing as a financing option. More opportunities
were created to "sell" tax shelters between lessors and lessees. The
result was a great increase in leasing activity.

The idea of a *safe-harbor lease* was created as a result of the tax law of
1981. The lease contract was entered into for the sole purpose of allow-
ing an unprofitable firm, which could not use the ITC since it had no
profits and therefore no taxes, to transfer its potential tax advantage to
another company. In practice, an unprofitable firm would purchase an
asset for which an ITC was allowed. Unable to use the ITC, the asset
was sold to another company that had profits and could make use of
the ITC. Such a benefit permitted the second company to act as lessor,
passing the ITC tax advantage along to the lessee in the form of reduced leased payments.

The ERTA leasing (tax) rules were especially favorable toward states
and localities.[5] Public-sector leasing rules under pre-ERTA tax laws

were restrictive. The primary benefit of ERTA, in that regard, was to liberalize depreciation provisions in order to make public-sector leasing more profitable. The new rules also included an incentive for rehabilitation of housing not suitable for occupation. Such incentives also facilitated the sale-and-leaseback arrangement. Local governments purchased the housing, sold it to private investors, then leased the housing from those investors. The point is that ERTA was a major demonstration by the Internal Revenue Service (IRS), private businesses, and local governments of leasing's flexibility and its contribution to the movement of capital and other resources in the economy.

In 1986, the Tax Reform Act (1986 TRA) was passed. The new law brought about two major changes relative to the 1981 law: the ITC was repealed and the rapid depreciation of assets was slowed. In addition, there are many facets to the 1986 TRA as it concerns leasing. While a full discussion and explanation of the 1986 TRA forms the basis for the bulk of this book, a brief list of its major implications and analytical concerns may be useful here.

The most visible effects of 1986 TRA upon the leasing industry include the following: corporate tax rates have been lowered, thus tax benefits will be less valuable; the ITC has been eliminated, and depreciation schedules for many assets have been lengthened; the tax deductibility of carrying costs for some municipalities will likely reduce tax-exempt leasing.

An additional aspect of the 1986 TRA that appears to be of considerable consequence to many firms is the Alternative Minimum Tax (AMT). Chapters 5 and 8 illustrate treatment of the AMT. Only the general characteristics of the AMT are provided here. The AMT is seen by some analysts as a potential boon to the leasing industry. The AMT represents an apparent attempt by Congress to enact a minimum tax for businesses. Prior to the 1986 TRA it was possible for some firms to avoid any level of tax payment; a minimum tax, in this case the AMT, essentially removes that possibility for many firms. The tax liability must be calculated based upon the regular tax and the AMT. The firm pays whichever amount is greater. One source offers the following as a rationale for imposition of the AMT:

Alternative minimum tax rules have been created to maintain a degree of tax equity between high-income taxpayers who are able to use income tax deductions, credits, and exemptions to generate large tax savings and lower-income taxpayers who are unable to make significant use of them. Some high-income taxpayers are able to avoid taxation entirely. By recapturing some of the tax breaks achieved through the use of a class of tax items known as "preference items," the high alternative minimum tax is an attempt to ensure that taxpayers with high incomes pay at least a minimum amount of tax.[6]

What other changes are on the horizon for the leasing industry post–1986 TRA?[3]

Aircraft Leasing. The growth in this large "leasing segment" is expected to continue for the foreseeable future as airlines around the world expand. In addition, 1986 TRA has favorable "transition rules," many of which apply directly to airlines. The effect of such rules is to maintain many pre–1986 TRA leasing benefits. The strength in the airline-leasing segment is such that many companies are being formed solely for the purpose of aircraft leasing.

High-Tech Leasing. Items such as used computers and new advances in technology, including telecommunications equipment, give rise to the leasing of advanced technology items.

Utilities. The opportunity for obtaining cash from completed construction projects (sale-and-leaseback, to be discussed in full detail in Chapter 8, provides an opportunity here) and the acquisition of additional plant or transmission capacity means leasing by utilities. Further, the more creative a utility can be with its financing the more the opportunity to keep costs and rates within present bounds. Such cost containment is a major concern for a closely regulated and closely watched industry.

Securitization. If lease receivables are converted to a "certificate" and sold to investors, such receivables are said to be securitized. Some of the most well-known investment banking companies in the United States are rapidly becoming involved in the packaging of securities backed by leases. Conceivably, such efforts could provide a major source of funding for lease deals in the next few years.

CONSOLIDATION AND CHANGES AMONG LESSORS

The 1986 TRA was greeted with some dread by the leasing industry, which is made up of lessors, lessees, and third-party suppliers of capital. The results of the tax law changes are now being more rationally assessed and most, if not all of the fear has subsided. There is much capital available for leasing activity, and benefits attached to the leasing arrangement appear plentiful.

A major change in the leasing industry, the importance of which is yet to become fully clear, is consolidation among lessors. Smaller lessors are being acquired by larger lessors. The desire to enter certain specialized markets and the desire to take full advantage of the tax law encourage the move toward consolidation. The ebb and flow of the number and size of the players on the leasing landscape appears directly related to the opportunities to specialize and be profitable given the existing tax laws.

Leasing will survive the present round of tax-law changes as it has survived previous changes. First and foremost, leasing is an economic activity and as such it is guided by occurrences and forecasts in the

macroeconomy. Interest rate levels, competition from overseas manufacturers and lenders, and advancements in technology all serve to
influence the level of leasing activity greatly and to determine who
participates in that activity. As specialization, product diversification,
and other microeconomic factors become more pronounced in the industry, the need for a straightforward and accurate mode of analysis
will become even more important.

Lessors and lessees, analysts, and investors will increasingly demand that the definition and evaluation of the various leasing arrangements be available and comprehensible. It is the purpose of this book
to offer that clarity and delineation. Leasing is a permanent part of the
U.S. financial substructure. It is an important and necessary part of
that substructure and its role, based upon leasing volume data, is
increasing in that regard. As a result of leasing's importance in the
modern financial environment, this book's purpose is to assist the analyst in the construction and use of a generally applicable method of
analysis.

LEASING CONCEPTS DEFINED

A *lease* is a written agreement between the lessor (the owner of the
property) and the lessee (the user of the property) concerning the use of
and payment for the property over a specific period of time. Therefore,
a lease is a rental agreement that will last for at least one year. There
are two broad categories of leases — the *operating lease* and the *financial lease*. A financial lease is sometimes referred to as a *capital lease*.
There are also at least two important special lease categories — the
leveraged lease and the sale-and-leaseback arrangement. These are discussed in detail in Chapter 8.

An operating lease is characterized by the following:

1. The duration of the lease is usually for a time period shorter than the
   economic life of the asset.
2. An operating lease is of shorter duration than a financial lease.
3. The lease is cancelable if the lessee gives proper notice. The financial value
   of assets placed in service under the operating-lease arrangement is lower
   than that of the financial lease. In general, the items placed in service
   through the operating lease are lower-cost items than those of the financial
   lease. Certain types of equipment are usually associated with the operating-
   lease arrangement. Office equipment and motor vehicles are two types of
   assets often placed into service via an operating lease.

The maintenance contract is also a distinguishing characteristic of
the operating lease. Often, under that arrangement, the lessor will

assume responsibility for the maintenance of the leased item. The particular aspects of the maintenance agreement may be separate from the lease contract or they may be a part of the lease contract. Operating leases are not capitalized, thus the lease payments represent expenses in the period in which they are incurred. An operating lease may be known as a *service lease*, an *IBM lease*, or a *maintenance lease*. The reference to IBM is due to that company's wide use and eventual popularization of the operating lease.

A financial lease (or capital lease) has certain characteristics that set it apart from the operating lease. These characteristics have implications for the firm's balance sheet and the resulting tax obligations of the firm. These characteristics are as follows:

1. A financial lease is usually a direct substitute for long-term borrowing. As a result, there are implications for the firm's capital structure decisions. These implications are illustrated in a subsequent section of this chapter.
2. The lease is fully amortized. The lessor's investment in the asset is totally recouped.
3. The lessee is usually responsible for insurance and property taxes.
4. The lease is not cancelable.
5. The lease term and the asset's useful life are usually identical or very similar. The special lease categories referred to above – the leveraged lease and the sale-and-leaseback arrangement – are types of financial leases.

LEASE FUNDS: SOURCES AND COSTS

Sources: The Small Firm

The popularity of leasing assets for business use has reached the small business. (There is no standard definition of the term "small business." For example, the Small Business Administration, or SBA, categorizes retail companies with sales less than $8 million per year as small businesses.) In general, a significant characteristic of the small firm, regardless of a strict definition, is its relative lack of access to the capital markets. As a result, the sources of funds to the small firm, including leasing, are very important.

For the small firm, for which leasing is seen as a necessary and viable means of acquiring assets, what are the possible sources of funds to finance the lease? Among the more reliable sources are independent leasing companies, commercial banks, insurance companies, and pension funds. The independent leasing companies usually specialize in operating or service leases, financial leases, or they act as brokers. The brokerage role is for the purpose of intermediating the lessee and lessor.

The commercial bank's role as a provider of funds for firms began in the 1960s and began to flourish in the mid-1970s. Commercial banks are heavily involved in the *leveraged lease*, wherein the lessor borrows the funds necessary to purchase the asset. The asset is then put into use by the lessee, whose payments compensate the lessor and allow repayment of the borrowed funds. Insurance companies are also providers of leasing funds. It is unlikely, however, that very many funds from insurance companies are obtained by small firms. The data on this are unclear; however, the size of insurance company loans for leased assets indicates a market among larger firms. The same may be said for pension funds as a source of funds for leasing.

Reilly[7] lists ten reasons why small (or large) firms may consider leasing an attractive means of asset acquisition relative to owning the asset: (1) long terms; (2) convenience; (3) improved return on investment; (4) no dilution of ownership; (5) loan covenants; (6) lower cost; (7) cash flow is improved; (8) lease rental payments are made from pretax rather than after-tax earnings; (9) on or off balance sheet financing; (10) impact on book earnings.

The essential element for small firms in the preceding list is flexibility. Financing flexibility is always important to businesses. It is especially so for firms whose ability to acquire funds may be restricted solely by its sales and asset size. Leasing, again, is a means of financing; it is relevant for the decision-maker only if it offers an attractive alternative to financing using debt or equity. The ten reasons shown above indicate that leasing is such an alternative. As is shown throughout this text, leasing provides financing flexibility for firms of any size. This is so because there are so many variations on the leasing theme. No doubt there are many more variations on the horizon as a result of tax law changes and the changing circumstances of many firms. Leasing's base is firmly rooted in the tax laws and, as the section that follows illustrates, those laws strongly dictate why a particular firm may decide on one type of lease over another.

Sources: The Large Firm

The supply of funds for leased assets for the large firm follows a more predictable and well-organized pattern. This is so because of the depth of financial management in the large firm and the economies of scale associated with seeking out alternative sources of financing. The large firm simply has more contact with funds providers than the small firm does and such contact is more sophisticated and more likely to bear fruit. Thus, the cultivating of sources of funds and the eventual acquiring of funds is an ongoing process in the large firm. By comparison, while small firm management is not inattentive to financial details, it is generally much less layered than that of the large firm; therefore, the ability to consistently target funds sources is reduced. In any case, the sources of funds noted for the small firm's leasing activities apply also to the large firm. The commercial bank source is likely deemphasized and the insurance companies and pension funds are relied upon more in the case of the large firm. Insurance companies and pension funds are in the position to make larger loans due to the size of their asset base and the maturity structure of the available funds. Those funds are of a long-term nature (insurance premiums and pension contributions), therefore they can be loaned for long periods and in large amounts.

Lease Payments

Leasing is often compared to borrowing. That is a commonplace comparison and it is used throughout this book. While the logic of this comparison is explored more fully in a subsequent section of this chapter, the repayment characteristics of the lease obligation and the term loan obligation are compared here. The calculation of the lease payment is highlighted by this comparison.

Consider a loan, the conditions of which are as follows: the principle is $50,000; the loan is an installment loan, which usually means interest is paid on the unpaid balance; the annual interest rate on the loan is 12%; and the loan has a three-year maturity. The periodic payments (assumed to be one payment per year) should be calculated in the following manner:

$$\text{Periodic Payments} = \text{Principal} \div \text{PVIFA}_{k,n}$$

The principal is $50,000; PVIFA, the present-value interest factor of an annuity, may be found by use of a financial calculator or through the use of financial tables. Assuming use of financial tables, once the PVIFA table is located (see the Appendix at the end of this book), the "number-of-payments" column (n) on the left side of the table is used to correspond to the loan's interest rate of 12% (k). Locating those two places on the table yields a PVIFA of 2.4018. Therefore, $50,000 ÷ 2.4018 = $20,817.72. The term loan described above requires three annual payments of $20,817.72. The payments include both principal and interest, as shown in Exhibit 2-1. Column 1 is the periodic payment found earlier; Column 2 is the interest at 12% on the principal. In Year 1 the interest is 0.12 × $50,000 = $6,000. In Year 2 it is 0.12 × $35,182.28; the balance of the principal in that year (Column 3) is the amount of the total yearly payment that applied to the principal.

The preceding example permits an assessment of the important cash

Exhibit 2-1
Calculation of Lease Payment

Year	Loan Payment	Interest	Principal Reduction	Remaining Balance
1	$20,817.72	$6,000.00	$14,827.72	$35,182.28
2	20,817.72	4,222.00	16,595.84	18,586.43
3	20,817.72	2,230.00	*18,587.43	-0-

*Difference due to rounding.

flow characteristics of the loan. That is, the interest, which is tax deductible, is highlighted for each year. Once a specific depreciable asset is purchased, the depreciation, maintenance charges, and additional tax-deductible expenses may be added to the interest payments to reveal the total tax-deductible amount available to the purchaser.

Continuing the assumption that the $50,000 of borrowed funds will be used to purchase an asset for use in normal business activities, the loan cash flows may be compared to those of lease financing. The conditions of the lease alternative to financing the asset may appear as follows: duration of the lease is 3 years; lease payments will be $25,000 per year, including maintenance. The situation concerning lease cash flows may be seen simply as payments of $25,000 per year, which are tax-deductible. The net cash outflow per year of the loan alternative may then be compared to that of the lease.

The primary question for the decision-maker is whether it is more beneficial to lease the asset or to borrow the funds and acquire the asset as a purchase. That question forms the basis for much of what is done in this book and involves the concept of discounted cash flow analysis (DCF). As a result of the DCF concept, the cost of each alternative, lease or buy, is the question that must be resolved in order to make a correct decision. Cash inflows and outflows and the related tax consequences are only a portion of the answer. Chapter 4 provides a more detailed introduction to the methods of financial analysis and the use of discounted cash flows in evaluating financial alternatives. In Chapters 7 and 8, after sufficient groundwork has been established, the lease-versus-buy analysis is presented.

FASB 13

The Financial Accounting Standards Board (FASB) was established in 1973 to establish and improve financial accounting standards for reporting and accounting. Such improvements were intended for the benefit of the public. In 1976, the Statement of Financial Accounting Standards Board No. 13 (FASB 13) was originated to set down rules for determination of a *capital lease*. The distinguishing feature of a capital lease is that it must be recorded on the firm's books as an asset and as a liability in an amount equal to the present value of the future lease payments. It is then called a capitalized lease, also known as a financial lease.

It is necessary to familiarize the reader of financial statements with the effect of lease contracts on the firm's financial condition. In terms of a firm's total-debt-to-total-assets ratio, a capital lease is very similar to debt and, therefore, its proper recording and disclosure is essential. The FASB 13, in essence, mandates the following: If a lease transfers substantially all of the benefits and risk of asset ownership to the lessee, the property should be capitalized on the firm's books.

If a leased asset meets one or more of the following criteria, then it must be capitalized on the firm's books according to the FASB:

1. The lease contains a bargain-purchase option.
2. The lease term is equal to 75% or more of the estimated economic life of the leased property.
3. The lease transfers ownership of the property to the lessee.
4. The present value of the minimum lease payments equals or exceeds 90% of the fair value of the leased asset.

Chapter 6 provides a detailed examination of accounting for lease transactions.

OTHER CONSIDERATIONS IN LEASING

It is on the basis of the preceding criteria that analysts may now more easily distinguish between the two primary types of leases – the financial lease and the operating lease. As mentioned above, there are special categories of the two primary types of leases, and these are illustrated and defined in Chapter 8.

Financial leases are used to acquire a wide range of assets – from real estate to barges. Based upon leasing's well-documented popularity, it is useful to enumerate the particular considerations relative to the lease-versus-buy (borrow) decision. Such considerations are noteworthy because they are often difficult to quantify. Their influence upon the lease-versus-buy decision is not clear cut. Each time the lease-versus-buy analysis is conducted, the following items may be included or omitted, and their influence may be significant or negligible:

1. *Technological Obsolescence.* If rapid obsolescence can be forecast for a given asset, leasing will likely be the favored means of acquiring the asset. This is especially true in the case of the operating lease, since such leases are cancelable.

2. *Inflation.* A forecasted rapid increase in the price level will affect the cost of money, the value of the asset at the end of its economic life, and the cost of the asset. Therefore, the anticipated level of inflation must be carefully considered in the lease-versus-buy decision.

3. *Residual Value.* The asset's residual or salvage value is often very uncertain. For the lessor, the level of the residual value is critical to the profitability of the lease. If the residual value of the asset is high, the lessor receives relatively more value at the end of the lease and less value if the residual value is low. For the lessee, the salvage value is foregone if the asset is leased. While the salvage value is probably the most uncertain cash flow item in the lease-versus-buy decision, it is very important for both lessee and lessor to use the most reliable information available to assess the asset's value at the end of the lease. An additional item, the use of which is often vague in the lease-versus-buy analysis, is that of the discount rate necessary to discount all relevant cash flows. The discount rate is not included in the preceding list of considerations because the manner in which it is used is not dependent upon the particular leasing situation. The proper discount rate to use in the lease-versus-buy analysis is, however, a controversial question.

In assessing financial leases versus borrowing funds and purchasing the asset, businesses should use the after-tax debt cost to discount the relevant cash flows. Discounting at that rate permits the inclusion of tax deductibility of interest in the analysis, and that rate corresponds to the relative certainty of the cash flows, excluding the salvage value. The salvage value may be discounted at the firm's weighted marginal cost of capital. The rationale behind this choice is provided in Chapter 7.

The preceding considerations are of great importance in the lease-versus-buy analysis. Their significance is due to the necessity of obtaining a direct comparison between the lease and buy (borrow) alternatives. It is necessary, however, to rely upon judgment in assessing the relevance of technological obsolescence, inflation, and residual value. Once the certain cash flows are correctly evaluated, the items requiring judgment appear as less of a problem. In the pages that follow, great attention is paid to a clear illustration of the correct handling of the more certain cash flows.

LEASING: FINANCING ALTERNATIVE OR INVESTMENT DECISION?

As a firm experiences growth in sales, the need to expand the pool of physical assets is a permanent part of that growth. In general, there are two ways in which the firm's physical assets may be expanded — through leasing or purchasing. Often, when the asset is purchased, the necessary funds must be borrowed. The choice between a lease or borrow (purchase) decision represents a financing choice for the firm.

In recent years, firms have experienced considerable growth in leasing as a means of acquiring assets. In 1988, leasing was the third largest source of funds for U.S. businesses. At that time, there were well over 1000 lessors to facilitate the asset acquisitions of firms.[1] The increase in the use of leasing as an asset acquisition alternative is due to several key factors. The most significant of these are as follows:

1. Technological changes and a changing economic environment. These factors serve to increase the uncertainty inherent in doing business.
2. Changes in the tax laws. The tax laws themselves influence the level of leasing activity, and, under any set of tax circumstances, lessors often adapt contract conditions to maintain the desired volume of business.
3. Constantly changing and improving analytical techniques for the lease-versus-buy decision.

Throughout this book, these and other topics directly related to the lease-versus-buy decision are discussed and illustrations are used that make clear the proper application of the modern theory of business finance as it relates to leasing.

The preferred approach to a cost-versus-benefit analysis of the lease-or-buy decision is the net advantage to leasing (NAL). The NAL analysis "is conducted independently of the primary capital budgeting evaluation of the asset."[8] It is very important to understand that the NAL approach is designed to view the decision to lease or purchase an asset as one of financing and not as an investment decision. This is because the investment decision should have been made by the time financing alternatives are considered. More accurately, the investment decision is conducted given a fixed- or optimal-capital structure. Therefore, the leasing alternative serves as a means of financing asset acquisition over and above the limits imposed by the firm's optimal debt and equity levels.

The lease-versus-buy decision is part of a larger body of theory generally referred to as internal-investment analysis, or capital budgeting. Cost-of-capital theory also assumes an important role in the discussion. The relationship among lease analysis, capital budgeting, and cost-of-capital theory is based on the following: Lease analysis is a part of the capital budgeting activities of the firm in that it represents an additional manner in which to finance a desirable capital investment opportunity. The relevant cash flows in the capital-budgeting analysis must be discounted at some marginal cost of funds to the firm, division, or other economic unit.

It is at this point in the decision process that the discount rate or cost of capital becomes an important part of the financing-versus-investment decision in the lease-versus-buy analysis. By the time the firm looks to the leasing alternative, its capital-budgeting decision (whether or not to acquire the asset) should have been made. Consideration of the leasing alternative should be for the sole purpose of a wider choice of financing arrangements over and above the usual debt or equity financing.

How do the preceding ideas relate specifically to the lease-versus-buy decision? Leasing is a specific means of financing a capital investment. Moreover, the cash flows that are relevant in the analysis have characteristics that warrant special attention. A major area in leasing cash flow analysis is the discount rate used to discount the cash flows. The cash payments by the lessee to the lessor are certain. That is, the cash flows are legally due and payable, and such cash flows are very similar to debt service payments. Bankruptcy ensues if the payments are not made; therefore the cost (discount factor) attributable to debt may also be used to discount the lease payments. The uncertainty surrounding the level of the asset salvage value may warrant a discount rate that is different from that used to discount the lease payments. The objective is to use a discount rate that is reflective of the uncertainty of cash flows.

In the lease-versus-buy decision, it is hazardous to oversimplify matters addressing any portion of the analysis. For example, if the argument for discounting cash flows on a "risk" basis is accepted – as it should be, based upon "perfect-market" principles – how should a series of short-term lease cash flows be discounted? The lessee often has a choice between long-term or short-term leases. If the need for the asset is long term and the asset is acquired through a series of short-term leases, the discount rate for the projected cash outflows (the lease agreement is not yet finalized) should reflect that uncertainty.

The intent here is not to resolve all issues dealing with the lease-versus-buy analysis, but to enumerate those issues. In this introductory chapter, the mix of tax laws, finance theory, and day-to-day business issues involving leasing has been raised. The mix need not present an analytical quagmire. Financial, economic, and accounting literature have contributed much to assist in the resolution of most of the difficulties encountered in the analysis. What follows are theoretical examples accompanied by realistic examples (to the extent possible) that should be sufficiently generalizable to allow a correct cost/benefit decision in most cases.

NOTES

1. *Leasing and Tax Reform: A Guide Through the Maze* (Stamford, CT: General Electric Credit Corporation, 1987, pamphlet).

2. H. M. Weingartner, "Leasing Asset Lives and Uncertainty: Guides to Decision Making," *Financial Management* 16, no. 2 (Summer 1987), pp. 5–13.

3. "Leasing: Proving the Predictions Wrong," *Institutional Investor* (November 1987) (special advertising section), pp. 3–24.

4. L. D. Schall, "Analytic Issues in Lease vs. Purchase Decisions," *Financial Management* 16, no. 2 (Summer 1987), pp. 17–21.

5. M. A. Willis, "Leasing – A Financial Option for States and Localities," *FRBNY Quarterly Review* 6, no. 4 (Winter 1981–82), pp. 42–46.

6. "Alternative Minimum Tax – Post-1986," (Chicago, IL: Commerce Clearing House, Inc., 1987).

7. R. F. Reilly, "Leasing: An Attractive Alternative Method of Asset Financing for Small Firms," *The National Public Account* 27 (November 1982), pp. 30–37.

8. T. J. O'Brien, and B. H. Nunnally, Jr., "A 1982 Survey of Corporate Leasing Analysis," *Financial Management* 12 (Summer 1983), pp. 30–36.

II

The Analytical Foundations of Leasing

3

The Benefits of Leasing

While the preceding two chapters have indicated there are two types of leases in commercial activity – the operating lease and the financial lease – there are subcategories within those two groups. The subcategories of leases come about as a result of the tax laws and the particular financing needs and wishes of the lessee or lessor; these often overlap (see Exhibit 3-1).

The purpose of this chapter is to discuss the advantages and disadvantages of leasing from the standpoint of the lessee. In order to assess such characteristics fully, the various types of leases must be understood. Referring again to Exhibit 3-1, the financial-lease category includes the following "subcategories":

1. *Sale-and-Leaseback.* A sale-and-leaseback arrangement exists when the owner of the asset sells the asset with the intention of leasing it back for normal business use. The advantage of a sale-and-leaseback arrangement is that it permits tailor-made construction of a commercial building, for example, then permits immediate recovery of the cash investment for the asset. There are few, if any, disadvantages for the lessee in the sale-and-leaseback arrangement. As with any lease, if the asset becomes obsolete, there may be difficulty in moving from one lease to the next, in terms of additional cost to the lessee.

2. *Leveraged Lease.* The leveraged lease is so called because generally the lessor borrows the funds necessary (thereby creating leverage) to purchase the asset. The asset is then let to the third party in the transaction. In Chapter 6, specific applications of the leveraged lease are illustrated.

3. *Direct Lease.* A direct lease is identical to a sale-and-leaseback arrangement except that the lessee does not necessarily own the property; the lessor provides both financing and the asset.

Exhibit 3-1
Leasing Categories

1. Financial Lease (Capital Lease)	2. Operating Lease (Service Lease)
Non-cancelable, full amortization of the lessor's cost for the asset.	Usually, maintenance and/or service is provided by lessor, and the costs of these services included in the lease agreement. Does not fully amortize lessor's cost.
Subcategories:	Subcategories:
(a) Sale-and-Leaseback	None.
(b) Leveraged Lease	
(c) Direct Lease - Identical to sale-and-leaseback, but lessee did not necessarily own the asset. Lessor provides financing and the asset.	
Tax Considerations:	Tax Considerations:
True Lease: Lessee may deduct lease payments fully; lessor retains depreciation. Five IRS guidelines must be met for true lease.	Conditional Sale Lease: Applies when any of the five IRS guidelines for true leases are not satisfied. IRS views this transaction as an installment purchase.

TAX CONSIDERATIONS AND LEASE CATEGORIES

Lease categories are, to a large extent, based upon or best understood relative to tax considerations. As has been maintained, the tax laws dominate the analytical/economic aspects of leasing. This is especially evident in lease-versus-buy analysis. Chapter 5 presents a comprehensive illustration of the tax-related nature of leasing. Here, the goal is to make clear the general influence that the tax laws have upon lease categories, and the resulting value of leasing to the firm.

In a report published by the General Electric Credit Corporation, under the heading "How Do I Account for a Tax-Oriented Lease?"[1] is an example that illustrates the tax/leasing symbiosis. This example reveals not only the direct relationship and dependency between taxes and leasing, but also the necessity of close attention to detail. The sentence, " . . . the liability is reduced and expensed according to the interest method. . . . " is interesting, but what does it mean? To the reader of the firm's financial statements it means the asset appears as an asset that is owned by the firm. To the lessee, the asset is, essentially, being depreciated. It is, in effect, an installment purchase. To the auditors of the company's accounting records, the asset is leased. To the IRS, the asset's acquisition may be an operating lease or capital lease. The IRS is concerned with whether the asset is a *true lease*, the requirements for which are as follows:

1. The lessee must have the right to purchase the asset at a "bargain price" (less than fair market value).
2. The estimated fair market value of the asset at the end of the lease must equal at least 20% of the asset's original cost.
3. The lessor must have at least a 20% equity interest in the leased asset.
4. The estimated useful life of the asset, beyond the lease term, must be at least 20% of the original estimated useful life of the asset.
5. The lessor must receive a reasonable return from the leased asset, usually as compared to the return on a loan.

The preceding explanation and Exhibit 3-1 describe the same type of lease – almost. The difference between the definition of a *true lease* and a *capital lease* is exemplified by the "residual" value restrictions inherent in each definition. The IRS mandates that a true lease have an estimated fair market value at the end of the lease that equals or exceeds 20% of the asset's original cost (excluding inflation and deflation effects). In the case of a capital lease, the lessor must recover at least 90% of the fair market value of the property, according to FASB 13. Thus, based upon Exhibit 3-2, a tax-oriented lease may be a capital lease or an operating lease. It is the idea of tax deductibility that is of importance to the lessee.

When a lease is only a lease in the minds of the lessor and lessee, it is a conditional sale lease. When the IRS guidelines for a tax-oriented lease are not met the transaction is an installment purchase; for tax purposes the user of the asset may deduct only the interest or equivalent interest on the loan.

In order to discern clearly the advantages and disadvantages of leasing, it is necessary to understand the important role the tax laws play in defining a particular transaction. Whether an asset acquisition is actually a lease depends upon the IRS guidelines prevailing at that time.

Exhibit 3-2
Taxes and Lease Categories

HOW DO I ACCOUNT FOR A TAX-ORIENTED LEASE?*

A tax-oriented lease - one that allows the lessor to use the tax benefits - may be either a
capital lease or an operating lease for book reporting purposes as defined in the FASB Statement
No. 13 published by the Financial Accounting Standards Board.

According to FASB 13, a capital lease must have one or more of the following characteristics:

1. a bargain purchase option;

2. transfer of ownership of the property to the lessee by the end of the lease term;

3. a term equal to 75% or more of the estimated economic life of the property; or

4. 90% or more recovery of the fair market value of the property through the present
   valuation of minimum lease payments.

A lease having none of these characteristics is an operating lease. This is the simplest type
of lease to account for, since the lessee only has to expense the rentals. There is no necessity to
add the asset to the balance sheet (other than footnoting the amount of firm lease rental
obligations in the notes to the financial statements).

On the other hand, in a capital lease the asset goes on the lessee's books as though it were
purchased. A corresponding liability, equal to the present value of the lease payments, is also
recorded. Each month the asset is amortized in accordance with the lessee's normal depreciation
procedure, and the liability is reduced and expensed according to the "interest method". In other
words, it's as though the asset were bought and financed with debt. For tax purposes, of course,
there is no balance sheet consideration, and monthly rentals are fully expensed.

Source: Leasing and Tax Reform: A Guide Through the Maze, (Stamford, CT: General
     Electric Credit Corporation, 1987), p. 12.

GENERAL ADVANTAGES OF LEASING

The advantages of leasing for commercial activity are many. As pointed out in an earlier chapter, all types and sizes of businesses have
access to these advantages. The increased flexibility that comes about
through leasing is an advantage often cited by business operators as a
key consideration in a leasing decision. What is the nature of such
flexibility?

When assets are acquired through a short-term lease arrangement, the threat of obsolescence is lessened. The short-term lease (operating or service lease) is cancelable by the lessee. Obsolescence is a particularly important concern for users of computing equipment where changes in technology are rapid and significant. The cancelable lease permits the lessee a rapid, relatively cost-effective move to the new equipment. Usually, the lessor encourages this action as such assets are updated in a predictable fashion.

An idea of the importance of such flexibility to the lessee and lessor is illustrated by the expenditures in the U.S. economy for advances in technology and the expectations of business managers from such expenditures. The end users of these newly developed products will likely desire financial arrangements where movement from one generation of productive assets to another is not restricted by the financing method of those assets. Leasing is an ideal method to gain such added flexibility.

The increased flexibility brought about by leasing influences the cost of leasing and the analytical considerations necessary to evaluate such costs. In an article by Cason,[2] a method of assessing long-term asset acquisition is shown. The asset may be purchased or leased, and its use is necessary for 20 years. Under the leasing alternative, the asset may be leased in five-year increments; lease terms are certain only for the first five-year lease period. The question for the analyst is how best to compare the two financing options – lease or borrow-and-purchase.

An appropriate comparison is heavily dependent upon the manner in which the cash flows are discounted. The more certain cash flows should be discounted at a rate that is different from the less certain cash flows. The implications for leasing flexibility is that the series of leases available to the user (lessee) firm permits an adjustment for the cost of money (which directly influences the value of the lease cash flows) at the specific period during which the cash flows occur. While this may be possible with an adjustable-rate loan, the leasing arrangement offers the added flexibility of reconsidering the entire decision, lease or borrow-and-buy, in five years. While not every borrow-versus-lease arrangement is as flexible as this example, it is often possible for the potential lessee to negotiate the lease terms so that a capital lease becomes an operating lease, gaining the flexibility offered by the shorter term lease.

Leasing activities by firms often become a means to reduce overall administrative costs. This is accomplished by avoiding purchasing and maintenance departments established for the sole purpose of overseeing productive asset acquisition and maintenance. An analogy to this potential cost saving is the factoring of accounts receivable, which often removes the need for a credit analysis function within the firm. The leasing of assets places some net costs with another party and the user firm (the lessee) realizes a savings on administrative costs.

It is likely that as leasing becomes more familiar to business operators and managers, the direct earnings attributable to the lease arrangement will lessen. The indirect savings, however, may be the major determinant of whether firms choose to lease or buy assets. Such indirect cost savings include those mentioned above: administrative costs, the tangible benefits of flexibility for financing and ease of asset exchange, and the option of altering the maturity of an asset acquisition by connecting a capital lease to an operating lease for the same asset.

ADVANTAGES OF OPERATING LEASES*

The Financial Accounting Standards Board describes an operating lease as any lease that does not meet the criteria of a capital lease. An operating lease differs from a capital lease in the following significant ways: operating leases are cancelable by the lessee and operating leases permit the lessor to benefit from the salvage value of the asset. What is the importance, if any, of those characteristics to the lessee? The lessee, in the words of Copeland and Weston, then has "equipment that can be laid off."[3] The lease contract is no longer a fixed cost (overhead) but is a variable cost under the operating-lease arrangement.

Most firms prefer to treat any lease as an operating lease whenever possible because the accounting is comparatively simple. Also, the belief in and need for "off-balance-sheet financing" is an important consideration for most firms. Referring again to the cancelability of operating leases, if an operating lease is not cancelable by the lessee, it takes on a major characteristic of the financial lease – a more complete disclosure in the firm's financial statements. In fact, in the case of noncancelability of a financial lease, a note is required in the financial statements to disclose the amount of lease payments due during each of the successive five years. Thus, the off-balance-sheet aspect of the operating lease is forfeited in that instance.

Much could be said about the aspects of the operating lease in regard to the challenge it poses for the analyst in terms of valuation. Pricing, salvage value, cancelability, and duration of the lease all work separately or in combination to make valuation of the operating lease interesting and difficult. Such valuation is especially important when the objective of the analysis is to compare leasing to borrowing funds and purchasing the asset. These more analytical issues are discussed in full detail in Chapters 7 and 8. Some preliminary comments to introduce those issues may be useful at this point.

Risk and return are the central considerations of financial analysis.

*Portions of this section were contributed by Greg M. Lipe, C.P.A., M.B.A. candidate at the University of North Carolina–Charlotte.

When assuming additional risk, the investor demands a "compensating" increment in expected return. What is the nature of the risk elements in the operating-lease arrangement? At the risk of being redundant, the issue of cancelability is at the heart of the risk-and-return aspects. For example, the lessor recognizes that the cancelability feature places the lease revenue at risk; moreover, the lessee may default on the lease payments. These risk considerations have direct implications for the pricing of operating leases, which has implications for the lease-versus-buy analysis conducted by the lessee.

The replacement costs and salvage value of a lease are extremely important risk components of the overall lease analysis. These concerns have to be factored into the lessor's assessment of the lessee's propensity to cancel the operating lease. If the replacement cost of the asset is increasing at a rate substantially greater than the nominal increase in the general price level, it is likely that the cancellation risk is reduced. This process is reversed when the replacement cost moves upward at a much lower rate, or actually declines. In the case of salvage value, it is not only influenced by the replacement cost of the asset, but is itself, in certain instances, a stochastic process.

What are the ramifications for the lessee of the uncertainty in an operating lease? The ramifications are, of course, closely connected to the prevailing tax laws. One of the things that is happening at present in the lessor–lessee relationship is the "management" of the asset over the life of the lease. The maintenance of the asset is monitored by the lessor and the lessee in an attempt to insure a more certain value for the asset at the end of the lease. As the changing tax laws serve to make the periodic cash flow benefits from the lease smaller, the total cash flow to the lessor becomes more important.

The use of operating leases by businesses offers several substantial advantages to the lessee. Chief among these is the short-term nature of the lease. The often-mentioned cancelability option is also highly valuable to the lessee. Indeed, the operating lease represents a variable cost to the user, in keeping with the idea of assets that may be laid off as the firm's business temporarily slackens.

The duration of an operating lease is dependent upon the type of asset in question. The 1986 TRA modified the depreciation schedule for most productive assets, and that modification caused certain changes in the duration of lease contracts for assets. The Modified Accelerated Cost Recovery System (MACRS) of the 1986 TRA has an influence on the leasing of assets, especially in relation to lease duration. Regardless of the manner in which depreciation practices have affected lease decisions, the primary advantage to the lessee is the flexibility provided by the cancelability of the lease and the tax deductibility of the lease payments.

When an asset is obtained through an operating lease, the lessee is not required to record the leased asset on its balance sheet, which results in no readily visible change in the firm's debt ratio. What becomes apparent to the more astute analyst is the change in the firm's fixed charge coverage (FCC) ratio. The ratio appears as follows:

$$\text{Fixed Charge Coverage} = (\text{EBIT} + \text{Leases} + \text{Interest}) \div (\text{Interest} + \text{Leases})$$

where EBIT = earnings before interest and taxes. What becomes important is not the amount of debt the firm has, but its level of fixed, legally binding obligations, including leases. In consideration of FASB 13, which modified or supplanted Accounting Principles Board (APB) opinion numbers 5, 7, 27, and 31, the belief in off-balance-sheet financing is not grounded in the reality of the post–1986 TRA. The essence of FASB 13, issued in 1976, is that a lease that transfers substantially all of the benefits and risks of ownership should be accounted for as the acquisition of an asset, tantamount to a purchase. The rulings by the accounting profession, separating operating and financial leases into more distinguishable financing options, have placed the operating lease in a much clearer focus, highlighting its advantages and the assets to which it is most amenable.

ADVANTAGES OF THE CAPITAL (FINANCIAL) LEASE

For the lessee firm entering into a capital-lease agreement, a choice appears between two financing alternatives. These alternatives are lease the asset or borrow the funds and purchase the asset. The ramifications of choosing the lease alternative, as Exhibit 3-2 illustrates, are far-reaching. When a capital lease option is chosen, the main considerations are shown in Exhibit 3-3.

In Exhibit 3-3, the asset and financing considerations are not intended to suggest that there are two sets of decisions or criteria involved in the capital lease-versus-borrow (buy) decision. The purpose of the exhibit is to demonstrate the nature of the decision process once the following necessary questions have been answered: is the asset needed and, if so, how should the asset be financed? If leasing is the financing option chosen, then the considerations in the exhibit are of great importance to the financial decision-maker. The purpose here is to discuss the advantages of the capital lease, and not to re-visit some of the more theoretical aspects of that financing option. Even a cursory reading of the literature, however, will indicate leasing's advantages can be assessed only in the context suggested by Exhibit 3-3.

There are several substantive reasons why a firm would enter into a

Exhibit 3-3
Capital Lease Implications for the Firm

---

1. Asset Considerations

    a. Obsolescence

    b. Salvage Value

    c. Inflation Effects

2. Financing Considerations

    a. Discounting Cash Flows

    b. Debt Displacement

---

capital-lease agreement. Primary among these reasons may be the following: (1) the tax deductibility of the lease payments; (2) the present-value cost of the lease alternative may be lower than the purchase alternative; or (3) leasing may greatly facilitate the made-to-order aspect of certain assets. The idea of the tax deductibility of lease payments is straightforward; these provide a tax shield for the lessee. The advantage is directly connected to (2) – the comparison of the present-value costs of leasing versus buying. The tax deductibility of the lease payments contribute to the net cost of the lease alternative and its proper comparison to the buy alternative.

A characteristic of the financial lease that has proven to be advantageous is the analytical comparison of the lease-versus-purchase option, which has developed from the finance literature. The analysis demands a clear delineation of the cash flows relative to each financing option; as a result the analyst is made more aware of the content, meaning, and value of each cash-flow component for each alternative.

Debt Capacity

A persistent question in the discussion of capital lease-versus-borrow (buy) is that of debt displacement. What is the amount of debt that is displaced by an "equivalent" (capital) lease? The question is not trivial; it bears directly upon a potential lender's perception of the borrowing firm's ability to repay debt. While the debt-displacement issue has been discussed at length in the finance literature, a plausible approach to the question and a reasonable answer appeared only recently.

In a 1986 article, researchers surveyed a broad range of lenders concerning the comparability of debt and lease obligations.[4] It is, after all, the lending segment of the economy that has the most influence over the debt-capacity question. The results of the 1982 study indicated that a capital-lease obligation, with its associated income tax benefits, displaced 10% to 20% more unused debt capacity than debt. The study addressed debt compared to a capital lease, not an operating lease of even the non-cancelable variety, although that restriction may be a mere technicality given the comparability of a non-cancelable operating lease and a capital lease.

Financial Statement Effects

In terms of the total financial consequences of leasing, regardless of the type of lease, the nature of such consequences are reflected in the firm's financial statements. The statements show the immediate effect of financing decisions as well as the soundness of past decisions. The financial statements, whether based upon accrual accounting or the more current attention to cash flow, provide necessary insight into the firm's financial decision-making. This is especially so if attention is paid to the attendant footnotes and notes to the financial statements.

Exhibits 3-4, 3-5, and 3-6 are financial statements for the Sihler Company, a contractor to municipal governments that wishes to monitor air quality in high-risk areas. Based upon its line of business, the need for the most up-to-date and often expensive equipment is fairly constant. Several portions of the exhibits allude to MACRS and other tax-related considerations. A full treatment of the tax laws as they relate to leases is provided in Chapter 5. In order to present the advantages, if any, of leasing realistically it was necessary to include the ramifications of the existing tax laws as they affect the financial statements. In the exhibits, no distinction is made between a capital lease and an operating lease. What is important is whether the lease is "tax-oriented"; that is, is the lessee able to deduct the lease payments for book-reporting purposes per FASB 13? If the lease payments are tax-deductible, then the lease is said to be a tax-oriented lease.

The purpose of the exhibits is to show the interrelationships among financing, profit after tax, and total cash flow. Exhibit 3-5 shows the effect upon profit after tax of the financing alternative chosen. The result is important for the tax position of the firm. In Exhibit 3-6, however, the firm's total cash flow is unaffected by its financing choice. That result is important to the day-to-day operations of the business.

Exhibit 3-4
Lease Payments versus Loan Amortization (Sihler Company)

Transaction Details

Initial Cost of Asset:	$100,000
Economic Life of Asset:	5 years
Term of Loan:	5 years
Annual Interest:	8 percent
Corporate Tax Rate:	35 percent
Annual Lease Payment:	$24,000

Financial Data

Year	Payment	Interest	Principal Payment	Remaining Principal Balance
1	$25,046	$8,000	$17,046	$82,954
2	$25,046	$6,636	$18,410	$64,544
3	$25,046	$5,164	$19,882	$44,662
4	$25,046	$3,573	$21,473	$23,189
5	$25,046	$1,855	$23,191	-0-

Therefore, the choice of financing is an important tax consideration. Changes in working capital may, however, make the choice of financing relevant for the cash flow position of the firm as well.

Exhibits 3-4, 3-5, and 3-6 indicate that the effect upon the income statement of the financing alternative chosen may be significant. Such significance depends upon the cost of the asset, the economic life of the asset, and the lease payments. They also show that profitability and cash flow may be vastly different in terms of absolute values and comparative values when the choice of financing is the issue.

Cash flow considerations in accounting and business finance are rap-

Exhibit 3-5
Income Statement, Tax Reporting Year 19X1
($000—No Prior Interest Payable) (Sihler Company)

Item	Acquisition of Asset with Borrowed Funds	Acquisition of Asset with a Tax-Oriented Lease*
Sales	$500	$500
Cost of Goods Sold	($300)	($280)
(Includes $20 in Depreciation)	========	========
Gross Profit	$200	$220
Operating Expenses	($50)	($74)
	========	========
Net Operating Income (EBIT)	$150	$146
Interest Expense	($8)	($0)
	========	========
Profit Before Taxes	$142	$146
Taxes @ 35%	($50)	($51)
	========	========
Profit After Tax	$92	$95

*A tax-oriented lease may be an operating lease or a capital lease. The criterion for a tax-oriented lease is that the lessee may use the tax benefits.

Exhibit 3-6
Cash Flow Effects of Financing Alternatives (Sihler Company)

(A) Definitions: <u>Operating Cash Flow</u> = EBIT plus depreciation minus current taxes.

<u>Total Cash Flow</u> = operating cash flow minus capital spending, plus (minus) changes in net working capital.

<u>Cash Flow Effects of the Financing Alternatives</u>

(A)	EBIT ($000)	150	146
	Depreciation	20	0
	Current taxes	(50)	(51)
	Operating cash flow	120	95
(B)	Operating cash flow	120	95
	Capital Expenditures (1st year pymt)	(25)	(0)
	*Add'n. to net working capital	(1)	(1)
	Total cash flow	94	94

*Calculations would indicate an increase of 5% of first year capital expenditures in year 1.

idly replacing the sources and uses of funds and accrual-versus-cash accounting concerns of the past. The issue, correctly, is how much cash does a firm have at the end of an accounting period? Or, of equal importance, what effect is brought about on that cash by various financing alternatives? Exhibit 3-6 summarizes the now-favored approach to answering that question. An outstanding feature of Exhibit 3-6 is that the reduced EBIT under the lease alternative does not change the firm's cash flow relative to the borrow (buy) financing alternative.

Exhibits 3-7A and 3-7B illustrate the interrelationship among cash flow, working capital, the financial plan, and the firm's strategic plan. The relationship between the advantages of leasing and cash flow and financial planning is represented by items 6A and 7C in Exhibit 3-7B. While the lease-versus-buy analysis is one way in which to assess whether there is an advantage to leasing, the "fit" of leasing in the

Exhibit 3-7A
Cash Flow and Financial Planning—Panel A

---

1) Cash flow, regardless of its frequent and varied usage, has a specific meaning. That meaning may be expressed in two parts:

   (A) Operating Cash Flow = EBIT plus depreciation minus current taxes.

   (B) Total Cash Flow = Operating cash flow minus capital spending, plus (minus) changes in net working capital.

2) A determination of total cash flow indicates the amount of cash generated by the business's expenditures and receipts for assets and liabilities.

3) Cash Flow Example:

A)	Earnings before interest and taxes	$350.00	
	Depreciation	100.00	
	Current taxes	(80.00)	
	Operating cash flow	$370.00	
B)	Operating cash flow	$370.00	
	Capital expenditures	(125.00)	
	Additions to net working capital	(50.00)	
	Total cash flow	$195.00	*(continued)*

Exhibit 3-7A
(Continued)

4)   Analysis of Working Capital Changes

    A)   Increase (decrease) in current assets

Cash	$125.00
Accounts receivable	20.00
Inventory	150.00
Total	$295.00

    B)   Increase (decrease) in current liabilities

Accounts payable	$125.00
Accrued wages and taxes	120.00
Total	$245.00

    C)   Increase in current assets $295.00

        Increase in current liabilities   245.00

        *Net change in working capital $ 50.00

* Cash flow is not the same as net working capital.

firm's financial planning is made clear by the exhibit. Leasing is a financing alternative, and the cash flow of an internal-investment (capital-budgeting) decision may be influenced by the chosen financing alternative. It can be seen how the leasing decision not only influences the firm's cash flow in a particular accounting period, but how leasing as a financing choice should be integrated into the firm's overall planning process. While the preceding aspects of the decision to lease assets are important, necessary, and represent a more global view of the possible advantages of leasing, the financial manager is concerned with the more specific and direct benefits and costs of the leasing alternative.

SUMMARY

It is useful at this point to summarize the intent of this chapter. To the commercial enterprise, what are the advantages of acquiring productive assets through lease financing? The alternative to lease financing is to borrow funds and purchase the asset. The lease offers the firm

Exhibit 3-7B
Cash Flow and Financial Planning—Panel B

5) The Forecast: Once cash flow is determined - the future can be more realistically considered.

    A) How much cash will be needed?

    B) Tools to answer part A: Pro-forma analysis; cash budget

    C) Refinements to the analysis constructed from part B: accurate profit prediction; interest payments on new borrowing; a clear idea of the source of funds.

6) The Financial Plan:

    A) Major elements:

        1) dollars needed per time period;

        2) source (banks, investors, etc.)

        3) the term or maturity of loans [lease-vs-borrow (buy) analysis]

    B) Use of the financial plan: Financial plan outlines detail of short-term and long-term expenditures in overall budget.

7) The Strategic Plan

    A) The strategic plan outlines company's specific competencies - relates directly to specific products and markets 5-10 years into the future.

    B) The strategic plan (of which the financial plan is an integral part) is implemented through the treasurer's function (planning for and acquiring funds) and the controller's function (allocation of capital through capital budgeting).

    C) Primary elements of capital budgeting:

        1) Cost estimation (fixed assets, installation, working capital)

        2) Cash inflow estimation (increased profit and/or cost savings)

        3) Required rate of return (based on capital costs)

        4) Post-audit

flexibility generally not available with the borrow-and-purchase alternative. This flexibility is most readily seen in the case of cancelable leases. As stated above, this type of lease offers the user the ability to "lay-off" machinery and equipment in the case of an economic downturn.

Administrative costs are attached to the purchase and use of assets and to leased assets as well; however, generally the costs are lower for the use of leased assets. The lessor is usually primarily responsible for the maintenance, record-keeping, and disposal of the asset. This advantage may be a very large one for those firms that use large numbers of assets that have the characteristics of "operating-lease type" of equipment. Examples include office machinery, motor vehicles, and similar, relatively short-duration assets.

Another leasing advantage of great importance to users of assets is low-cost maintenance. The maintenance of leased assets is often the responsibility of the lessor, or a maintenance contract is offered at a known cost. Either maintenance alternative reduces uncertainty for the user. In periods of economic uncertainty either for the lessee or within the general economy such reduction of uncertainty is very important, as it permits added flexibility in cash-flow concerns and other critical matters of a firm.

An essential part of the advantage of leasing is the cost of leasing relative to the cost of the borrow (purchase) alternative. As we note throughout this chapter, the cost of leasing is often vague and difficult to specify. In this instance, we refer to the equivalent of a loan's annual percentage rate (APR) for the lease alternative. The lease-pricing evidence indicates no logical and consistent practice. Therefore, the lessee is left to pay whatever the lessor imposes as a lease note in most instances. It is precisely due to confusion about the pricing issue that the lessee is under considerable pressure to ensure equitable treatment in a lease transaction in order to reap leasing's full advantage.

NOTES

1. *Leasing and Tax Reform: A Guide Through the Maze* (Stamford, CT: General Electric Credit Corporation, 1987, pamphlet), p. 12.

2. R. L. Cason, "Leasing, Asset Lines and Uncertainty: A Practitioner's Comments," *Financial Management* 16 (Summer 1987), pp. 13–17.

3. T. E. Copeland, and J. F. Weston, "A Note on the Evaluation of Cancellable Operating Leases," *Financial Management* 11 (Summer 1982), pp. 60–67.

4. M. E. Bayless, and J. D. Diltz, "An Empirical Study of the Debt Displacement Effects of Leasing," *Financial Management* 15 (Winter 1986), pp. 3–60.

4

Techniques of Financial Analysis*

The analysis of financial leases, including comparison of the financial lease to the buy-borrow alternative, is dependent upon two interrelated ideas: the "mathematics of finance" and capital budgeting. The mathematics of finance includes the concepts of present and future value analysis. Capital budgeting includes the important concept known as discounted cash flow analysis. This chapter is a primer or practical guide, intended to review or introduce these important concepts.

In making financial decisions, we often face questions that require us to employ methods to account for the time value of money. For example, what amount would we have in one year if we accepted $100 and invested it at 6%? Or, if given a choice between having $100 a year from now and a sum of money today that we could invest at 6%, what would that amount be? Or, if we invest $100 today and receive $115 two years from now, what rate of return are we earning? Solutions to problems like these can be obtained by methods that we collectively call the mathematics of finance. In this book, few topics are more important because many of the financial decision-making techniques we present in the chapters that follow employ these methods. For this reason, it is extremely important to understand thoroughly the materials in this chapter before proceeding to other topics.

COMPOUND VALUE

Future value (or, as it is sometimes called, *compound value*) simply means that interest is paid on any interest that has accumulated in the account or investment. To illustrate this concept, consider a $1000

*A portion of this chapter was contributed by William F. Kennedy, Ph.D.

deposit in a bank account that pays 6% interest annually, but does not compound the interest. (This is sometimes called *simple interest*.) How much would you have in the account in two years? The interest would be $1000 times 6%, or $60 per year. Thus, in two years you would have your original $1000 deposit plus $120 in interest, for a total balance of $1120.

Now suppose the bank compounded the interest annually. In other words, at the end of one year, the $60 interest was credited to your account, and interest was paid on this in future periods. How much would you have in your account at the end of two years? We can calculate the balance as follows:

At the End of:	Beginning Balance	+	Interest	=	Ending Balance
Year 1	1,000	+	(1,000 x .06)	=	$1,060.00
Year 2	1,060	+	(1,060 x .06)	=	$1,123.60

Because the interest was compounded, we ended the two-year period with $3.60 more than if it were not compounded. While this may seem like a relatively small difference, we shall see that compounding can have a very profound effect over a number of years.

In calculating compound value, we are essentially trying to determine what amount we will have in an account or investment after a specified period of time has passed. The basic formula for this calculation is:

$$FV = PV(1 + k)^t \qquad\qquad (1)$$

where
  FV = the balance in the account after t periods have passed
  PV = the present value, or initial investment
  k = the interest rate
  t = the number of years the balance remains in the account.

To illustrate the computation of compound value, assume that you deposited $1000 in a bank account today paying 6% interest compounded annually. How much would you have in the account four years from now? The calculations are:

$$
\begin{aligned}
FV &= PV(1 + k)^t \\
&= 1000\,(1 + .06)^4 \\
&= 1000\,(1.2625) \\
&= \$1262.50.
\end{aligned}
$$

While these calculations are relatively straightforward, they could become extremely cumbersome if you were computing compound value for a long period of time. Imagine how difficult it would be if, in the preceding example, we were interested in finding the compound value of $1000 earning 6% over a period of 15 years!

Fortunately, many handheld calculators are preprogrammed to calculate compound interest easily. In addition, tables (such as those contained in the Appendix to this book) are readily available and greatly simplify the calculations. To illustrate the use of these tables, consider the question just posed: How much would you have in an account after 15 years if your initial deposit was $1000 and interest was compounded annually at the rate of 6%? The appropriate formula is:

$$FV = PV \,(FVIF) \tag{2}$$

where FVIF is the future-value interest factor for the indicated years and the interest rate is the value of $(1 + k)^t$.

Now turn to Table A-4 in the Appendix. To find the appropriate FVIF, look across the columns until you find the interest rate, in this case 6%. Now look down this column until you find the FVIF associated with 15 periods, in this case FVIF = 2.3966. Thus, the compound value of $1000 at 6% after 15 years will be:

$$FV = 2.3966 \,(1000) = \$2396.60.$$

After 15 years at 6% compounded annually, you would have roughly 2.4 times your original investment in your account.

The Miracle of Compound Interest

The amount an investment will be worth after a period of time depends on three factors: initial investment, interest rate, and the time it is permitted to compound. Even a relatively small initial investment will grow to huge proportions if left to compound for a long enough period.

To illustrate, consider the following often-told story concerning the sale of Manhattan Island by the Canarsee Indians to Dutch explorers in 1626. The Indians have often been criticized for selling this valuable real estate for only $24 worth of trinkets. However, they may have suffered a "bum rap" for a couple of reasons. First of all, so the story goes, these Indians did not really own the island, and were merely fishing there when the explorers arrived. No one can be accused of a lack of shrewdness in selling something he or she does not own! But even had the Indians owned the island, they might not have made such a bad deal. If they had deposited the $24 in an investment earning 8%, and allowed this amount to compound annually until 1990, they would be worth approximately $35 trillion! They probably would be able to buy back not only Manhattan Island, land and buildings included, but perhaps the rest of New York State as well.

Present Value

The concepts of compound value presented in the preceding section are designed to help answer this type of question: How much will a deposit or investment be worth at some future time if interest is compounded annually at a given rate? Sometimes, however, we may be interested in a somewhat different question: How much will I need to invest today, earning a stated rate of interest, in order to have a certain amount at a future time? For example, how much would I need to deposit in an account, today earning 8% interest compounded annually, in order to have $1000 three years from now?

This problem may be solved by use of the following formula:

$$PV = \sum_{t=1}^{N} \frac{FV}{(1 + k)^t} \qquad (3)$$

All of the terms are defined in the preceding section. As a matter of fact, it is easy to see that the above equation is merely a rearrangement of Eq. (1).

Now to answer our question, What is the initial investment required to accumulate $1000 three years from now if we are paid 8% interest?

$$PV = \frac{1000}{(1 + .08)^3}$$

$$= \frac{1000}{(1.2597)} = \$793.84$$

Let us check this answer by using the compound value tables from the Appendix:

$$FV = PV(FVIF)_{8\%, \text{ 3 years}}$$
$$= 793.84 \ (1.2597)$$
$$= \$1000.00$$

Again, we would rarely have to use Eq. (3) in computing present values. Tables such as Table A-2 in the Appendix make these computations relatively easy. One need only multiply the future sum by the appropriate present-value interest factor (PVIF). To illustrate, assume that you need to have $10,000 ten years from now. How large a deposit must you make in an account earning 6% in order to have this amount at the end of 10 years? The formula is

$$PV = FV(PVIF) \qquad (4)$$

where PVIF is the present-value interest factor from Table A-2. The calculations are

$$PV = 10,000 \ (.5584)$$
$$= \$5584.$$

The PVIF was found in Table A-2 by looking across the 10-year row to the 6% column. Equation (4) represents the discounting process.

We can see the power of compound interest again by using the same table to find out how a relatively large sum can result from a relatively small investment today, if allowed to compound for a long enough period. Let us say that you have determined that you plan to chuck the workaday world in 30 years and spend the remainder of your days as a beach bum. Since your needs will be relatively modest (although you will have heavy expenses for surfboard wax), you could probably achieve your goal if you could amass $100,000. How much would you need to invest today in a government security paying 12%, compounded annually, to have your $100,000 in 30 years? This is the same as solving for the present value of $100,000 30 years from now at 12%, and the solution is

$$PV = \$100,000 \ (.0334)$$
$$= \$3340.$$

Yes, a mere $3340 investment today would do it!

Compound Value of an Annuity

We are often interested in knowing how much we will accumulate over a given period of time if we make regular periodic payments to an account or investment. We refer to this regular, even stream of payments for a definite period of time as an *annuity*. If the payments occur at the end of each period, it is termed an *ordinary annuity*. If payments are made at the beginning of each period, it is called an *annuity due*.

Ordinary Annuities

Let us say that you have decided to embark on a regular savings program. Each year, when you receive your tax-refund check, you plan to place $100 in a bank account paying 6% interest, compounded annually. Your first contribution will be made one year from today, thus you have established an ordinary annuity. The stream of payments to this account for the first three years is illustrated by the time line in Exhibit 4-1.

The first payment remains in the account for two years, so at the end of the annuity period it has earned a total of $12.36 in interest. The second payment is in the account long enough to earn one year's interest, so it is worth $106. The final payment of $100, of course, earns no interest. Thus, the total value of our stream of payments is $318.36.

We can easily solve this sort of problem using Table A-3 in the Appendix. The formula for the future value of an ordinary annuity is

$$FV_a = PMT\,(FVIF_a) \tag{5}$$

where
$\quad$ FV_a = compound value of an annuity
$\quad$ PMT = annual payment
$\quad$ $FVIF_a$ = compound value interest factor for an annuity (from Table A-3).

Using this formula to solve our example,

$$
\begin{aligned}
FV_a &= 100\,(FVIF_{a,\ 6\%,\ 3\ \text{yrs}}) \\
&= 100\,(3.1836) \\
&= \$318.36.
\end{aligned}
$$

Exhibit 4-1
Payment Time Line, Ordinary Annuity

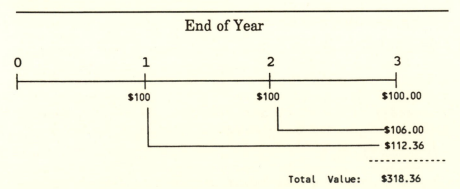

Total Value: $318.36

The $FVIF_a$ was obtained from the 6% column, period row 3, in Table A-3. Let us use this concept to illustrate again the power of compound interest. Assume that you can make a $2000 annual contribution to an Individual Retirement Account over the next 25 years. If this account will earn you 12% compounded annually, how much will you have in the account at the end of 25 years?

$$FV_a = 2000 \, (FVIF_{a, \, 12\%, \, 25 \text{ yrs}})$$
$$= 2000 \, (133.33)$$
$$= \$266,660$$

Thus, a contribution of $2000 per year to an IRA earning 12% would make you a quarter-millionaire in 25 years.

Annuities Due

On occasion, the annual annuity payment will be made at the beginning of the period rather than at the end. If this is the case, an annuity is due and a slight adjustment is required to the compound-value formula. The formula for an annuity due is

$$FV_a \text{ due} = PMT \, (FVIF_a) \, (1 + k) \qquad (6)$$

where k is the rate of interest.

To illustrate, return to the example used in the preceding section. We were interested in knowing how much we would accumulate in three years if we made a $100 annual contribution to a bank account paying 6%, compounded annually. Before, however, we assumed that the payments would be made at the end of each year. In this instance, we assume that the payments are made at the beginning of each period. The time line now resembles the one appearing in Exhibit 4-2. Because contributions to the account have a longer period to accrue interest, we end with a total value of $337.46, compared to $318.36 if we make payments at the end of the period. To solve this problem using our formula,

$$FV_a = \$100 \, (3.1836) \, (1 + .06)$$
$$= \$100 \, (3.3746)$$
$$= \$337.46.$$

Present Value of an Annuity

In finance we are often faced with the present value of an annuity problem similar to the following example. An investment will pay

Exhibit 4-2
Payment Time Line, Annuity Due

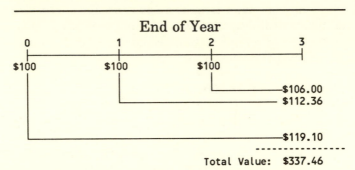

$1000 per year for 10 years. If you desire a 12% annual rate of return, what would you be willing to pay for this investment? Notice that we are talking about the present worth of a stream of even payments, that is, the present value of an annuity. The formula for this type of problem is

$$PV_a = \sum_{t=1}^{N} \frac{PMT}{(1 + k)^t} \tag{7}$$

where
  PV_a = the present value of an ordinary annuity
  PMT = the annual payment or receipt
  t = the year
  k = the discount.

The solution to our problem, then would be

$$PV_a = \frac{1000}{(1 + .12)^1} + \frac{1000}{(1 + .12)^2} + \ldots + \frac{1000}{(1 + .12)^{10}} = \$5650.$$

If we paid $5650 for an investment providing us $1000 per year for 10 years, we would be earning a 12% annual rate.

Fortunately, we have tables, such as Table A-4 in the Appendix, that make calculations quite simple. We can solve the problem using the following formula:

$$PV_a = PMT\,(PVIF_a) \tag{8}$$

where $PVIF_a$ is the present value interest factor for an annuity (Table A-4). Thus, the solution to the problem is

$$PV_a = 1000\ (PVIF_{a,\ 12\%,\ 10\ years})$$
$$= 1000\ (5.650)$$
$$= \$5650.$$

Obviously, as the required return on the investment increases, the present value of the annuity will decline. For example, what if we demanded a 14% rate of return on this stream of payments, rather than 12%? The present value then becomes

$$PV_a = 1000\ (PVIF_{a,\ 14\%,\ 10\ yrs})$$
$$= 1000\ (5.216)$$
$$= \$5216.$$

Since we wanted a higher rate of return, the amount we were willing to pay for the investment declined. It is important to remember that as the desired return on the investment increases, the present value will decrease.

In the example above, we assumed that the annual receipts would come at the end of each year, again an ordinary annuity. What if the receipts were to come at the beginning of each period? Then we would have an annuity due, and once again we would need to make an adjustment to our formula

$$PV_a\ due = PMT\ (PVIF_a)\ (1 + k). \qquad (9)$$

For our problem, if the payments were received at the beginning of each year, the present value would be

$$PV_a = 1000\ (5.216)\ (1 + .12)$$
$$= 1000\ (5.8419)$$
$$= \$5841.90.$$

The present value of an annuity due will always be more than that of an ordinary annuity because of the compounding of each of the payments.

Perpetuities

On occasion we may come across an annuity where the annual payments will last forever. This stream of payments is called a *perpetuity*. An example would be a preferred stock issue that has no maturity, but promises to pay a stated annual dividend forever. How could we determine the present value of this type investment? One need only divide the annual payment or receipt by the required discount rate

$$PV_{\text{perpetuity}} = \frac{PMT}{k}.$$ (10)

For example, suppose we offered an investment that would pay us $100 per year forever. What would be the present value of this perpetual stream of income if we required a 10% rate of return? The solution is

$$PV_{\text{perpetuity}} = \frac{100}{.10} = \$1000.$$

This technique may also be used when the period of payments is very long, though perhaps not forever, and will provide a good approximation of the present value when all cash flows have been discounted. For example, the present value of an annuity of $100 per year for 50 years at 10% would be $991.48, very close to the $1000 computed if the stream of income were to last forever.

Review

We have looked at five basic types of problems involving the interest factor in financial decisions. These problems are summarized in Exhibit 4-3. We are now in a position to use these basic concepts to solve other types of problems, such as determining rates of return or loan payments.

EFFECTIVE RATES OF RETURN

Let us say you have the opportunity to purchase an acre of land for $2000. You believe that in 10 years you can sell this property for $6000, or three times your investment. Is this a good investment? The answer depends, of course, on how your rate of return compares to other investments of similar risk. But how can you determine what your rate of return is? Remember that the formula for future value is

$$FV = PV \, (FVIF).$$

In this problem, we know what the future value is (FV = $6000) and we know what the present value is (PV = $2000). We need to solve for the FVIF.

$$6{,}000 = 2{,}000 \; (\text{FVIF})$$

$$\text{FVIF} = \frac{6000}{2000} = 3.$$

Now, we can go to the FVIF table (Table A-1) and look across period row 10 until we find the factor 3.000. We do not have a factor of exactly 3.000 in the table, but we can see that it is between the factor for 10%, where the FVIF = 2.5937, and 12%, where the FVIF = 3.1058. Thus,

Exhibit 4-3
Interest Factor Sample Problems

Type of Problem	Example Problem	Formula	Contained in:
Compound Value	How much will I have in three years in a bank account paying 6% interest if I deposit $1000 today? FV = $1000 x (1.1910) = $1,191.00	FV = PV(FVIF)	A-1
Present Value	How much must I deposit today in an account earning 6% interest in order to have $1191 three years from now? PV = $1191 x (0.8396) = $999.96 or $1000	PV = PV(PVIF)	A-2
Future Value of an Ordinary Annuity *	How much will I have in a bank account paying 6% interest if I deposit $1000 a year for three years? FVA = $1000 x (3.1836) = $3183.60	FVA = PMT(FVIFA)	A-3

(continued)

**Exhibit 4-3
(Continued)**

Present Value of an Annuity*	What is the value today of a stream of payments of $1000 per year for three years if the required return is 6%? PVA = $1000 x (2.6730) = $2673	PVA = PMT(PVIFA)	A-4
Perpetuities	What is the value of a stream of payments of $1000 per year forever if the interest rate required is 6%? $PV_{perpetuity}$ = $1000 /.06 = $16,666.67	$PV_{perpetuity}$ = PMT / k	

*These formulas are for ordinary annuities. If we are dealing with an annuity due we must multiply the right side of each equation by $(1+k)$.

the rate of return we would earn on a $2000 investment that returned us $6,000 ten years later would be between 10% and 12%. Of course, we would like to be a bit more precise about our rate of return so that we could intelligently compare it with alternative investments. The use of linear interpolation would help us find the "approximate exact" rate.

Linear interpolation involves setting up a proportion and solving for the value that would, when added to the lowest interest rate in our range, provide us with the rate of return. As a first step in this process, set up the relationship in the following manner:

Interest Rate	FVIF
10%	2.5937
k	3.0000
12%	3.1058

Our rate of return is k, which would have an FVIF of 3.000. There is some value x that, when added to 10%, would give us the return. Look at the relationship again:

	Interest Rate	FVIF	Difference in FVIFs
	10%	2.5937	
x%			.4063
2%	k	3.0000	.5121
	12%	3.1058	

There is an x% difference between our rate of return k and 10%, and a difference of 2% between our "bracket" of 10% and 12%. On the other side, there is a difference of .4063 between the FVIFs for 10% and x%, and a .5121 difference between the FVIFs for 10% and 12%. We can set up a proportion.

$$\frac{x}{2} = \frac{.4063}{.5121}$$

We are saying that x is to 2 as .4063 is to .5121. Cross-multiplying we have

$$.5121x = .8126$$

$$x = \frac{.8126}{.5121} = 1.59\%.$$

Thus, our rate of return on the property investment is 10% + 1.59% = 11.59%. We would compare this rate of return with that offered by alternative investments of similar risk. If we could get a better return elsewhere, we would not be interested in this purchase.

The process for determining the interest rate on annuities is similar. For example, you are offered an investment for $10,000 that will pay you $3000 per year for five years. What rate of return will you be earning? We can use the basic formula for the present value of an annuity to solve for the PVIF:

$$PV_a = PMT\,(PVIF_a)$$
$$10,000 = 3000\,(PVIF_a)$$
$$PVIF_a = 3.3333.$$

We now refer to Table A-4 and look along the 5-year row. We find that the rate is between 14% and 16%. By interpolation, we find that the "approximate exact" rate is

	Interest Rate	PVIF	Difference in PVIF
	14%	3.4331	.0998
x%			
2%	k	3.3333	.1588
	16%	3.2743	

$$\frac{x}{2} = \frac{.0998}{.1588}$$

$$x = 1.25$$

$$k = 14\% + 1.25\% = 15.25\%.$$

We would compare this rate to that available on alternative investments of similar risk.

INTRODUCTION TO CAPITAL BUDGETING

Attention now turns to a specific application of present- and compound-value concepts: capital budgeting. Lease financing is a sub-set of the capital budgeting process. It is only within the context of capital budgeting that the analysis of financial leases becomes relevant. Capital budgeting provides the framework for determining which assets will add the most value to the firm. Leasing is a possible means of financing the assets.

The process of capital budgeting, also referred to as "asset expansion" or "internal-investment analysis," is intended to provide the firm with an optimum pool of fixed assets. Capital budgeting is of critical importance for that reason. The capital budgeting techniques developed in this chapter are used in those other managerial decisions that require cost/benefit analysis, for example, bond refunding and advertising decisions.

The capital budgeting process generally involves the following stages: origination of beneficial expenditure ideas; classifying the expenditure idea; estimating relevant cash flows that are directly related to the expenditures; and determining which expenditure is best for a particular objective. The discussion that follows elaborates upon these steps and additional concerns.

Origin of Capital Budgeting Ideas

In a typical U.S. firm, there are individuals engaged in marketing, cost-accounting, planning, and other managerial functions. Each of the functions is a potential source of capital-expenditure ideas. Marketing personnel meet the firm's customers, and information is exchanged concerning the best way to serve the ultimate consumer. This information will find its way to the firm's "product-creating" areas, which include accounting, marketing, and engineering (or product development, in the case of a non-manufacturing firm). If the idea has merit, in a cost/benefit sense, it may become a capital budgeting "project" to be evaluated by top-level financial management. *Project* is a term that means an investment idea intended for a specific business objective.

The firm's engineers or product-development staff also share the responsibility of adding to the firm's list of potentially profitable expenditure ideas. Product-development personnel review production processes and plant layout as a normal part of their daily duties. As a result, opportunities for cost-reduction through improvements in the production process are located and studied. Such cost-reduction activities usually require cash outlay. The expenditure will be worthwhile, however, if the discounted expected savings exceed the discounted implementation cost. Project evaluations by the product-development staff will usually involve the firm's cost-accounting personnel. Accountants typically provide the data from which the cost-saving estimates can be made.

Capital budgeting, then, is the sum of all the firm's activities that relate to the economic evaluation of a proposed asset acquisition. Capital budgeting activities determine the relative merits of different asset-acquisition proposals by estimating the cash inflows of different projects, estimating the cash outlays, and estimating the overall rate of return from the proposed asset and how much value it adds to the firm, if any. The section that follows describes the entire set of capital-budgeting activities in a sequence closely related to that typically found in actual practice.

The flow of capital expenditure ideas in the firm is represented in Exhibit 4-4.

Classification of Capital Projects and Estimation of Relevant Cash Flows

Capital investment projects may not share the same risk characteristics. Great effort is undertaken by corporate management to measure the risk inherent in the projects' expected cash-flow streams accurately. One method of assessing the risk of capital projects is to classify them according to broad-risk categories. For example, a firm may have capital outlays for new products, cost-reduction expenditures, and expenditures for improving existing products. Each of these vary according to their risk. The economic evaluation is adjusted to reflect the differences in risk.

Exhibit 4-4
Origin of Capital-Budgeting Ideas and the Evaluation Process

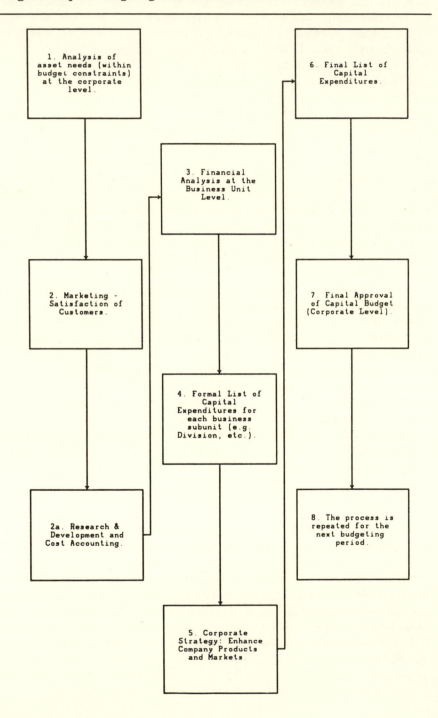

The following list is useful in understanding classifications according to risk:

Highest risk	→	New products for new markets
Next highest risk	→	New products for existing markets
Average risk	→	Improve existing products for existing markets
Low risk	→	Replacement expenditures
Risk neutral	→	Pollution abatement, employee safety, etc.

The list represents only one way of classifying capital projects based on historical or predicted risk characteristics. The purpose here is to point out management's awareness of the relative risk among cash flow streams. These risks bear directly on the return. The expected return from an expenditure means that the cash flows are weighted relative to a probabilistic estimate. That estimate can be "adjusted" based upon the risk classification of the expenditure. This adjustment may be an increased or decreased discount rate, depending on the level of uncertainty, or a more quantitative approach to the risk/return relationship. The more quantitative approaches may include the use of certainty-equivalents or the use of simulation, topics that are beyond the scope of this book.

It becomes the top-level financial manager's responsibility to conduct an analysis of the proposed expenditure, or project. This standard analysis begins with verification of the project's cash flows. The outlay of cash for property, plant and equipment, and such items as working capital need to be estimated, along with estimates of the most likely cash flows resulting from project approval and implementation. In the simplest sense, such funds may be thought of as profit-after-tax or cash inflows. As is pointed out below, however, project cash flow involves more than cash receipts in excess of costs.

Independent Projects and Mutually Exclusive Projects

There is more than one way to perform a task. Capital expenditure analysis often involves comparing different alternatives, one of which can be accepted. The accepted alternatives are called mutually exclusive projects. Accepting one alternative automatically means that the others are rejected. The projects that remain are independent; in a typical firm with many levels of financial, accounting, and marketing management, the mutually exclusive projects are easily determined at one level or another before the final capital budget is approved.

EVALUATION OF PROJECT CASH FLOWS

The economic benefit of a capital project is of great importance to a firm. Further in our discussion, it is apparent that some projects are classified as beneficial for reasons other than their providing an economic return. At present, however, it is important to understand how a firm decides whether the positive flow from an independent project provides an economic benefit.

For example, consider a project the cost of which is $10,000, and the annual undiscounted cash inflows are $3000 per year for six years. The evaluative techniques described below illustrate the economic (cost-versus-benefit) analysis of such a capital expenditure proposal.

Payback

One of the ways in which the economic benefit of an expenditure may be assessed is the time necessary to recoup the cash outlay from the project's inflows of cash. The technique is called *payback*. Referring to the preceding simple cash expenditures and receipts, the payback period for that stream of cash is three years and four months. The payback period was determined as follows:

$$\begin{aligned}
\text{Cash (outflow)} &= (\$10,000) \\
\text{Inflows (per year)} \quad &\ 3,000 \\
&\ 3,000 \\
&\ 3,000 \\
&\ 3,000 \\
&\ 3,000 \\
&\ 3,000.
\end{aligned}$$

In three years, $9000 of the project's cost will be returned to the firm. In one-third year, or four months of Year 4, the remaining $1000 will be received, assuming cash inflows are received evenly throughout each year. If the cash-inflow stream were not an annuity, the payback period would still amount to an accumulation of the inflows of cash until such flows equaled the project's cost.

There are two weaknesses of the payback approach: first cash receipts beyond the payback period are not considered, and second, the cash receipts considered in the calculations are not discounted. The payback method does not consider the time value of money.

Recent research into actual financial practices of firms, however, indicates that the payback method is often used by many firms. The reason for its continued use is understandable. The method has appeal because it is simple and easy to understand. More important, however, is its significance for a firm whose investment dollars are severely limited. In this instance, the question of how soon the dollars invested in one project become available for investment elsewhere is most critical in the investment decision process. Projects with faster payback will likely be preferred and chosen in such firms.

Discounted Cash Flow Methods of Project Evaluation

The following discussion outlines the net present value (NPV) and internal rate of return (IRR) methods of cash expenditure and receipt evaluation. Discounted cash flow methods are necessary because cash received or spent in the future must be valued in present-value dollars, based on when it will be received in the future and the relevant opportunity cost of money. In the use of discounted cash flow methods, NPV provides a result in dollars and is relatively easy to interpret. IRR is expressed in percent terms and may be compared directly to opportunity cost, or the cost of capital. In selection of capital expenditure proposals, both methods provide equivalent and reliable results. When expenditure proposals are being ranked, finance literature generally agrees that NPV is the superior discounted method. The reasons for IRR's inferiority are beyond the scope of this book. The two methods, however, are closely related. The following discussion illustrates the two methods.

Net Present Value (NPV) Method

The evaluation of cash flows expected in the future requires consideration of the time value of money. We know that a dollar received today has more value (its value is more certain) than a dollar expected to be received in the future. The net present value method of expected future cash evaluation permits a time-value evaluation of cash expenditures and receipts. As shown previously, the time-value adjustment is accomplished by discounting these flows at some rate that (it is hoped) adequately reflects the uncertainty of the flows.

The NPV formula is as follows:

$$\text{NPV} = \sum_{t=1}^{N} \frac{\text{CF}_t}{(1 + k)^t} - I. \tag{11}$$

The net present value of a series of cash inflows X is equal to the sum of those flows discounted at a rate k minus the initial investment (I). The initial investment, in Period 0, usually represents the outlay necessary to obtain the cash inflows.

Returning to the numerical example used in the payback discussion, a discount rate of 10% is assumed. From the data presented in Exhibit 4-5, an example of the NPV can be calculated. Assume that the cost- and cash-inflow data have been forecast through the combined effort of marketing, accounting, engineering, and finance personnel, and represents their best estimate. The sum of the discounted cash inflows is $13,065.60, the cost of the project is $10,000; thus the NPV is equal to $13,065.60 minus $10,000 or $3,065.60. How do we interpret this figure? The net present value represents dollar value added to the firm. That is, NPV is the excess of cash received over cost.

We assume that the firm is interested in incremental flow rather than the accounting profit from a capital expenditure. Cash flow for a company called Microplunk is determined in Exhibit 4-6, using the company's estimate of sales and cost data for a new type of computer. Depreciation expense is a non-cash charge; it reduces the amount of taxes paid, but no cash is paid out by the firm for depreciation. Therefore, accounting income understates cash flow from operations by the amount of the firm's depreciation expense.

The Internal Rate of Return (IRR) Method

The return received from a capital expenditure may be expressed in terms of a percentage amount. The return earned on a production facility, a new piece of machinery, or some other expenditure can be viewed in the same manner as that earned on a bank account. Another technique for a time-value evaluation is called the internal rate of return (IRR). The formula for the IRR reveals the formula's similarity to the NPV method.

$$\sum_{t=1}^{N} \frac{CF_t}{(1 + k_{IRR})^t} - I = 0 \qquad (12)$$

Exhibit 4-5
Sample Data, Calculation of Net Present Value

Period	Cash Flow (1)	Present Value Factor at 10% (2)	Present Value [(1) x (2)] (3)
0	($10,000)	1.0000	($10,000.00)
1	3,000	0.9091	2,727.30
2	3,000	0.8264	2.479.20
3	3,000	0.7513	2,253.90
4	3,000	0.6830	2,049.00
5	3,000	0.6209	1,862.70
6	3,000	0.5645	1,693.50
TOTAL			$13,065.60

Exhibit 4-6
Determination of Cash Flow (Micro-plunk Company)

Microplunk Company	($000)
Sales (annual)	10,000
*Cost of goods sold	(7,500)
Gross profit	2,500
Selling expense	(500)

*Includes depreciation expense of $500.

Earnings before interest and taxes	2,000
Interest charges	(200)
Profit before tax	1,800
Taxes @ 50%	(900)
Profit after tax	900
Add back depreciation	500
	$1,400 = Cash flow

The formula requires finding the discount rate r, which, when applied to the cash flows, will make them equal to zero. To return to the earlier example, the IRR for the $10,000 expenditure, which yields the $3000 cash inflow for each of six years, is found as follows:

$$0 = \frac{\$3000}{(1 + r)} + \frac{\$3000}{(1 + r)^2} + \frac{\$3000}{(1 + r)^3} + \frac{\$3000}{(1 + r)^4}$$

$$+ \frac{\$3000}{(1 + r)^5} + \frac{\$3000}{(1 + r)^6} - \$10,000$$

The trial-and-error method provides a solution to the preceding problem. Application of a 20% rate provides a discounted cash inflow stream of $23.50. Interpolation permits a determination of the exact discount rate necessary to cause the cash inflows to equal the outflows.

First, however, it may be useful to discuss a significant aspect of our example. It is clear that the cash inflows constitute an annuity. In such a case, the IRR can be found through the use of present-value tables. For example:

$$\frac{\$10,000}{3,000} = 3.333$$

Referring to Table A-5 in the Appendix, the PVIFA of 3.333 represents a rate of return that closely approximates 20%. It is useful to know the exact return that the cash flow represents.

When the cash inflows in each period are not equal (hence, not an annuity), the IRR must be found by trial and error. Certain handheld calculators and computer programs permit direct computation of the IRR.

NPV and IRR are closely related in terms of informational content. In the on-going example, the discount rate initially applied to the cash inflows produced an NPV of $3,065.60. Since the NPV is greater than zero, the IRR for that series of flows must be greater than 10% – the discount rate in the NPV calculation. Indeed, the IRR was approximately 20%. An NPV of zero implies that the IRR is equal to the discount rate that produced the zero NPV. This idea may be more clearly illustrated by Exhibit 4-7. The graph and table in the exhibit point out the internal rates of return realized at varying levels of net present value. The relationship between these two measures is very close. One or the other is chosen based on whether information is desired in terms of dollars or percents.

Exhibit 4-7
Relationship between Internal Rate of Return and Net Present Value

```
   NPV ($)                                          IRR or Discount Rate          NPV
10,000   |
         |                                              0%                  $8,000.00
 8,000   |
         |                                              5%                   5,227.10
 6,000   |
         |                                             10%                   3,065.60
 4,000   |
         |                                             15%                   1,353.50
 2,000   |              IRR = 19.80%
         |                                             20%                  Approx. 0
     0   |---------------------------->  Discount Rate (IRR)
             5   10   15   20   25
```

Application of Discounted Cash Flow

The discounted cash flow methods presented above are used by business firms to select the desired projects and, once selected, to rank those projects. The need for ranking projects becomes most important for companies that are short of investment funds. Therefore, the projects ranked highest in terms of return or NPV may be implemented first. Of course, certain projects may have to be implemented regardless of return, such as pollution-control expenditures. These expenditures are not discretionary in nature and are classified on a "must do" basis.

When the firm considers two expenditure proposals or projects, it may wish to evaluate them with both NPV and IRR. If the evaluation includes ranking of the projects, a conflict may occur between the rank of one project and another. That is, the IRR and NPV may rank two or more projects differently. This conflict occurs because of the different reinvestment assumptions implicit in the two techniques. NPV is calculated based on a known reinvestment rate; IRR implicitly assumes reinvestment at the IRR itself, which may be unrealistic. The NPV has a more objective economic meaning (a positive NPV means that marginal revenue exceeds marginal cost, all else being equal), and it is sometimes more easily understood than IRR. The NPV amount represents value in dollars added to the firm.

The following example helps to summarize the ideas surrounding the techniques. We use data and information for the Andrea Knitting Company, a manufacturer of high-fashion leisurewear for men and women. Andrea needs an additional press to smooth large pieces of fabric before it is cut into smaller pieces. Company management has found a suitable machine that can be purchased for $15,000. The faster production process provided by the machine will produce positive cash flows each year for five years. Exhibit 4-8 contains the results of Andrea's cost accounting and financial analysis data concerning the project.

Column 2, Exhibit 4-8, shows the cost of the machine in Time Period 0 (the present) to be $15,000. In Column 3, the $500 is for the increase in inventory (fabric) necessary to accommodate additional press capacity. The depreciation in Column 5 represents straight-line depreciation on the new press. No salvage value will remain. Column 6 shows total cash flows each year—profit after tax plus the depreciation tax shield of $3,000 per year. Also, in Column 3, Year 5, the working capital will be recaptured; the inventory will be sold down to its old level and not replaced at the end of the project's life. The working-capital expenditure represents a cash inflow, or savings, of $500 in Year 5.

All of the figures in Exhibit 4-8 are incremental—these numbers, or cash flows, come about as a result of implementing only this project.

Exhibit 4-8
Financial Data (Andrea Knitting Company)

1	2	3	4	5	6
Time	Cost of Machine	Working Capital	Profit After Tax	Depreciation	Total Cash Inflow
0	($15,000)	-	-	-	-
1	-	(500)	1,000	$3,000	$3,500
2	-	-	2,500	3,000	5,500
3	-	-	3,000	3,000	6,000
4	-	-	4,800	3,000	7,800
5	-	500	5,000	3,000	8,500

With this information, the NPV, IRR, and payback for the machine can be calculated as follows:

Payback = 2 years, 11 months:
Cumulative Inflows = $4,000 Year 1
$9,500 Year 2
$15,500 Year 3.

Andrea needs $15,000 to totally recapture the cost of the machine. Only $5500 of Year 3 cash flows are needed to reach the $15,000 plateau. Thus, 5500/6000 = 92% of Year 3's flows = approximately 11 months. Two years and 11 months is the payback period.

The NPV of the project may be found as follows, assuming Andrea's discount rate or cost of capital is 12%:

Year			
0	($15,000)	$(PVIF_{.12,0})$ =	($15,000)
1	3,500	$(PVIF_{.12,1})$ =	3,125.15
2	5,500	$(PVIF_{.12,2})$ =	4,360.95
3	6,000	$(PVIF_{.12,3})$ =	4,270.80
4	7,000	$(PVIF_{.12,4})$ =	4,956.90
5	8,500	$(PVIF_{.12,5})$ =	4,822.90

The NPV, then, is $21,536.70 − 15,000 = $6,536.70.

The IRR must be found for this uneven cash-inflow stream by the trial-and-error method. It is clear that the IRR will be greater than 12% because the NPV is positive at 12%! Since it is often useful to begin the trial-and-error process between 15 and 20%, the highest point on that range may be of assistance. A hasty calculation indicates 20% is too low as the IRR. At 20%, the values of the cash flows equal $17,000.20. A larger discount rate is needed, so 26% is arbitrarily selected. At a discount rate of 26%, the sum of the discounted cash inflows is $15,410. Thus, 26% is very close to the discount rate that satisfies our IRR equation. Interpolation or a calculator solution, discussed above, would provide a number more exact than our approximation of 26%.

Based on the preceding example, Andrea Knitting should accept the project because of the favorable discounted cash flow results.

SUMMARY

This chapter presents one of the most important topics in finance: the time value of money. Many of the topics discussed in subsequent chapters build on the concepts presented here. While these concepts may at first appear confusing, there is no need for them to be. There are really only five basic types of problems to remember, and they are presented in Exhibit 4-9 for review. Using these five basic concepts, we are able to solve a number of types of financial problems. For example, we are able to determine the amount we will accumulate if we invest a given sum today, or over a period of years. Or, we can determine how much

Exhibit 4-9
Formulas—Compounding and Discounting

Type of Problem	Formula	Appendix
Compound Value	$FV = PV \times (FVIF)$	A-1
Present Value	$PV = FV \times (PVIF)$	A-2
Compound Value of an Annuity	$FV_a = PMT \times (FVIF_a)$	A-3
Present Value of an Annuity	$PV_a = PMT \times (PVIF_a)$	A-4
Perpetuities	$PV = PMT \div k$	

we need to invest today in order to have a certain sum in the future, or to withdraw a certain amount each year over a period of time. We can also use these concepts to find the rate of return we are earning on a given investment. The chapters that follow show how these important concepts can also be used to determine the value of investments and to make decisions regarding the acquisition of long-term assets.

The purpose of capital budgeting is to provide a means for asset expansion by a firm. A major task for the firm is to generate a steady stream of beneficial capital-budgeting ideas. The sources for these ideas include marketing personnel, strategic planning, production and engineering personnel, and various other sources of product/market information and data.

A primary concern within the capital budgeting process is the determination of relevant, incremental after-tax cash flows. Project cash flows may be evaluated through the use of several quantitative techniques. Among these techniques are payback, net present value, and internal rate of return.

REFERENCES

Brick, I. E., and D. G. Weaver. "A Comparison of Capital Budgeting Techniques in Identifying Profitable Investments." *Financial Management* 13 (Winter 1984): 29–39.

Brigham, E. F., and T. C. Tapley. "Financial Leverage and the Use of the Net Present Value Investment Criterion." *Financial Management* 14, no. 2 (Summer 1985): 48–53.

Cissell, R., and Helen Cissell. *Mathematics of Finance*. 4th ed. Boston, MA: Houghton Mifflin Company, 1973.

Hart, W. *Mathematics of Investment*. 5th ed. Lexington, MA: D. C. Heath and Company, 1975.

III

Reporting for Leases

5

Tax Reporting for Leases

Chapters 2 and 3 analyzed three primary factors responsible for fueling the explosive growth in the leasing industry. First, leases provide companies with a means of financing when traditional sources of financing are unattractive or unavailable. Second, leases minimize the risks of holding assets subject to technological obsolescence. Finally, leases present a variety of tax benefits.

The tax consequences relevant to a lease–buy decision include the effect of a swap of tax benefits, such as accelerated depreciation, for reduced lease payments. Other consequences include depreciation recapture, the alternative minimum tax, the tax treatment of rental payments, and the passive-activity-loss and at-risk rules.

Leasing is an attractive alternative for companies with exposure to the alternative minimum tax. The 1986 Tax Reform Act (1986 TRA) made the alternative-minimum-tax rules applicable to corporations, and included other provisions that affected the tax benefits of leasing. It repealed the investment tax credit, decreased the amount of accelerated-depreciation deductions, and repealed safe-harbor and financing leases. In the wake of 1986 TRA, many commentators lamented the questionable vitality of equipment leasing. However, their dire predictions have not necessarily been realized.

As Exhibit 5-1 shows, by replacing the Accelerated Cost Recovery System (ACRS) with Modified Accelerated Cost Recovery System (MACRS), repealing the investment tax credit, and imposing the alternative minimum tax, 1986 TRA increased the cost of asset ownership. As a result of the alternative minimum tax rules, leasing may be an even more attractive option, as this chapter and Chapter 8 explain. Another reason equipment leasing is still attractive is that equipment leasing offers advantages, independent of tax consequences.

Exhibit 5-1
Net Present Values of the Cost of Corporate Ownership for Selected Assets
Based on Accelerated Depreciation
(Expressed as a Percentage of Original Purchase Price)

Asset	A ACRS ITC	B ACRS No ITC	C MACRS No AMTS	D MACRS AMTS	E (C-A)/A	F (D-A)/A	G (D-C)/C
Passenger Cars	54.4	58.8	71.4	83.8	31.3	54.0	17.4
Computers	53.3	60.8	71.4	83.8	34.0	57.2	17.4
Typewriters	53.3	60.8	71.4	84.1	34.0	57.8	17.8
Heavy Trucks	53.3	60.8	71.4	84.9	34.0	59.3	18.9
Files, Cabinets Tables	53.3	60.8	72.8	87.2	36.6	63.6	19.8
Desks	53.3	60.8	72.8	87.9	36.6	64.9	20.7

Source: J. Burns, K. Hreha, and S. Luttman, "Corporate Leasing versus Property Ownership under the Tax Reform Act of 1986," *The Journal of the American Taxation Association* (Fall 1989), p. 109.

Tax consequences are one of many complex factors that influence
whether a company should lease or purchase an asset. While tax considerations may weigh in favor of a lease decision, other factors may
tip the scales in another direction. Tax considerations alone cannot determine whether a firm should purchase or lease an asset. Decision-
makers should consult business and tax advisors for the overall implications regarding the particular transaction.

This book approaches the lease–buy decision primarily from the lessee's perspective. This chapter, however, addresses both lessor and lessee tax consequences because, in certain cases, the Internal Revenue
Service (IRS) may look beyond the form of a lease. Tax law looks
beyond the forms of transactions, and imposes tax benefits based on
their economic substance. A lease has economic substance to the extent that it subjects the lessor to the burdens and benefits of the leased
property. Accordingly, if the IRS determines a lessor retains only nominal ownership rights in the property, the IRS will treat the lease as a
conditional, deferred-payment sales contract. Thus, the lessor will be
treated as having sold the leased asset. The lessee is treated as a
purchaser of the leased property. This chapter emphasizes the criteria
used by the IRS to determine whether or not lessors retain nominal
ownership rights, and highlights the ensuing tax consequences. Exhibit 5-2 delineates the tax issue relevant to the lease–buy decision. A
more detailed analysis of the consequences could fill several hand-
books.

Exhibit 5-2
Tax Issues Relevant to the Lease–Buy Decision

LESSEE	LESSOR
Passive activity rules	Passive activity rules
Rent expense	Rent income
Depreciate leasehold improvements	Depreciation
Interest expense deductions	Interest expense deductions
Alternative minimum tax	Alternative minimum tax
	Section 179 immediate expensing
	Recapture

CONSEQUENCES OF LEASE TRANSACTIONS NOT QUALIFYING AS TRUE LEASES

As indicated in Chapter 2, parties may enter into leases as a means of transferring tax benefits to the party most able to utilize them. For example, a company that needs a new machine has the option to lease or purchase it. If the company purchases the machine, it would be entitled to deduct depreciation. However, the value of the deduction is reduced or eliminated if the company is in a low marginal tax bracket or has no taxable income. Therefore, a "loss company" might seek to "sell" those benefits to a more profitable company. The profitable company may purchase the asset and lease it to the loss company. The profitable company could utilize the tax benefits, and pass the tax savings to the loss company, in the form of reduced lease payments. This transaction is in substance an installment sale. Depending on the lease terms, the lessee in reality owns the asset, and, from a tax perspective, all that occurred was the wholesaling of tax benefits to the lessee.

The Internal Revenue Service is sensitive to transactions, such as the one described, that are structured solely for tax considerations. Accordingly, the IRS may disregard the form of certain transactions and recast transactions to reflect economic reality. A lease transaction lacks economic reality if the lessor is merely a nominal property owner that does not retain the benefits and burdens of property ownership. Benefits of property ownership include the use of the asset and potential for gain on disposition. Ownership burdens include responsibility for maintenance and repair costs, impairment of working capital, and the risk of loss on disposition.

Chapter 2 introduced the concepts of financing and operating leases. The terms of financing leases are quite similar to provisions found in conditional-sales agreements: the lessee bears responsibility for taxes and maintenance and the lease term generally coincides with the asset's useful life. Because the substance of the financing lease is a sale, tax law treats the lessee under a financing lease as the owner of the property. Under an operating lease, the lessor is treated as the economic owner of the property. Parties must be sensitive to this issue – IRS recasts of transactions subject the parties to unexpected tax consequences.

Tax law, generally accepted accounting principles, and general contract law have developed different criteria for determining the substance of a lease. Chapter 6 enumerates the tests used for accounting purposes to determine the validity of a lease. Both tax and generally accepted principles provide that a lease that transfers benefits and burdens of ownership is in substance a financing transaction. However, the criteria used to determine the existence of a lease for accounting purposes do not always conform to that used for tax purposes. Therefore, parties cannot trigger application of the most favorable tax consequences by casting the transaction in the form of an otherwise enforceable lease or sale.

Several major consequences face the lessor when a lease is recast as a conditional sales contract.[1] First, amounts received by the supposed lessor as rent, taxable as ordinary income, instead represent payments on the sales price of the property. The gain on disposition may be accorded capital-gain status.[2]

Not only does recast affect the nature of the contract's proceeds, it also has an impact when the proceeds are reportable as taxable income. The period in which the gain is taxable may differ from the period in which the rent is taxable. Generally, rent income is taxable when received. Therefore, if the lease provided for annual rentals, the lessor would have reported the income annually. However, in two instances, gains realized on sales of assets are fully taxable in the year of the sale, despite the fact that the contract provides that the lessor receive the payments annually. In the first case, dealers of inventory recognize gains on the sale of inventory in the year of sale. In the second case, sellers recapture the tax benefits of depreciation as ordinary income in the year of sale.

The IRS could also impute interest income arising from the conditional sales contract. Deferred-payment contracts are subject to imputed interest rules. The IRS may restate the selling price of property that is sold under a recast lease to reflect unstated interest. The effect of these imputed interest rules is to convert capital gains into ordinary income. Because capital gains are currently taxed at ordinary income rates, the effect of interest imputation has little significance today. However, there exists a real possibility that capital gains will again be taxed at favorable rates, and this issue could again become meaningful.

The lessee is also subject to unexpected consequences. The lessee may not deduct rent expense. Instead, the lessee capitalizes the cost of the lease. The total of all "rent payments" is treated as payments on the purchase of the asset and interest on the debt. The total of all such amounts payable over the full term of the lease becomes the basis of the asset. The lessee, as the true owner of the property, is entitled to deduct all necessary and ordinary business expenses with respect to the property, including depreciation, interest, state and local taxes, and maintenance. The holding period of the asset begins when the lessee acquires possession of the asset or is entitled to possession.

DETERMINING THE TRUE LESSOR AND LESSEE

The preceding section of this chapter illustrates why parties must be sensitive to lease provisions that indicate that a conditional sales agreement exists. This section analyzes types of lease provisions that indicate that the transaction is a financing agreement. The rules used to determine whether a lease will be treated as a conditional sales agreement have been modified over the past several years. Prior to 1981, the IRS and case law employed a facts-and-circumstances approach to determine if a lease transfers the benefits and burdens of ownership.

In 1981, Congress supplanted the facts-and-circumstances test with safe-harbor rules. Essentially, those rules allowed nominal lessors the tax benefits traditionally accorded to property owners. In 1981, Congress modified the treatment of safe-harbor leasing. The Tax Reform Act of 1984 further altered safe-harbor leasing. The 1986 Tax Reform Act completely repealed safe-harbor leasing, returning the issue of determining ownership to pre-1981 analysis. Because safe-harbor leasing treatment is no longer available, the discussion of it is brief and is included here solely for historical perspective.

Pre-1981 and Current Analysis

Prior to 1981 and currently, common law determines whether a transaction will be treated as a "true lease" by ascertaining the intent of the parties.

The test should be not what the parties call the transaction nor even what they may mistakenly believe to be the name of such transaction. What the parties believe the legal effect of such a transaction to be should be the criterion. If the parties enter into a transaction which they honestly believe to be a lease but which in actuality has all the elements of a contract of sale, it is a contract of sale and not a lease no matter what they call it nor how they treat it on their books. We must look, therefore, to the intent of the parties in terms of what they intended to happen.[3]

The provisions that the IRS and the courts look at to determine the parties' intent can be distilled into four general areas. For tax purposes, a valid lease is predicated upon (1) business motives; (2) there must exist a reasonable expectation of profit, independent of tax benefits; (3) the lessee cannot have an equity interest in the property; and (4) the lessor must retain benefits and burdens of ownership. Listed below are examples of lease provisions that satisfy or violate the business motive test, reasonable expectation of profit test, and the equity interest test. Equipment leasing, leveraged leasing, and sales-and-leaseback transactions are also vulnerable to recast on the additional ground that such transactions can be used as tax shelters.[4] These provisions may also indicate that the transaction is used as a tax-shelter device.

Lease Provisions Used to Determine Intent

The transaction is predicated upon business motives and there is a reasonable expectation of profit

Taxpayers must investigate the profitability of the transaction and act in accordance with reasonable business practices by maintaining accurate business records in order to satisfy these tests.[5] Case law and the IRS find that a transaction lacks business purpose if the lease property is not suitable for leasing (e.g., a sprinkler system).

The lessee does not have an equity interest in the property

The courts and the IRS have found that the following types of lease terms indicate that the parties intended that the lessee will acquire an equity interest in the property.

1. The existence of a bargain-purchase option.[6] However, the presence of a purchase option will not invalidate a lease if the option permits the lessee to purchase the property for its expected fair market value at the time the option becomes exercisable.
2. The agreement designates some portion of the rental as interest.[7]

3. The lessee acquires title upon payment of a stated number of rentals.

4. The lease payments materially exceed the current fair rental value.

5. The presence of bargain renewal options. One court recast a transaction because the renewal option permitted a lessee to renew a lease for a rent equal to 3% of the rent payable under the first lease term.[8] Another objectionable option provided that the annual rent for the renewal periods equaled the monthly rent applicable to the first lease term.[9] On the other hand, bargain options do not invalidate a lease if the renewal periods do not exceed the property's economic life.[10]

6. The lease term coincides with most of the asset's useful life, but rentals received over a relatively short period approximate the price at which the asset could have been purchased.[11]

7. Total rental payments divided by the asset's total value exceed the lease term divided by the asset's useful life.

8. Portions of periodic rental payments are specifically applied to an equity interest.[12]

9. Lease payments are excessive compared to amounts ordinarily required for securing title.[13]

10. The total of the rental payments and any option price approach the price at which the equipment could have been acquired by purchase at the time of lease inception.

Safe-Harbor Leasing

Congress enacted a "safe harbor" as part of the Economic Recovery Tax Act of 1981 (ERTA), which sanctified the form of certain leasing transactions. Under safe-harbor leasing rules, lessors were entitled to depreciation deductions even if the lease contained provisions that effectively transferred benefits and burdens of ownership to lessees.[14]

In order to be accorded bona fide lease treatments, leases had to meet these safe-harbor requirements:

1. The property under lease was depreciable under the ACRS.

2. The lease was written, and named one party lessor and one party lessee.

3. The lessor, at all times during the lease term, had to be "at risk" for at least 10% of the cost of the property.

4. Generally, the lease term could not exceed 90% of the estimated useful life of the property.

5. Both the lessor and lessee had to elect safe-harbor treatment by the timely filing of certain documents with the IRS.

To illustrate the beneficial nature of safe-harbor leasing, assume Lessee Company, having little taxable income, purchases new equipment.

Immediately, Lessee sells it to Lessor for the same amount Lessee paid. Lessor is in the 34% tax bracket. Lessor finances 90% of the purchase price with an interest-bearing note. Lessee makes lease payments to lessor in an amount equal to the amount of the loan payments. At the end of the lease term, Lessee purchases the asset for $1. Exhibit 5-3 compares the tax consequences of this scenario under the benefits of safe-harbor leasing, and in the absence of special treatment.

Not surprisingly, the ever-resourceful business community engaged in a substantial amount of safe-harbor leasing transactions. Congress, concerned with the amount of activity under the rules, substantially modified safe-harbor leasing in 1982 and 1984. For safe-harbor leases entered into prior to January 1, 1983, the Tax Equity and Fiscal Responsibility Act (TEFRA) limited the benefits of safe-harbor leasing. Among its modifications, TEFRA reduced the term of a safe-harbor lease, limited the amount of property that could be leased, eliminated safe-harbor leasing between related parties, lengthened the period of depreciation, and limited the types of lessees. TEFRA also provided

Exhibit 5-3
Tax Consequences of Safe-Harbor Leasing

LESSEE CONSEQUENCES	LESSOR CONSEQUENCES
WITHOUT SAFE-HARBOR LEASING:	WITHOUT SAFE-HARBOR LEASING:
1. The lease is ignored for tax purposes.	1. The lease is ignored for tax purposes.
2. The lessee depreciates the asset but does not benefit from the deduction because the lessee has little taxable income.	2. The lessor is treated as selling the leased property to lessee.
SAFE-HARBOR LEASING:	SAFE-HARBOR LEASING:
1. The lessee deducts the rent due and includes in income the interest from the note.	1. The lessor depreciates the asset. The depreciation and interest expense reduce lessor's tax liability. The lessor includes rent payments in income which is partly shielded by the above deductions.

that deductions attributable to safe-harbor leasing could reduce tax liability by no more than 50%, repealed safe-harbor rules for leases entered into after 1983, and replaced safe-harbor rules with finance-lease rules. Finance-lease rules never became effective; the Tax Reform Act of 1984 postponed their effective date, and the Tax Reform Act of 1986 repealed the advantageous treatment accorded leases between 1981 and 1984.

As a result of safe-harbor leasing repeal, all lessors and lessees must currently refer to pre-1981 case-law lease criteria to determine whether the lease in question will be respected for tax purposes: the lessor must demonstrate a profit motive, exclusive of tax benefits, and must further bear the burdens of ownership. There are some special rules with respect to leveraged leases, sale-leasebacks, and motor vehicle leasing activity; the next sections in this chapter analyze the criteria for determining whether the lease transaction transfers the benefits and burdens of ownership with respect to these specific types of leases.

Leveraged Leases

Case-law criteria may be difficult to apply with respect to leveraged leases because many of their provisions look suspiciously similar to a financing agreement. Leveraged leases involve three parties; the lessor, the lessee and the lessor's lender, who advances funds on a nonrecourse basis. Generally, the term of a leveraged lease coincides with most of the useful life of the leased property. The rent payments are structured to effectively compensate the lessor for payments to the lender.

Taxpayers contemplating questionable leveraged-leasing transactions involving substantial amounts of tax dollars may wish to obtain additional guidance regarding whether or not the IRS will respect the form of the transaction. These taxpayers are advised to request private-letter rulings. Private-letter rulings describe how the IRS will treat the transaction upon subsequent audit. The IRS requires taxpayers to comply with certain requirements before it will issue a ruling. These conditions have significance concerning whether or not the IRS will issue a private ruling, and indicate the position the IRS will take upon audit. Taxpayers who fail to receive letter rulings may nevertheless complete the transaction. However, taxpayers who fail to receive letter rulings may be playing the audit lottery by completing the transaction.

The IRS will issue advance rulings recognizing the validity of certain leveraged-lease transactions, providing the proposed transaction respects the six conditions that follow:[15]

1. At the inception of the lease, the lessor must have paid or personally incurred a liability equal to at least 20% of the cost of the property. The lessor must maintain this investment throughout the entire lease term, and the

investment must remain at the end of the lease term. The lessee or related parties may not in any way, or at any time, reimburse the lessor with respect to this 20% "at-risk" investment. Rental payments cannot be a disguised form of reimbursement. Rental payments have the effect of reimbursing the lessor for his investment in the property if projected cumulative lease payments less projected disbursements by lessor to maintain ownership of property exceed lessor's "at-risk" investment minus 20% times the cost of the property plus the cumulative pro-rata portion of projected profits from the lease transaction. Profits in this instance are equal to the amount obtained by subtracting the lessor's aggregate disbursements required to be paid in connection with the ownership of the property plus "at-risk" investment from the sum of the aggregate rental payments and the value of residual interest. The following example calculates rental payments.

EXAMPLE 1

A lessor purchases equipment costing $1,000,000. The lessor pays $250,000 cash and finances the balance. The estimated residual value is $400,000 and the lease term is 25 years. The lease was entered into 10 years ago. Total rental payments equal $800,000. This taxpayer cannot obtain a private letter ruling because the lessor has not maintained his 20% investment. The rental payments exceed $430,000, as determined below. While the taxpayer cannot receive IRS assurance, the transaction may nevertheless be respected providing common law tests are met. The calculations are as follows:

$$\text{lessor's at-risk investment} - (20\% \times \text{cost of property})$$
$$= \$250,000 - 200,000 = \$50,000 \text{ plus pro-rata profit}$$

Pro rata profit equals the following: [(rental payments + residual interest − at-risk investment) (divided by the lease term)] × number of lease periods from lease inception to current period.

$$[(\$800,000 + \$400,000 - \$250,000/25 \text{ years})] \times 10 \text{ years} = \$380,000.$$

Total rent payments cannot exceed $430,000.

2. At the end of the lease term, the fair market value of the property must equal at least 20% of the original cost of the property. The property must have a remaining useful life equal to the longer of either one year or 20% of the original estimated useful life.

3. The lease must not contemplate bargain purchase options, require any party to purchase the asset, nor permit the lessor to abandon the property.

4. The lessee cannot pay for permanent improvements unless the lessor recognizes rental income equal to the fair market value of the improvements. The lessor cannot have a contractual right to purchase several improvements made by the lessee.

5. The lessee may not in any way provide the lessor with funds necessary to acquire the property or guarantee lessor debt.

6. The lessor must establish that the transaction is profitable apart from the tax attributes. Further, the transaction must provide the lessor with estimated positive-cash flow.

Motor Vehicle Leasing

Automobile dealers often lease motor vehicles under an agreement that contains a terminal rental adjustment clause (TRAC). TRACs generally permit the rental price to be increased or decreased to compensate the lessor for unanticipated declines in the property's residual value. Because this provision shifts to the lessee one risk of ownership (the risk that the property will decline in value), one court held, in a 1981 decision, that an agreement that contained a TRAC was a conditional sales contract rather than a lease.[16] Currently, however, agreements that otherwise qualify as leases are not invalidated merely because they contain TRACs.

Congress, finding that TRACs are grounded in non-tax, business purposes, enacted IRC Sec. 7701(h). This section provides that leases will not be recast merely because they contain a TRAC. In order to fall within the protection of Sec. 7701(h), the lease must be a qualified motor vehicle operating agreement. The agreement must meet the following requirements in order to be classified as a qualified motor vehicle operating agreement:

1. The lessor must be personally liable to pay any amounts borrowed to finance the acquisition of the property subject to the agreement.
2. The lessee must intend that more than 50% of the use of the property subject to such agreement will be in the lessee's trade or business.
3. The lessee will not be treated as the owner of the property for federal income tax purposes.

Sale-and-Leaseback

In the sale-and-leaseback, a taxpayer sells property to an unrelated investor, and immediately leases the property back from the investor. The chief advantage of this type of transaction is that the lessee can raise cash and be entitled to a rent deduction. The rent deduction is often higher than the depreciation deductions to which the lessee is entitled, had the lessee mortgaged the property. On the other hand, a sale-and-leaseback subjects the seller to tax on any gain generated by the sale or recapture, and a potential loss of appreciation on the asset.

As is the case with other types of leases, this type of arrangement is vulnerable to IRS upset if the seller/lessee retains an equity interest or if the transaction is motivated primarily by tax-avoidance purposes.

As discussed above, a valid lease must have economic substance. Economic substance means the lease is motivated by non-tax motives: the lessor retains benefits and burdens of ownership, the lessor has a realistic expectation for profit, and, in the case of a sale-and-leaseback transaction, the transaction involves at least three parties.

Courts employ a case-by-case approach in deciding whether a sale-and-leaseback is valid. The Supreme Court respected a sale-and-leaseback where the rent payments equaled the lessor's mortgage payments.[17] In addition, the lease contained a repurchase option. The IRS had argued that the lease was in substance a financing arrangement. The Court, however, found that the transaction was grounded in business motives: state and federal regulations precluded the lessee from obtaining financing on its own. Furthermore, the Court found that the repurchase option did not shift the risk of loss because the option provided that the lessee could purchase the property for an amount equal to the unpaid mortgage balance and interest.

In contrast to that case, one court disregarded the form of a transaction because the buyer/lessor did not have an equity investment in the property. The lease in this case provided that the price of the asset would be paid in installments, the seller bore no personal liability for payment of the purchase price, and the rent payments equaled the mortgage payments.[18] Another court disregarded the form of a sale-and-leaseback where the residual value of the leased property was so low that the buyer/lessor could not recover its initial investment plus interest.[19] The court found the transaction lacked economic substance because there was no investment.

In a computer equipment sale-and-leaseback, an additional case held that the residual value of the equipment, if any, at the end of the lease term determines whether or not the lessor can expect to profit from the transaction. The court reasoned that the lessors realize profit from the value of the equipment at the termination of the lease, not from the rent payments received.[20]

In order to demonstrate that the transaction has economic substance, based upon case law, a sale-and-leaseback transaction should include the following:

1. Written documents to provide for a sale-and-leaseback
2. No repurchase options
3. Consistent treatment of the transaction as a sale-and-leaseback by all parties
4. Assumption of the underlying indebtedness and substantial mortgage payments by the buyer

5. No resale of the property to the seller or lessor by the buyer

6. Non-tax reasons for the form of the transaction

7. A residual value for the property at termination of the lease

To summarize the common law indicia of a "true" lease: the benefits and burdens of ownership remain with the lessor; the transaction rests upon non-tax motives and does not transfer equity to the lessee; there must exist a reasonable expectation of profit, exclusive of tax benefits. Leveraged leases, motor vehicle leases, and sale-and-leasebacks are no exception. Exhibit 5-4 summarizes the additional guidance available with respect to these types of leases.

The most important hurdle to overcome is whether or not the lease will be respected for tax purposes. Once the parties determine that their transaction has economic effect, they can focus on the ensuing tax consequences. The following discussion is intended to introduce these tax consequences, and subsequent sections of this chapter provide more detail regarding them.

Tax laws embody, in part, policy decisions that encourage property ownership. The tax laws provide owners of certain types of tangible property used in a trade or business with depreciation deductions,

Exhibit 5-4
Additional Tax Guidance for Leases

TYPE OF LEASE	ADDITIONAL GUIDANCE
1. LEVERAGED LEASE	1. Advisable to obtain a ruling from the IRS. To obtain a ruling, lessor must comply with several requirements.
2. MOTOR VEHICLE LEASE	2. TRAC provisions will not necessarily invalidate the lease; lease must be a qualified motor vehicle operating agreement.
3. SALE-LEASEBACK	3. Property must have a residual value at lease termination, agreement should be written, transaction involves three parties.

interest-expense deductions, and, prior to 1986, investment tax credits. Furthermore, owners of tangible personal property may elect immediately to expense part of the cost of such assets. Lessors, who retain property ownership, benefit from these deductions and credits. Lessors may also deduct all ordinary and necessary expenses paid or incurred during the taxable year that are attributable to earning the rent income. Transactions that do not qualify as true leases shift these consequences to the lessee.

In some cases, deductions and credits enabled taxpayers effectively to avoid income taxation. So, what Congress giveth in the form of these deductions and credits, Congress taketh away in the form of recapture, the alternative minimum tax, at-risk rules, and the passive-activity rules. Accounting methods may also affect the owner/lessor's ability to utilize these deductions. The nemesis of many taxpayers, the passive-activity-loss rules and the at-risk rules may curtail the attractiveness of certain leasing activities and are difficult to apply.

DEPRECIATION, RECAPTURE, AND SECTION 179 EXPENSING

Lessors often find leasing advantageous because lessors are entitled to depreciation deductions with respect to property they own and lease. Generally, only owners of certain types of property used in their trade or business are entitled to depreciation deductions. Consequently, lessees may not depreciate the property under lease. However, in some cases, lessees may depreciate the cost of improvements they make to the leasehold. Lessees calculate depreciation on leasehold improvements over the improvement's recovery period. Often, this period exceeds the lease term; at lease termination, the lessee, who does not retain the improvement, removes the asset from his accounting records and computes gain or loss based on the adjusted basis of the improvement.

For both tax- and financial-accounting purposes, depreciation represents a process of allocating the cost of an asset to the periods benefited by its use. Unlike financial accounting, however, tax law often views depreciation as a mechanism to accomplish certain objectives. As a result of the different objectives underlining depreciation, lessors use different methods to calculate depreciation for accounting and for tax purposes.[21] Furthermore, tax depreciation changes as tax policy changes over time. Prior to January 1, 1981, taxpayers recovered the cost of certain property over its useful life. In 1981, Congress introduced the ACRS, to spur the economy. ACRS allowed property owners to recover the cost of capital assets, using an accelerated method of depreciation, over a short recovery period. In 1986, Congress modified this system in an effort to increase Treasury revenues. In order to accomplish this objective, under modified ACRS (MACRS) the periods over which the costs are recovered lengthen.

Modified Accelerated Cost Recovery System

The Tax Reform Act of 1986 represents an extensive overhaul of the federal income tax system in an effort to provide a simpler, fairer, and more efficient system. As a result, 1986 TRA repealed the investment tax credit and modified ACRS (MACRS). MACRS lengthened the depreciation period of certain assets to reflect the actual useful life of these assets.

Generally, taxpayers calculate depreciation under MACRS by applying certain percentages to the basis of property. The percentages are based on a 200% declining balance, with a later change to straight-line depreciation. Exhibit 5-5 illustrates the new recovery periods and percentages under MACRS.

Under MACRS, tangible personal property is subject to a half-year convention. This convention confers a half year of depreciation in the year the asset is first placed in service, and a half year of depreciation in the year the property is removed from service. The half-year convention permits a half year of cost-recovery deduction regardless of when the asset is placed in service. Therefore, taxpayers should consider accelerating year-end asset acquisitions.

The advantage to this strategy is lessened in the event the basis of all personal property placed in service in the last quarter of the tax year exceeds 40% of the basis of all personal property placed in service during the entire year. In this case, a mid-quarter convention applies to all personal property placed in service or disposed of during the year.

Leasing represents an attractive way for companies to avoid the mid-quarter convention. Companies that expect to purchase a substantial amount of property during the last three months of the tax year should consider leasing the property. In this way, the lessee can use the half-year convention for asset acquisitions made earlier in the year. Taxpayers cannot use, or may not want to use, MACRS to depreciate certain types of property. In lieu of MACRS, taxpayers depreciate property under the straight-line method.

Alternative Depreciation System and Listed Property

The Alternative Depreciation System (ADS) provides for straight-line depreciation. It ignores salvage value, and the half-year and mid-quarter conventions discussed above apply to ADS as well. Taxpayers may elect to depreciate assets under this system in lieu of MACRS. Taxpayers *must* use ADS to depreciate certain types of property.

Exhibit 5-5
MACRS for Selected Types of Property (Assuming Half-Year Convention)

Type of Property	Recovery Period	Percentage per Year							
		1	2	3	4	5	6	7	8
Tractors	3	33.33	44.45	14.81	7.41				
Autos, light trucks, computers	5	20.00	32.00	19.20	11.52	11.52	5.76		
Office furniture, equipment	7	14.29	24.49	17.49	12.49	8.93	8.92	8.93	4.49

Note: Straight line depreciation must be used if business use of certain types of property does not exceed 50%. Property subject to this rule includes automobiles and computers. Lessors engaged in the business of leasing this type of property are excepted from this rule. Lessees of this type of property include in income an amount determined under IRS regulations.

ADS may be advantageous if the taxpayer faces alternative minimum tax. This is because accelerated depreciation increases the amount of income subject to alternative minimum tax. Depreciation computed under ADS does not increase the amount of income subject to alternative minimum tax. The alternative minimum tax is discussed in a subsequent section of this chapter.

With one exception, ADS must be used to calculate depreciation of certain types of "listed" property that are used 50% or less for business. Listed property includes automobiles, cellular telephones, property used for entertainment or recreational purposes, and computers. The reason that taxpayers cannot use MACRS to depreciate these types of properties is that Congress did not want to underwrite the personal use of these types of assets through accelerated-depreciation deductions. Lessors who are regularly engaged in the business of leasing are excepted from this requirement, and may use MACRS to depreciate listed property.

In the absence of special rules, taxpayers could circumvent the prohibition against using an accelerated method to depreciate listed property. They could lease the asset and deduct the accelerated depreciation in the form of rent payments. To prevent this result, lessees who lease listed property for 30 days or more must include in income an amount that approximates the excess accelerated-depreciation deduction. This has the effect of reducing the rent deduction by an amount that approximates the difference between depreciation calculated under the accelerated and straight-line methods. The IRS provides tables for determining the amount of income inclusion.

Section 179 Expensing

Internal Revenue Code Section 179 permits owners of recovery property to elect to expense up to $10,000 per year of the cost of such property. This amount is reduced to the extent that the total cost of property placed in service in the year exceeds $200,000. The amount that is expensed is not part of the depreciable basis of the property.

Recapture

Gain realized on disposition of depreciable property is "recaptured" as ordinary income under IRC Sec. 1245. The purpose of Sec. 1245 is to prevent taxpayers from converting depreciation deductions that offset ordinary income into capital gains upon disposition of the property. Section 1245 provides that gain recognized on the sale of depreciable personal property is treated as ordinary income to the extent of depreciation deductions taken on the property, or depreciation that could have been taken on the property. Section 1245 may also recapture Sec. 179 deductions.

ALTERNATIVE MINIMUM TAX

The alternative minimum tax (AMT) is imposed in addition to regular income tax. All entities, with the exception of S corporations and partnerships, have potential exposure to the AMT. The purpose of the tax is to insure that corporations having substantial economic income do not avoid paying tax. The alternative minimum tax accelerates recognition of income by requiring corporations to increase or decrease taxable income by certain preferences and adjustments.

The starting point in calculating AMT is the corporation's taxable income. Taxable income is increased by tax-preference items, and increased or decreased by certain adjustments. The total is called the alternative minimum taxable income (AMTI). AMTI is reduced by recomputing net operating losses. The tentative minimum tax equals 20% of the difference between the AMTI and a $40,000 statutory exemption.[22] The alternative minimum tax is the difference between the tentative minimum tax and the regular tax liability. While the AMT is 20%, compared to the highest marginal income tax rate for most corporations of 34%, the AMT generally results in a corporation paying higher taxes because the AMT base is broader than the tax base used to calculate regular income tax. Exhibit 5-6 illustrates the mechanics of the AMT calculation.

The preferences and adjustments relevant for leasing transactions are depreciation, installment sales, and the adjusted-current-earning (ACE) adjustment. For purposes of computing the regular tax, corporations may reduce taxable income by MACRS deductions. However, for purposes of the AMT, depreciation on tangible personal property placed in service after 1986 must be recomputed under ADS.[23] Corporations facing AMT liability should therefore consider depreciating tangible personal property using the straight-line method for income tax purposes. While this election will increase the corporation's regular tax liability, it may result in a reduction of total tax liability.

Taxpayers facing imposition of the alternative minimum tax may also find that leasing certain types of assets is attractive because lessees do not depreciate leased property, and therefore are not subject to this adjustment. An excellent study on the effect the AMT has on equipment leases holds that

the corporate lessee in an AMT position may benefit by leasing certain assets from a corporate lessor that is not subject to the AMT. The tax advantages of leasing tend to increase for those assets that have longer economic lives. Thus,

Exhibit 5-6
Alternative Minimum Tax Computation—Taxable Income

PLUS OR MINUS ADJUSTMENTS- Selected adjustments include:

-depreciation of tangible property placed in service after 1986
-installment sales of certain property
-ACE adjustment = 75% of the difference between ACE over
AMTI. ACE equals AMTI adjusted for the following selected items:
   ADS depreciation
   tax-exempt interest

PLUS PREFERENCE ITEMS- Selected preferences include:
-accelerated depreciation of leased personal property placed in service before 1987 (this
preference is applicable to personal holding companies)

LESS RECOMPUTED NET OPERATING LOSS DEDUCTION

EQUALS ALTERNATIVE MINIMUM TAXABLE INCOME

LESS EXEMPTION

TIMES 20%

LESS RECOMPUTED FOREIGN TAX CREDIT

EQUALS TENTATIVE ALTERNATIVE MINIMUM TAX

LESS REGULAR TAX LIABILITY

EQUALS ALTERNATIVE MINIMUM TAX

---

the corporate lessee subject to the AMT should benefit from purchasing those assets with shorter economic lives and AMTs lives (e.g., cars and computers) and leasing those with longer economic and AMTs lives.[24]

The tax advantages of leasing also increase depending on whether you lease from a corporate or noncorporate lessor, as Exhibit 5-7 illustrates.

With respect to lessors, depreciation on leased property placed in service prior to 1981 may be a preference item. The preference equals the difference between depreciation taken and depreciation calculated under the straight-line method. For purposes of the AMT, dealers must recognize income from installment sales in the year of sale. Therefore, it is vitally important that a lease transaction is not vulnerable to recast as a conditional sale.

Prior to 1990, corporations increased their regular taxable income by 50% of the difference between income reported on the corporation's applicable financial statement[25] over AMTI. For taxable years begin-

Exhibit 5-7
Minimal Annual Lease Payment Required by Corporate and
Noncorporate Lessors Based on Accelerated Depreciation
(Expressed as a Percentage of Original Purchase Price)

	CORPORATE LESSOR		NONCORPORATE LESSOR	
Asset	A MACRS No AMTS	B MACRS AMTS	C MACRS No AMTS	D MACRS AMTS
Passenger Cars	31.7	31.6	31.6	31.8
Computers	31.7	31.6	31.6	31.8
Typewriters	31.7	31.7	31.6	32.0
Heavy Trucks	19.8	20.4	19.9	20.3
Files, Cabinets Tables	12.9	13.8	13.1	13.7
Desks	11.0	12.1	11.3	11.8

Source: J. Burns, K. Hreha, and S. Luttman, "Corporate Leasing versus Property Ownership under the Tax Reform Act of 1986," *The Journal of the American Taxation
Association* (Fall 1989), p. 110.

ning in 1990, that adjustment is replaced by the ACE adjustment. The
ACE adjustment requires regular C corporations to increase regular
taxable income by 75% of the excess of ACE over AMTI.

The starting point to determine ACE is AMTI. AMTI is then adjusted for certain items, one of which is depreciation. The specific depreciation adjustment depends upon when the property is placed in service.
If property is placed in service in 1990 or after, ADS must be used to
calculate the depreciation deduction for purposes of ACE. ACE is increased for certain items that are not taxable for purposes of computing the regular income tax — for example, interest on tax-exempt bonds.
The IRS is expected to issue guidance regarding other items that will
increase or decrease ACE.

In addition to leasing, strategies to reduce exposure to the corporate
AMT include making the election to be taxed as an S corporation,
accelerating income into the current year, and deferring deductions
until a later taxable year.

This discussion has focused on how the alternative minimum tax
affects the lessee's decision. Exhibit 5-7 shows the effect of the combination of the alternative minimum tax and depreciation on corporate
and noncorporate lessors, and illustrates the amount of the lease payment required in order for both corporate and noncorporate lessors to
recover their investment in the leased asset.

The remainder of this chapter highlights three provisions that limit
the ability of taxpayers to use deductions to reduce taxable income.
Basically, these rules have impact on a taxpayer not engaged in a

business. Because it is assumed that a lessee will use the leased property in his or her business, the discussion is brief.

PROVISIONS THAT LIMIT THE ABILITY OF A LESSOR OR LESSEE TO REDUCE TAXABLE INCOME

Tax Treatment of Lease Payments

Tax law allows taxpayers to deduct ordinary and necessary business
expenses incurred or paid in a taxable year. Accordingly, lessees are
entitled to deduct rent paid or incurred as a condition of the continued
use or possession of property used in the lessee's trade or business,
providing the lessee does not have any equity interest in the leased
property. Lessors report rents received as ordinary income.

The taxable year in which the lessee deducts the rent, and the taxable year in which the lessor reports the rental income, is a function of
the taxpayer's method of accounting. Generally, taxpayers compute
taxable income under the method of accounting regularly employed in
keeping books and records. Most individuals and small business entities account for income using the cash method of accounting. Most
large corporations are required to use the accrual method of accounting. Normally, cash-basis taxpayers deduct expenses in the year paid
and report income in the year received; accrual-basis taxpayers deduct
expenses in the year the liability is incurred and recognize income in
the period in which the income is earned. With respect to accrual-basis
lessees, the liability is "incurred when all events have occurred which
determine the fact of liability and the amount of such liability can be
determined with reasonable accuracy."[26]

Regardless of the method of accounting employed, lessees must account for deferred and advance rentals under the accrual method of
accounting. In some cases, lessors must report rental income using the
same method.

Lessors generally report the full amount of prepaid rent in the taxable year received. However, expenses of one year cannot reduce the
income of a subsequent year.[27] Regardless of which accounting method
the lessee uses, the lessee may not deduct the full amount of advance
rent payments. Instead, advance payments are deductible over the
entire lease term. For example,[28] a lessee enters into a six-year lease.
Rent is payable over three years. A portion of the rent is deemed to be
an advance payment for the last three years of the lease. Therefore, the
lessee may deduct in each of six taxable years only 1/6 of the payments
due under the lease.

Generally, the IRS will not adjust deductions for prepaid or deferred income over the life of the lease when the annual rent does not vary by more than 10% from the annual average aggregate rent for the entire lease term.[29]

Section 461(h) of the 1984 Tax Reform Act limits the ability of accrual-basis taxpayers to deduct advance payments before "economic performance" occurs. With respect to lease transactions involving tangible property, economic performance occurs as the lessee uses the property. Lessees may deduct rental in advance of economic performance if the property will be used within 8½ months after close of the taxpayer's year, and the expense amount is immaterial. In addition, the expense must be recurring in nature and treated consistently.

In general, effective tax planning dictates that the taxpayer accelerate deductions to the current taxable year and defer income recognition to later years. Leases often provide this tax-planning opportunity: rent payments may be accelerated or deferred in order to shelter income. In the absence of legislation, a lessee might accelerate payments of rent at year-end in order to minimize taxable profits. Conversely, the lessor may wish to defer recognition of taxable income to later years, by accepting reduced rental payments. To curb this potential abuse with respect to the timing of certain large rent payments, Congress, in Section 467, requires both lessors and lessees to account for rent under the accrual method. Refer to Exhibit 5-8 for an application of Section 467 to rents.

This code section applies to leases for the use of tangible property that cover terms of more than one year and involve total payments exceeding $250,000. Under the terms of such leases (1) there is at least one amount allocable to the use of property during a calendar year that is to be paid after the close of the calendar year following the calendar year in which such use occurs, or (2) there are increases in the amount to be paid as rent under the agreement. This section also applies in the case of agreements in which rents decrease during the term of the agreement.

With respect to leases that fall within the purview of this section, Section 467 forces three consequences:

1. Unequal rent payments may be leveled. The unequal rent payments are leveled and any rent to be paid after the close of the period is taken into account in accordance with present-value concepts. The method used to level rents depends on whether the agreement allocates an equal amount of rent each period.
2. Both the lessor and lessee are treated as accrual-method taxpayers with respect to the rental income and deductions.
3. Interest may be imputed as a result of the consequences above.

How is it decided in which taxable year rent is deductible or included in income? Accrual-basis taxpayers deduct rent when all events that determine the fact of the liability have occurred, and the amount of such liability can be determined with reasonable accuracy. Regardless of which method of accounting is used, the accrual method of accounting must be used by lessees to account for advance payments (note the exceptions from the economic performance test), and by lessees and lessors to account for certain leases involving the use of tangible property where the lease payments exceed $250,000.

Passive-Activity Rules

Prior to 1986, lessees could magnify the effect of favorable tax consequences by conducting the leasing activity through a limited partnership that financed the equipment with nonrecourse debt. By conducting the activity through this vehicle, investors would be entitled to large depreciation deductions because nonrecourse financing increases the depreciable basis of the property. Investors would also be entitled to significant interest-expense deductions on the nonrecourse debt. These deductions would shelter cash distributions to the partners from taxation. Prior to 1986, investors could shelter income with deductions from other activities.

The Tax Reform Act of 1986 enacted passive-activity-loss rules that significantly blunted the benefits of the transaction described above. The passive-activity rules arose out of Congressional concern about extensive tax-shelter activity. The rules limit individuals, partners, S corporation shareholders, trusts, estates, closely held corporations,[30] and personal-service corporations[31] from using deductions, losses, and credits from a "passive" activity to shelter "active" and interest and dividend income. By limiting the tax advantages of an investment, Congress believed the rules would encourage investors to make decisions based on the economics of the investment.[32]

A passive activity is one in which the taxpayer does not materially participate, a rental activity,[33] or any limited-partnership activity. Material participation means the taxpayer engages in an activity in a regular, continuous, and substantial manner.[34] Limited partners of an equipment-leasing partnership, therefore, can only use losses and deductions from the partnership to offset income from passive activities.

Passive-activity-loss rules divide all income and losses into three types: active, passive, and portfolio. Generally, passive losses can only be used to offset income from passive activities. Unused losses and credits are carried forward to successive taxable years and may be used to offset passive income generated in those years. "Suspended" losses

Exhibit 5-8
Application of IRC Section 467 to Rents

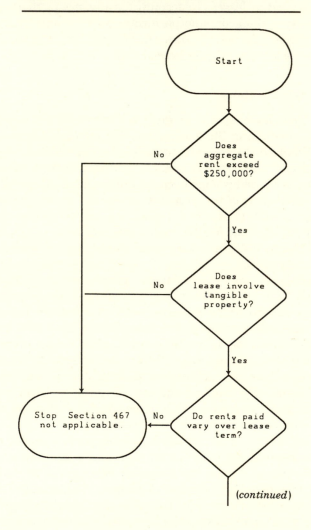

94

**Exhibit 5-8
(Continued)**

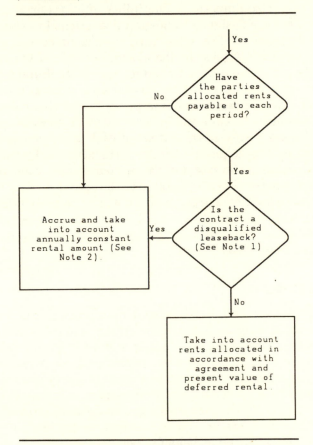

Notes: *1*. A disqualified leaseback is a leaseback to a person who had an interest in the leased property within the past two years, or an agreement for a term in excess of 75% of the MACRS recovery period.

2. The constant rental amount equals an amount that, if paid at the close of each lease period, would result in an aggregate present value equal to the present value of the aggregate payments required under the lease (Sec. 467).

and credits are also allowed in the year the taxpayer disposes of the activity.

At-Risk Rules

At-risk rules also limit the deductibility of losses arising in certain activities. They are designed to prevent deductions in excess of actual economic investment. The rules have significant consequences with respect to leveraged leases. In the absence of special tax rules, leveraged leases entitle taxpayers to deduct losses attributable to leasing activities despite the fact that the taxpayers are not at risk for repayment of the leased asset's purchase price. The at-risk rules curb this abuse by permitting lessors and lessees to deduct losses attributable to equipment leasing only to the extent of cash and recourse borrowing contributed by the taxpayer to finance the activity. Deductions may also be permitted to the extent of the net fair market value of property used to secure borrowing attributable to the activity.

Equipment leased for purposes of the at-risk rules includes computers, automobiles, and furniture. Closely held corporations[35] that receive more than 50% of gross receipts from equipment-leasing transactions are excepted from the at-risk rules.

Interest Expense

Generally, lessors and lessees may deduct interest expense incurred to finance the leasing activity. However, the amount of the deduction may be limited, depending on whether or not the leasing activity is in the nature of a trade or business, investment, or personal activity. Interest on indebtedness incurred to acquire property used in a trade or business may be fully deductible. With respect to the proceeds of debt incurred in or after 1990 used to acquire investment property, interest-expense deductions are limited to net investment income. Generally, interest expense incurred on behalf of personal activities is not deductible. The limitations on the deductibility of interest expense make crucial the determination of whether or not a lessor's leasing activity constitutes that taxpayer's trade or business, and whether or not the lessee uses the leased property in his or her trade or business.

SUMMARY

"The Tax Reform Act of 1986 may not have altered equipment leasing benefits, but it has changed the playground in which leasing decisions are made."[36] The essence of the tax impact on the leasing decision is the effect of exchanging depreciation and interest-expense deductions for rent deductions. While the new tax laws may have added additional complexity to the lease–buy decision matrix, the traditional benefits associated with equipment leasing have not changed. Leases are a flexible means of acquiring the use of an asset while preserving capital.

The decision to lease or buy cannot be made or structured solely by reference to favorable tax consequences. A decision must be made based on the overall financial effect of the transaction. Furthermore, the IRS can overlook the form of the transaction and impose unexpected consequences.

From a tax perspective, when does leasing make sense? Lessees must consider the effect that the alternative minimum tax, passive-activity-loss rules, the at-risk rules, and marginal tax bracket have upon the value of the deductions. Leasing certain types of assets make sense if you have exposure to the alternative minimum tax because depreciation increases the amount of income subject to that tax. Leasing is also attractive if you have acquired a substantial amount of property in the beginning of a year and expect to need more equipment in the last part of that year. Unless you lease the equipment that you expect you will need, you must use the mid-quarter convention for all the assets. If you have unused passive losses, you may wish to consider generating passive income by investing in a limited leasing partnership. If you are in a low tax bracket, you may consider trading your deductions to a lessor in exchange for lower lease payments.

NOTES

1. Rev. Rul. 72-408, 1972-2 C.B. 87.

2. Congress repealed the capital-gains deduction in 1986. However, capital-gain status remains important today for at least two reasons. First, capital gains are offset by capital losses. Second, Congress is considering reenacting the capital-gains deduction.

3. *Walburga Oesterreich*, 48 AFTR 335, 55-2 USTC Par. 9733, at 55-2 USTC 56,025.

4. CCH Internal Revenue Manual, Vol. 1, M.T. 4236-1.

5. *Johnson v. U.S.*, No. 310-84T (Cl. Ct. 1896).

6. Rev. Rul. 55-540, 1955-2 C.B. 39.

7. Rev. Rul. 55-540.

8. *Estate of Starr v. Comr.*, 30 T.C. 856 (1958); revised on other grounds, 274 F.2d 294 (9th Cir. 1959).

9. *Mt. Mansfield Television, Inc. v. U.S.*, 239 F.Supp. 539 (D. Vt. 1964), aff'd. per curiam, 342 F.2d 994 (2d Cir.), cert. denied 382 U.S. 818 (1965).

10. *Lockhart Leasing Co. v. U.S.*, 446 F.2d 269 (10th Cir. 1971).

11. Rev. Rul. 55-540.

12. Rev. Rul. 55-540.

13. Rev. Rul. 55-540.

14. Section 168(f)(8) of the Internal Revenue Code of 1986.

15. The IRS will not issue rulings with respect to limited-use property, including smokestacks and sprinkler systems.

16. *Swift Dodge v. Comr.*, 692 F.2d 651 (9th Cir. 1982), rev'g. 76 T.C. 547 (1981).

17. *Frank Lyon Co. v. U.S.*, 435 U.S. 918 (1978).

18. *Estate of Franklin v. Comr.*, 64 T.C. (1975), aff'd. per curiam, 241 F.2d 288 (9th Cir. 1976).

19. *Rice's Toyota World, Inc. v. Comr.*, 81 T.C. 184 (1983), aff'd. in part revd. and remd. in part, 55 AFTR2d 85-580.

20. *Goldwasser v. Comr.*, P-H T.C. Mem. Dec. ¶88,522.

21. The differences between tax and accounting treatment give rise to deferred tax liability. Discussion of deferred taxes is beyond the scope of this book.

22. The exemption is reduced by 25% of the difference between AMTI and $150,000. The exemption is fully phased out when AMTI exceeds $310,000.

23. The method used to recompute depreciation on real property is the straight-line method.

24. J. Burns, K. Hreha, and S. Luttman, "Corporate Leasing versus Property Ownership," *The Journal of the American Taxation Association* (Fall 1989), p. 111. It should be noted that these results are based, in part, on a prior provision of the AMT. Prior to 1990, one-half of the difference between tax and book depreciation increased the amount of income subject to the AMT. In the early years of an asset, the tax depreciation usually exceeds the book depreciation. Therefore, in the early years, the difference between book and tax depreciation is greater than in the later years, and accordingly, income subject to the AMT is higher in the early years.

25. The book income reported on the financial statement was adjusted to disregard federal income taxes and certain other taxes.

26. Section 461(h)(4) of the Internal Revenue Code of 1986.

27. Reg. 1.461-1(a)(3).

28. Rev. Rul. 60-122, 1960-1 C.B. 56.

29. Rev. Proc. 75-21, 1975-21 C.B. 715.

30. A corporation is closely held if not more than five individuals own more than 50% of the value of the outstanding stock.

31. A corporation is a personal-service corporation if more than 10% of its stock is owned by owner-employees. The corporation performs personal services in the fields of health, law, engineering, architecture, accounting, actuarial science, performing arts, or consulting. The services are substantially performed by owner-employees.

32. The rules and regulations are complex. The purpose of this section is to discuss the general concepts relating to passive activity loss rules that have impact on the lease–buy decision.

33. The rules regarding rental activities differ from the general concepts presented here. Discussion of how the passive activity rules affect rental activities is beyond the scope of this book.

34. The regulations under Section 469 provide seven tests that measure whether a taxpayer materially participates in an activity.

35. For this purpose, a closely-held corporation is a corporation that, at any time during the last half of the year, not more than five individuals owned more than 50% in value of the corporation.

36. T. Ozark, "Leasing Strategies after Tax Reform," *Cashflow* (October 1987), pp. 47–49, at p. 47.

REFERENCES

Bierman, H. "Buy versus Lease with an Alternative Minimum Tax." *Financial Management* (Winter 1988): 87–91.

Burns, J., K. Hreha, and S. Luttman. "Corporate Leasing versus Property Ownership under the Tax Reform Act of 1986." *The Journal of the American Taxation Association* (Fall 1989): 105–13.

Endres, J. "Leasing After the Tax Reform Act of 1986." *The Tax Advisor* (August 1988): 536–50.

Grossman, J. "RRA '89 Eases Corporate Alternative Minimum Tax Somewhat." *The Journal of Taxation* (March 1990): 140–45.

Haight, G., and K. Smith. "Equipment Leasing: Residual Values and Investor Returns." *Tax Notes* (December 4, 1989).

Internal Revenue Code of 1986.

Ozark, T. "Leasing Strategies after Tax Reform." *Cashflow* (October 1987): 47–49.

Thompson, K. "Business Rentals Can Provide Hefty Deductions if the Deal is Structured Well." *Taxation for Accountants* (February 1988): 114–18.

Volpi, J., and P. DeAngelis. "Using E&P to Compute AMT." *The Tax Adviser* (July 1989): 441–52.

Walthall, T. M. 12-6th, "Equipment Leasing." *1989 Tax Management Inc.*

6

Accounting for Lease Transactions

The accounting profession's sensitivity to the importance of lease transactions as financing devices dates back to the 1940s. Since then, accounting standards have been continuously issued, revised, and amended in an attempt to conform the accounting and reporting for lease transactions and to recognize the underlying economic effect of the many varied, and often complex, lease transactions. For example, a lease that contains a bargain-purchase option may shift to the lessee one of the risks of property ownership — the risk that the residual value of the property will decline. This type of lease could be characterized as an installment purchase and is accounted for as an acquisition of an asset through a financing arrangement. Conversely, operating leases do not typically transfer the benefits and burdens of ownership and are, therefore, accounted for as rental agreements.

As discussed in Chapter 5, the tax consequences of lease transactions also depend on whether the lease has shifted the benefits and burdens of ownership. However, the standards used to determine if the lease arrangement has effectively transferred those benefits and burdens may differ for tax and accounting purposes.[1] Tax law looks primarily to the intent of the parties as evidenced by the terms of the lease agreement. The tests used to evaluate the nature of a lease transaction for accounting purposes are more quantitative than the tests used for tax purposes. Exhibit 6-1 summarizes and compares the standards used for tax and accounting purposes.

The Financial Accounting Standards Board currently governs financial accounting and reporting for leases. FASB Statement No. 13, Accounting for Leases, and its various amendments and interpretations delineate the tests contained in Exhibit 6-1 that are used to determine whether a lease agreement has effectively transferred the benefits and burdens of ownership. Leases that shift the benefits and burdens of ownership to the lessee are capitalized. All other leases are operating leases. This chapter examines the accounting treatment and reporting standards required by FASB 13 for leases of tangible personal property.[2] The remainder of this introduction highlights the lessee and lessor consequences that ensue from lease transactions that satisfy or fail the FASB 13 tests.

Lessees' Consequences

For accounting purposes, lessees classify leases in one of two ways. A lease that satisfies at least one of the FASB 13 criteria must be capitalized. Capital leases typically transfer the benefits and risks of ownership to the lessee. Therefore, lessees account for capital leases in much the same way as purchasers record asset acquisitions financed through debt obligations. The lessee records the lease as an asset (capitalization) and the corresponding obligation on the balance sheet and amortizes the cost of the asset either over its useful life or the lease term. All other leases are operating leases, whereby the lease payments are recorded as rental expense. Generally, lessees recognize this rent expense on a straight-line basis over the lease term. Operating leases do not have an impact on balance-sheet reporting.

Many companies, believing that capital leases may adversely affect their financial position, structure lease transactions to purposely fail the FASB 13 criteria because capital leases create liabilities that are reported on the balance sheet. Capitalization may result in unfavorable debt-to-equity ratios, whereas leases that do not transfer the risks or benefits of property ownership are not reported on the balance sheet. Operating leases permit the lessee to borrow capital without recording the liability – a concept referred to as "off-balance-sheet" financing. However, the perceived advantages of off-balance-sheet financing may be illusory for three reasons. First, many financial statement users factor off-balance-sheet financing arrangements into financial decisions. Second, capital and operating leases have the same cumulative effect on both cash flow and net income over the total lease term.[3] Third, while lease obligations are not always recognized on the balance sheet, such transactions are not necessarily hidden because FASB 13 requires disclosure of all material-leasing transactions and obligations in notes to the financial statements.

Lessors' Consequences

For accounting purposes, lessors classify leases in one of four ways: direct-financing, sales-type, leveraged, or operating. Direct-financing,

Exhibit 6-1
Criteria of Lease Classification for Accounting and Tax Purposes

ACCOUNTING		TAX
LESSEE	LESSOR	
Lease is capitalized if it satisfies one of the following:	Lease is capitalized if it satisfies one of the following:	Lease may be treated as a conditional sales contract if it:
1. transfers ownership	1. transfers ownership	1. transfers ownership
2. contains bargain purchase option	2. contains bargain purchase option	2. has a bargain purchase option
3. lease term is for at least 75% of asset's useful life	3. lease term is for at least 75% of asset's useful life	3. is for a term equal to most of asset's useful life

4. present value of minimum lease payments exceed 90% of fair market value of the property	4. present value of minimum lease payments exceed 90% of fair market value of the property and in addition, satisfy both of the following: 1. collectibility of minimum lease payments is reasonably assured 2. no important uncertainties surround the amount of unreimbursable costs	4. lease payments are inordinately large (Other indicia are listed in chapter of this text)
Treatment: Capitalize the lease (report the lease on the balance sheet)	Treatment: Record a receivable and remove the asset from the balance sheet	Treatment: Lessee capitalizes rents that are payments on the purchase price
ALL OTHER LEASES ARE OPERATING	ALL OTHER LEASES ARE OPERATING	

sales-type, and leveraged leases transfer substantially all the benefits and burdens of ownership; they are similar to sales. With respect to these types of leases, lessors remove the leased asset from the accounting records, and record a receivable on the balance sheet. Operating leases are reported as rental income on the income statement, in a straight-line manner, over the lease term.

Generally, leasing transactions with banks, insurance companies, and lease-finance companies produce direct-financing leases. In a direct-financing lease, the fair market value of the leased asset equals its carrying value at the inception of the lease, and either the leased asset or anticipated lease payments collateralize the financing agreement.

Sales-type leases are commonly used by manufacturers or dealers to market their equipment. In a sales-type lease, the fair market value of the leased asset differs from its carrying value at the inception of the lease.[4] The difference between the asset's fair market value and its carrying value produces profit or loss. For accounting purposes, the difference between direct-financing leases and sales-type leases is accounting for the profit or loss generated by a sales-type lease, which is similar to installment-sale profit recognition.

A leveraged lease is a direct-financing lease that satisfies additional criteria. Most notably, the lease involves three parties: a lessor, a lessee, and a long-term creditor who provides substantial nonrecourse financing.

All other leases are operating leases. Under an operating lease, the lessor transfers the use of property, but not the benefits and burdens of ownership. Lessors report rent income and depreciate the leased asset.

While some lessees prefer to classify leases as the operating type, lessors generally prefer classifying leases in their accounting records as other than operating leases. As is illustrated below in this chapter, capital-lease classification provides higher income flows for lessors in the early years of a lease. However, disclosure requirements may mitigate the impact different classifications have upon the lessor's financial position.

LESSEES' ACCOUNTING ISSUES

Lessees classify all leases as either operating or capital leases. Different accounting consequences are attached to each classification. Capital leases are similar to asset acquisitions, while operating leases are rental agreements where the lessee acquires only the right to use the property for a specified period of time. This section first examines the capitalization criteria under FASB 13, and then explains the accounting rules and disclosure requirements applicable to lessees.

Capitalization Criteria

FASB 13 requires capitalization of lease transactions if the lease satisfies at least one of the following tests:

1. For both tax and accounting purposes, the asset under a lease that transfers ownership is capitalized.

2. Leases that contain a bargain-purchase option must be capitalized. A bargain-purchase option permits the lessee to purchase the leased property for a price that is significantly lower than the expected fair value of the property at the date the option becomes exercisable. Because the option price is so low at the inception of the lease, exercise of the option is reasonably assured.

3. Both tax and accounting standards recognize that lease terms that are large in relation to the asset's life effectively transfer the risks and rewards of ownership to the lessee. FASB 13 provides that leases must be capitalized if the lease periods equal or exceed 75 % of the asset's life. This rule is grounded in the belief that, due to obsolescence and wear and tear, more than 75 % of the benefit from use of the property accrues to the lessee within the first 75 % of the asset's life.

For purposes of this test, the lease term is the fixed, noncancelable term of the lease and all periods covered by bargain-renewal options.[5] The lease term is also extended when the lessee is subject to substantial penalties for failure to renew the lease.

A lease is considered noncancelable for purposes of this definition if it is cancelable only on the occurrence of a remote contingency, only with the permission of the lessor, only if the lessee enters into a new lease with the same lessor, or only on payment by the lessee of a substantial penalty.

Bargain-renewal options allow the lessee, at his option, to renew the lease for a rental that is substantially lower than the fair rental. The price is so low that, at the lease inception, exercise of the option appears to be reasonably assured.

4. For both tax and accounting purposes, lessees must capitalize the lease if cumulative lease payments have the effect of reimbursing the lessor for his investment in the asset. FASB 13 provides that payments should be capitalized if the present value of the minimum lease payments equal or exceed 90 % of the asset's fair market value. The amount of the asset and the liability that is recorded on the balance sheet is the lesser of the present value of the minimum lease payments or the fair market value of the leased property at the date of lease inception. The application of this test rests on lease payments, residual value, and executory costs.

Minimum lease payments include rent payments required under the lease, bargain-purchase options, penalties for failure to renew or extend the lease, and guaranteed residual value. *Residual value* is the estimated fair market value of the asset at lease termination. Unguaranteed residual value is the excess of the residual value over the amount guaranteed, if any, by the lessee. Because guaranteed residual value is, in effect, an additional lease payment that the lessee pays in the event the value of the property declines below a stated amount at the termination of the lease, lessees include the present value of only guaranteed lease payments in the calculation of minimum lease payments. *Executory costs* include insurance, maintenance, and taxes incurred in connection with the leased property. Lessees include executory costs in the calculation of minimum lease payments unless the lessor pays such costs.

With one exception, the lessee computes the present value of the minimum lease payments using the lessee's incremental borrowing rate. This is "[t]he rate that, at the inception of the lease, the lessee would have incurred to borrow over a similar term the funds necessary to purchase the asset."[6]

The following example illustrates the use of FASB 13 criteria to decide if a lease should be capitalized.[7]

EXAMPLE 1

1. Lessor and Lessee Companies enter into a lease on January 1, 1990. Under the lease terms, Lessor leases equipment to Lessee for 30 months at a monthly rent of $135, payable on the first of every month.

2. At the inception of the lease, the equipment has a carrying value to the lessor and a fair market value of $5000.

3. The expected residual value at the end of the lease is $2000. The lessee guarantees the residual value at the end of the lease term in the amount of $2000.

4. Lessor does not pay any executory costs.

5. Lessee depreciates all its property using the straight-line method.

6. Lessee's incremental borrowing rate is 10.5%. Lessor's rate of return on this lease is 12.036%.

Analysis

1. Does this lease transfer ownership? No.

2. Does this lease contain a bargain-purchase option? No.

3. Is the lease term at least 75% of the estimated economic life of the property? No. The 30-month lease term is 50% of the economic life (5 years) of the asset.

4. Is the present value of the minimum lease payments at least 90% of the fair value of the leased property? Yes, as calculated below:

Minimum Lease Payments:
Minimum rental payments over the lease term	$4050	
+ Guaranteed residual value	2000	
= Total minimum lease payments		6050

Present Value of Minimum Lease Payments:
Present value of minimum rental payments, using incremental borrowing rate	$3580	
+ Present value of guaranteed value	1540	
Total		5120
Fair market value of the property at inception of the lease		5000
Minimum lease payments as a percentage of fair value		102%

Because the present value of the minimum lease payments, using the lessee's incremental borrowing rate, exceeds 90% of the fair market value of the property at the inception of the lease, Lessee classifies this lease as capital.

The section that follows explains and illustrates how a lessee would record this lease in his or her financial books and records.

Accounting for Capital Leases—General

Because the substance of a capital lease is the same as a financing arrangement, the lessee accounts for the transaction as a financing transaction: the lessee records a capital lease on the balance sheet as an asset and a liability. The amount of the asset and liability is the lesser of the present value of the minimum lease payments, or the fair market value of the leased asset at the inception of the lease.

For accounting purposes, lessees amortize the cost of capital leases using one of the methods permitted under generally-accepted accounting principles. These methods include straight line, sum of the years' digits, declining balance, and units of production. The amortization period is a function of whether or not the lease transfers ownership of the asset or contains a bargain-purchase option. Capital leases that contain one of these provisions are amortized over the asset's useful life because the lessee will most likely use and own the asset for that period. If the capital lease does not contain the provisions above, it is amortized over the lease term.

Because rent payments under capital leases are in the nature of installment payments made under financing agreements, lessees must allocate each rent payment between principal and interest. Lessees allocate payments using the effective-interest method. This method applies the discount rate used to determine the present value of the minimum lease payments to the outstanding balance of the obligation.

The example that follows illustrates the accounting entries Lessee makes to record the lease described in Example 1, and uses the amortization table in Exhibit 6-2 for calculations.

EXAMPLE 2

1. On January 1, 1990, Lessee makes the following accounting entry to record the asset and liability:

Leased Equipment under Capital Lease   5000

    Obligations under Capital Lease   5000

(Note: The amount that is capitalized is the lesser of the present value of the minimum lease payments or the fair market value of the leased asset.)

2. Lessee makes the following journal entry to record the first lease payment on January 1, 1990:

Obligations under Capital Lease   135

    Cash   135

3. On January 31, 1990, Lessee makes the following journal entry to record interest expense for the first month of the lease:

Interest Expense   49*

    Accrued Interest on Obligations under
       Capital Lease   49

4. On January 31, 1990, Lessee makes the following entry to record amortization expense on a straight-line basis over 30 months to a salvage value of $2,000 (the estimated residual value to the lessee):

    Amortization Expense – Capital Leases   100

    Accumulated Amortization – Capital Leases   100

Accounting for Sales-Leaseback Transactions

In a sales-leaseback transaction, a property owner (lessee) sells an asset and simultaneously leases it back from the purchaser. Chapter 8 discusses the advantages and disadvantages of this type of lease. Accounting for sales-leaseback transactions reflects the substance of the

*See amortization table, Exhibit 6-2.

transaction. Lessees initially record a sale, and the leaseback is separately accounted for depending upon whether the leaseback is determined to be a capital or ordinary lease.[8]

The lessee determines the amount of profit or loss on the sale portion of the transaction as though the lessee did not enter into the leaseback. The profit or loss is the difference between the sales price of the asset and its carrying value to the lessor on the date of the sale. Such executory costs as insurance, maintenance, and taxes are excluded from the calculation of profit, regardless of whether the lessor or lessee pays these costs.

The full amount of profit or loss is not immediately reported on the lessee's income statement; it is believed that the profit or loss is a function of a sales price that is inflated to create a larger gain and increased basis for depreciation. Instead, the profit or loss is deferred and amortized. The amount of the profit or loss that is recognized on the income statement for each accounting period depends on whether the leaseback is treated as a capital or operating lease.[9]

If the leaseback is treated as capital, any profit or loss realized on the sale is deferred and amortized over the lease term or economic life of the asset. The lessee uses the same method to amortize the profit or loss as is used to depreciate the capital lease. The example that follows is an illustration of this principle.

EXAMPLE 3*

1. On January 1, 1990, Seller sold equipment having a sales price of $300,000, book value of $100,000, and estimated remaining economic life of 20 years. Seller immediately leased back the equipment for 16 years. In the year of sale, Seller recognizes profit equal to $12,500.

2. Since the lease term exceeds 75% of the estimated useful life of the lease, the lease qualifies as a capital lease. Therefore, the $200,000 profit is deferred and amortized over the useful life of the asset.

If the leaseback is treated as an operating lease, any profit or loss on the sale is amortized in proportion to the rental payments. Generally, lessees amortize and recognize profit or loss quicker under a leaseback classified as an operating lease. The nature of the leaseback affects the amount of earnings lessees report annually, and, consequently, equity ratios.

There are two exceptions to the rules above regarding profit or loss recognition: (1) lessees recognize losses at the time of sale if the carrying value of the asset exceeds it fair market value at the time of the

*Adapted from the Certified Public Accounting Exam, May 1987.

Exhibit 6-2
Amortization of Lease Obligation

Date	Column A Monthly payment	Column B (1.003% * Column D) Interest-1.003% per mo.	Column C (Column A - Column B) Reduction of obligation	Column D (Column D - Column C) Unpaid balance of obligation
Lease inception				5,000.00
1/90	135.00	0.00	135.00	4,865.00
2/90	135.00	48.80	86.20	4,778.80
3/90	135.00	47.93	87.07	4,691.73
4/90	135.00	47.06	87.94	4,603.79
5/90	135.00	46.18	88.82	4,514.96
6/90	135.00	45.29	89.71	4,425.25
7/90	135.00	44.39	90.61	4,334.63
8/90	135.00	43.48	91.52	4,243.11
9/90	135.00	42.56	92.44	4,150.67
10/90	135.00	41.63	93.37	4,057.30
11/90	135.00	40.69	94.31	3,962.99
12/90	135.00	39.75	95.25	3,867.74
Total	1,620.00	487.74	1,132.26	
1/91	135.00	38.79	96.21	3,771.53
2/91	135.00	37.83	97.17	3,674.36
3/91	135.00	36.85	98.15	3,576.22
4/91	135.00	35.87	99.13	3,477.09

110

5/91	135.00	34.88	100.12	3,376.96
6/91	135.00	33.87	101.13	3,275.83
7/91	135.00	32.86	102.14	3,173.69
8/91	135.00	31.83	103.17	3,070.52
9/91	135.00	30.80	104.20	2,966.32
10/91	135.00	29.75	105.25	2,861.07
11/91	135.00	28.70	106.30	2,754.77
12/91	135.00	27.63	107.37	2,647.40
Total	1,620.00	399.66	1,220.34	
1/92	135.00	26.55	108.45	2,538.95
2/92	135.00	25.47	109.53	2,429.42
3/92	135.00	24.37	110.63	2,318.78
4/92	135.00	23.26	111.74	2,207.04
5/92	135.00	22.14	112.86	2,094.18
6/92	135.00	21.00	114.00	1,980.18
7/92		20.00	(20.00)	2,000.18
Total	810.00	162.78	667.22	

Note- the obligation equals the residual value of the asset at lease termination.

sale-leaseback and (2) lessees immediately recognize gain if the present value of the lease payments do not exceed 10% of the fair market value of the asset.

Accounting for Termination, Renewal, or Modification of Capital Leases

Leases that do not contain bargain-purchase options or do not transfer ownership of the asset require the lessee to remove the asset and obligation upon termination of the lease. This may result in the lessee recognizing gain or loss.

The accounting consequences of renewals and modifications depend on whether or not the renewal or modification qualifies as an operating or capital lease, independent of the original lease.[10] If the modification or renewal is classified as an operating lease, the asset and obligation is removed, gain or loss is recognized, and the new agreement is accounted for as an operating lease.

If a renewal or extension merits capitalization, the lessee adjusts the existing balances of the asset and the obligation by an amount equal to differences between the present value of the future minimum lease payments under the revised agreement and the present balance of the obligation.

Accounting for Operating Leases

Leases that do not satisfy any of the four tests described by FASB 13 are classified as operating leases. Lessees record rent expense on a straight-line basis – the lessee divides the total of the lease payments under the lease by the number of lease periods. The example that follows illustrates accounting for operating leases.

EXAMPLE 4
If the lease described in Examples 1 and 2 were an operating lease, Lessee would make the following entry to record monthly rent expense:

Rent expense	135	
Cash		135

The straight-line method of recognizing rent expense prevents lessees from manipulating net income from year to year by structuring lease payments that vary from year to year.[11]

Lessees may face two accounting issues related to entering into new leases. One is accounting for lease incentives; the other relates to expenses incurred in connection with any preexisting lease. Some lease agreements may include incentives for the lessee to sign a new lease — for example, the lessor may pay certain costs or assume the lessee's preexisting lease in order to induce the lessee to enter into the lease. Lease incentives are considered reductions of rental expense by the lessee, recognized over the lease term on a straight-line basis. Expenses incurred in connection with changing from an original lease to a new lease require immediate recognition. When the leased property has no substantive future benefit to the lessee, lessees charge remaining rent payments under the preexisting lease and related capitalized leasehold improvements associated with the preexisting lease to expense.

Exhibit 6-3 contains key accounting concepts of capital and operating leases for lessees.

The "Real" Impact of Classification on Accounting Records

Should you intentionally structure your lease transactions to meet one classification or the other? Classification affects reported net income on an annual basis (see Exhibit 6-4, which shows the effect the lease described in Example 1 has upon reported net income, depending upon its classification). Capital leases result in lower reported net income than operating leases in the earlier years because the sum of depreciation and interest will exceed the periodic rental payment, recognized on a straight-line basis. In the later years of a lease, reported net income under a capital lease is higher than under an operating lease.

Classification also affects debt-to-equity ratios and the rate of return on assets — capital leases generate reportable liabilities, operating leases do not. If a company has loan covenants that require maintenance of a specified debt-to-equity ratio, then that company may structure the leasing arrangements to avoid capital classification.

On the other hand, lease classification has no impact on cumulative net income or cash flow over the lease term (Exhibit 6-4). Furthermore, any advantages of off-balance-sheet financing may be more theoretical than real because FASB 13 requires companies to disclose information about leasing transactions.

There is no one type of classification that is advantageous in every circumstance. While classifications do affect earnings ratios, debt-to-equity ratios, and asset ratios, sophisticated financial-statement users do factor operating leases into their decisions.

Disclosure Requirements

Financial accounting is designed to provide useful information to users of financial statements and responds to user needs by requiring

Exhibit 6-3
Key Accounting Concepts of Capital and Operating Leases—Lessees

From a lessee's perspective all leases are classified as capital or operating.

Capital Leases

1. Capital leases transfer ownership benefits and burdens to the lessee. FASB 13 requires capitalization if the lease satisfies at least one of four tests.

2. A capital lease gives rise to an asset, usually called Leased Equipment under Capital Lease, and a liability, usually called Lease Obligations.

3. The amount of the asset equals the lesser of the present value of the minimum lease payments or the fair market value of the asset. Minimum lease payments are the sum of total lease payments, guaranteed residual value, bargain purchase options, and penalties for failure to renew the leases.

4. Lessees amortize the cost of the asset over the lease term or useful life of the asset, depending on certain lease provisions.

5. Each lease payment partly represents a reduction of the liability and interest expense.

6. Lessees record a sales-leaseback as a sale and a capital or operating lease.

Operating Leases

1. Operating leases give the lessee the right to use tangible property for a specified period of time.

2. Lessees recognize rent expense.

3. Incentive payments made by the lessor reduce rent expense.

Exhibit 6-4
Effect of Lease Classification on Net Income

Year	Capital lease Depreciation	Interest	Total	Operating lease Rent expense	Difference in net income due to classification
1990	1,200	488	1,688	1,620	68
1991	1,200	400	1,600	1,620	(20)
1992	600	163	763	810	(47)
Totals	3,000	1,051	4,051	4,050	1 (rounding error)

Source: Adapted from D. Kieso and J. Weygandt, *Intermediate Accounting*, 6th ed. (New York: Wiley, 1989).

Note: Depreciation: $3,000/2.5 years = $1,200 per year; interest – see amortization table, Exhibit 6-2.

entities to provide information about their economic resources, claims to those resources, and the effects of transactions that change resources and claims to those resources. Generally-accepted accounting principles require the disclosure of certain transactions in order to provide more complete information to financial statement users. FASB 13 requires that lessees disclose certain information about their leasing transactions.

FASB 13 requires lessees to disclose the following information about capital leases:

1. Gross amount of assets recorded under capital leases as of the balance-sheet date
2. Future minimum lease payments as of the latest balance sheet date, in the aggregate, and for each of the five succeeding fiscal years
3. Assets recorded under capital leases and accumulated amortization that is separately identified in the balance sheet or in footnotes.

FASB 13 requires lessees to disclose the following information about operating leases having a remaining noncancelable lease term in excess of one year:

1. Future minimum rental payments required as of the balance sheet date in the aggregate, and for each of the five succeeding fiscal years
2. Rental expense for each period for which an income statement is presented, excluding rental payments under leases having terms not in excess of one month.

FASB 13 requires all lessees to describe the leasing arrangement, including renewal or purchase options, escalation clauses, and restrictions imposed by the lease.

Exhibit 6-5 illustrates how a lessee may satisfy these disclosure requirements.

LESSORS' ACCOUNTING ISSUES

Lessors classify all leases in one of four ways: sales-type, direct-financing, leveraged, and operating. Leases are classified as sales-type, direct-financing, or leveraged if they meet certain tests.

First, the lease must satisfy at least one of the following FASB 13 criteria:

1. The lease transfers ownership of the property to the lessee by the end of the lease term.
2. The lease contains an option to purchase the leased property at a bargain price.
3. The lease term is at least 75% of the estimated economic life of the leased property.
4. The present value of rental and other minimum-lease payments is at least 90% of the fair value of the leased property.

Criteria 3 and 4 are not applicable if the beginning of the lease term is within the last 25% of the total estimated economic life of the leased property. The lease must also satisfy both of the following FASB 13 criteria:

1. Collectibility of the minimum lease payments is reasonably predictable.
2. No important uncertainties surround the amount of unreimbursable costs yet to be incurred by the lessor under the lease.

The first set of criteria is identical to that used by lessees for determining lease classifications. Because lessors are subject to two criteria that are not applicable to lessees, it is possible a lessee may classify and treat a lease as capital, while the lessor classifies the same lease as operating. In such cases, both lessors and lessees record depreciation on the asset.

In the view of FASB 13, a lease that satisfies the criteria above effectively transfers the benefits and burdens of ownership to the lessee, and is in the nature of an installment sale. Therefore, accounting for these types of leases parallels accounting for installment sales. While direct-financing, sales-type, and leveraged leases all satisfy the criteria, there are some specific differences in accounting for them.

Exhibit 6-5
Lessee's Disclosure (Company X)

BALANCE SHEET

ASSETS			LIABILITIES		
	December 31,			December 31,	
	1990	1989		1990	1989
Leased Property under capital leases, less accumulated amortization	XXX	XXX	Current: Obligations under capital leases	XXX	XXX
			Noncurrent: Obligations under capital lease (Note 3)	XXX	XXX

FOOTNOTES

Note 1 - Description of Leasing arrangements

The Company conducts a major part of its operations from leased facilities which include a manufacturing plant, 4 warehouses, and 26 stores. The plant lease, which is for 40 years expiring in 1999, is classified as a capital lease. The warehouses are under operating leases that expire over the next 7 years. Most of the leases of store facilities are classified as capital leases. All of the leases of store facilities expire over the next 15 years.

Most of the operating leases for warehouses and store facilities contain one of the following options: (a) the Company can, after the initial lease term, purchase the property at the then fair value of the property or (b) the Company can, at the end of the initial lease term, renew its lease at the then fair rental value for periods of 5 to 10 years. These options enable the Company to retain use of facilities in desirable operating areas. The rental payments under a store facility lease are based on a minimum rental plus a percentage of the store's sales in excess of stipulated amounts. Portions of store space and warehouse space are sublet under leases expiring during the next 5 years.

In addition, the Company leases transportation equipment (principally trucks) and data processing equipment under operating leases expiring during the next 3 years.

In most cases, management expects that in the normal course of business, leases will be renewed or replaced by other leases.

The plant lease prohibits the Company from entering into future lease agreements if, as a result of new lease agreements, aggregate annual rentals under all leases will exceed $XXX.

Note 2 - Capital Leases

The following is an analysis of the leased property under capital leases by major classes:

Classes of Property	Asset Balances at December 31,	
	1990	1989
Manufacturing plant	$XXX	$XXX
Store facilities	XXX	XXX
Other	XXX	XXX
Less: Accumulated amortization	(XXX)	(XXX)
	$XXX	$XXX

(continued)

**Exhibit 6-5
(Continued)**

The following is a schedule by years of future minimum lease payments under capital leases together with the present value of the net minimum lease payments as of December 31, 1990:

Year ending December 31:

1977	$XXX
1978	XXX
1979	XXX
1980	XXX
1981	XXX
Later years	XXX
Total minimum lease payment	XXX

Less: Amount representing estimated executory costs (such as taxes, maintenance, and insurance), including profit thereon, included in total minimum lease payments.	(XXX)
Net minimum lease payments	XXX
Less: Amount representing interest	
Present value of net minimum lease payments	$XXX

Note 3 - Operating Leases

The following is a schedule by years of future minimum rental payments required under operating leases that have initial or remaining noncancelable lease terms in excess of one year as of December 31, 1990:

Year ending December 31:

1990	$XXX
1991	XXX
1992	XXX
1993	XXX
1994	XXX
Later years	XXX
Total minimum payments required*	$XXX

The following schedule shows the composition of total rental expense for all Operating leases except those with terms of a month or less that were not renewed:

	Year ending December 31,	
	1990	1989
Minimum rentals	$XXX	$XXX
Contingent rentals	XXX	XXX
Less: Sublease rentals	(XXX)	(XXX)
	$XXX	$XXX

Source: Reprinted from FASB Statement No. 13, Appendix C, par. 121.

Accounting for Direct-Financing Leases

In the direct-financing lease, the asset's cost to the lessor and its fair market value are the same. Therefore, these types of leases do not give rise to any profit or loss.[12] Lessors initially record a receivable. Each lease payment received by the lessor represents a reduction of the receivable and interest revenue. The amount of the receivable is equal to the present value of the minimum lease payments. With one exception, lessors and lessees calculate similarly the present value of minimum lease payments. As stated previously, minimum lease payments are payments the lessee makes in connection with the leased property, including the rent payments required under the lease, bargain-purchase options, penalties for failure to renew or extend the lease, and residual value. Unlike lessees, however, lessors include in the calculation both unguaranteed and guaranteed residual value accruing to the lessor at the end of the lease term, reduced by executory costs borne by the lessor. The reason that lessors include both guaranteed and unguaranteed amounts in the calculation of minimum lease payments, while lessees do not, is that lessors recover the investment regardless of whether the residual is guaranteed or unguaranteed. This is because lessors calculate the amount of the lease payment in order to earn a certain return on investment that takes into account the residual value of the property.

The difference between the gross investment (the receivable) and the fair market value of the property is the lessor's unearned interest revenue. The gross investment in the lease less unearned interest revenue is the net investment in the lease. Unearned interest revenue is amortized over the life of the lease using the effective-interest method. This method applies the lessor's implicit rate to the balance in the gross-investment account. Examples 1 and 2 illustrate lessee accounting for capital leases. The example that follows presents lessor accounting for the same lease. The pertinent information is repeated at the beginning of the example.

EXAMPLE 5

Facts

1. Lessor and Lessee Companies enter into a lease on January 1, 1990. Under the lease terms, Lessor leases equipment to Lessee for 30 months at a monthly rent of $135, payable on the first of every month.

2. At the inception of the lease, the equipment has a carrying value to the lessor and a fair market value of $5000.

3. The expected residual value at the end of the lease is $2000. The lessee guarantees the residual value at the end of the lease term in the amount of $2000.

4. The lessee pays $1000 of property taxes annually. Lessor does not pay any executory costs.

5. Lessee depreciates all its property using the straight-line method.

6. Lessee's incremental borrowing rate is 10.5%. Lessor's rate of return on this lease is 12.036%.

7. Collectibility of the minimum lease payments is reasonably predictable.

8. No important uncertainties surround the amount of unreimbursable costs yet to be incurred by the lessor under the lease.

Analysis

1. Does this lease transfer ownership? No.

2. Does this lease contain a bargain-purchase option? No.

3. Is the lease term at least 75% of the estimated economic life of the property? No. The 30-month lease term is 50% of the economic life (5 years) of the asset.

4. Is the present value of the minimum lease payments at least 90% of the fair value of the leased property? Yes, as calculated below:

Minimum Lease Payments:

Minimum rental payments over the lease term	$4050	
+ Guaranteed residual value	2000	
= Total minimum lease payments		6050

Present Value of Minimum Lease Payments:

Present value of minimum rental payments, using lessor's implicit rate	3517	
+ Present value of guaranteed value	1483	
Total		5000
Fair market value of the property at inception of the lease		5000
Minimum lease payments as a percentage of fair value		100%

5. Is collectibility reasonably assured? Yes.

6. Are there uncertainties surrounding unreimbursable costs? No.

Because the present value of the minimum lease payments, using the lessor's implicit rate, exceeds 90% of the fair market value of the property at the inception of the lease, because collectibility is reasonably assured, and because there are no uncertainties, Lessor classifies this lease as a direct-financing lease. This is a direct-financing lease as opposed to a sales-type lease because the fair market value of the asset equals its carrying value at the lease inception.

Lessor makes the following entries to record the lease above:

1. To record the investment in the direct financing lease:

Minimum lease payments receivable	$6050	
Equipment		5000
Unearned income		1050

2. To record receipt of first month's rent:

Cash	135	
Minimum lease payments receivable		135

3. To recognize the portion of unearned income that is earned during the first month of the lease:

Unearned income	49	
Earned income		49

(Net investment outstanding for month × implicit rate in the lease.)

Accounting for Sales-Type Leases

In most respects, accounting for sales-type leases is the same as for direct-financing cases: under both types of lease, lessors record the gross investment in the lease and unearned interest revenue. Lessors under sales-type leases, however, also recognize a sale. The difference between accounting for direct-financing and sales-type leases relates to recording profit or loss.[13]

In accounting for financing leases, the difference between guaranteed and unguaranteed residual value is irrelevant. For sales-type leases, the difference is significant: the amount of the sale and cost of goods sold differ, depending on whether the residual value is guaranteed or unguaranteed. Lessors record a sale for the present value of the minimum lease payments and the present value of guaranteed residual value. Unguaranteed residual value does not increase sales revenue. Cost of goods sold is recorded at an amount equal to the asset's cost to the lessor, less the present value of unguaranteed residual value.

Accounting for Sales-Leaseback Transactions

When accounting for sales-leaseback transactions, the lessor records the transaction as a purchase and a direct-financing lease, or a purchase and an operating lease, depending on the terms of the leaseback.

Accounting for Leveraged Leases

Leveraged leases are simply direct-financing leases that involve three parties—lessee, lessor, and creditor—and are accounted for as direct-financing leases. Generally, the lessor purchases the property from a third party, financing some of the purchase price and obtaining non-recourse debt to finance the balance of the purchase price. Leveraged leases offer the lessor tax advantages because the interest expense incurred by the lessor and depreciation deductions on the asset offset part of the revenue generated by the transaction.

Lessors enjoy economic benefits that are unique to leveraged leases. "[T]he combination of nonrecourse financing and a cash flow pattern that typically enables the lessor to recover his investment in the early years of the lease and thereafter affords him the temporary use of funds from which additional income can be derived produces a unique economic effect."[14] Therefore, lessors account for leveraged leases in a manner consistent with that economic effect. Generally, lessors account for these leases in the same manner as they account for other direct-financing leases, except that the lease receivable is recorded net of the nonrecourse liability.[15]

Accounting for Termination, Renewal, or Modification of Capital Leases

At the termination of a lease, the lessor removes the net investment from the accounts, and records the leased asset at the lower of its original cost, current fair market value, or present carrying amount. The net adjustment is charged or credited to income for the period of the change.

Lessors test modifications and renewals under the FASB criteria, independent of the original lease. If a lease modification is classified as an operating lease, the net investment account is removed from the books; the leased asset is recorded as an asset at the lower of its original cost, current fair market value, or present carrying amount; and the new agreement is accounted for as an operating lease. If a renewal, extension, or modification is not classified as a direct-financing lease, the present balance of the lease receivable is adjusted through the unearned-income account to reflect the change.

Accounting for Operating Leases

Lessors recognize rental income upon the receipt of rents under operating leases. Incentives that are paid to induce lessees to enter into leases reduce rental income on a straight-line basis over the life of the lease. Because lessors retain ownership of the leased asset, lessors also record depreciation on the asset. The example that follows is an illustration of accounting for operating leases.

EXAMPLE 6

Assume in Examples 1 and 5 that collectibility of lease payments is not reasonably assured. The lessee still accounts for the lease as capital. However, because collectibility of lease payments is not reasonably assured, Lessor accounts for the lease as an operating lease. Lessor makes the following entries to record receipt of the rent payment and depreciation on the asset:

Cash	135	
Rent revenue		135
Depreciation expense	60	
Accumulated depreciation		60

The cost of the asset net of salvage value (3000) divided by useful life (5 years) equals $60. It should be noted that both Lessor and Lessee depreciate the asset in this case. Lessor depreciates the asset over its useful life, while Lessee amortizes the asset over the life of the lease.

Exhibit 6-6 contains key accounting concepts of capital and operating leases for lessors.

The "Real" Impact of Classification on Accounting Records

Regardless of how a lease is classified, lessors have the same overall financial consequences. Unlike lessees, however, lessors will generally prefer that the lease not be classified as an operating lease, since an operating lease will result in lower reported net income in the earlier years of the lease.

Disclosure Requirements

FASB 13 requires that lessors disclose information about lease transactions. It requires lessors to disclose the following information about sales-type and direct-financing leases:

1. The components of the net investment as of the balance-sheet date
2. Future minimum lease payments to be received for each of the five succeeding fiscal years

FASB 13 requires lessors to disclose the following information about operating leases:

Exhibit 6-6
Key Accounting Concepts of Capital and Operating Leases—Lessors

Lessors classify leases as either direct-financing, sales-type, leveraged, or operating.

Lessors account for a sale-leaseback as a purchase and either financing or operating lease.

Direct-Financing

1. Direct-financing leases generate a receivable and unearned interest income.

2. Lessors record a receivable equal to the sum of the minimum lease payments. Unearned interest income equals the difference between the receivable and the present value of the minimum lease payments.

3. Lessors remove the leased asset from the accounting records.

Sales-Type

The only difference between sales-type and direct-financing leases is the former generates profit or loss. The difference between the cost and fair market value of the asset is the profit or loss.

1. Lessors record a receivable equal to the sum of the minimum lease payments. Unearned interest income equals the difference between the receivable and the present value of the minimum lease payments.

2. In addition to recording a receivable, lessors record a sale equal to the present value of the minimum lease payments. The carrying value of the asset less present value of unguaranteed residual value is charged to cost of sales.

Leveraged Leases

1. Leveraged leases are direct financing leases that involve three parties. The lessor obtains nonrecourse financing from the creditor.

2. Accounting for leveraged leases is the same as accounting for direct-financing leases except the lessor records the receivable net of the nonrecourse liability.

Operating Leases

1. Operating leases yield rent revenue, reported on the straight-line basis over the life of the lease.

2. Incentive payments reduce rent revenue.

3. Lessors own the asset under an operating lease and therefore are entitled to depreciate the asset.

Exhibit 6-7
Lessor's Disclosure (Company X)

<hr>

BALANCE SHEET

	December 31	
	1990	1989
Current assets:		
Net investment in direct financing and sales-type leases (Note 2)	XXX	XXX
Noncurrent assets:		
Net investment in direct financing and sales-type leases (Note 2)	XXX	XXX
Property on operating leases and property held for leases (net of accumulated depreciation of $XXX and $XXX for 1976 and 1975, respectively) (Note 3)	XXX	XXX

Footnotes appear (below and) on the following pages.

FOOTNOTES

Note 1 - Description of Leasing Arrangements

The company's leasing operations consist principally of the leasing of various types of heavy construction and mining equipment, data processing equipment and transportation equipment. With the exception of the leases of transportation equipment, the bulk of the Company's leases are classified as direct financing leases. The construction equipment and mining equipment leases expire over the next ten years and the data processing equipment leases expire over the next eight years. Transportation equipment (principally trucks) is leased under operating leases that expire during the next three years.

Note 2 - Net Investment in Direct Financing and Sales-Type Leases

The following lists the components of the net investment in direct financing and sales-type leases as of December 31:

	1990	1989
Total minimum lease payments to be received	$XXX	$XXX
Less: Amounts representing estimated executory cost (such as taxes, maintenance, and insurance), including profit thereon, included in total minimum lease payments	(XXX)	(XXX)
Minimum lease payments receivable	XXX	XXX
Less: Allowance for uncollectibles	(XXX)	(XXX)
Net minimum lease payments receivable	XXX	XXX
Estimated residual value of leased property (unguaranteed)	XXX	XXX
Less: Unearned income	(XXX)	(XXX)
Net investment in direct financing and sales-type leases	$XXX	$XXX
	====	====

Note 3 - Property on Operating Leases and Property Held for Lease

The following schedule provides and analysis of the Company's investment in property on operating leases and property held for lease by major classes as of December 31, 1990:

(continued)

Exhibit 6-7
(Continued)

```
        Construction equipment                    $XXX
        Mining equipment                           XXX
        Data Processing equipment                  XXX
        Transportation equipment                   XXX
        Other                                      XXX
                                                   XXX
        Less: Accumulated depreciation             XXX
                                                  $XXX

                                                  ====
```

```
Note 4 - Rentals under Operating Leases
```

The following is a schedule by years of minimum future rentals on noncancelable operating leases as of December 31, 1990:

```
        Year ending December 31:
             1991                                 $XXX
             1992                                  XXX
             1993                                  XXX
             1994                                  XXX
             1995                                  XXX
             Later years                           XXX
                                                   ===
```

Source: Reprinted from FASB Statement No. 13, Appendix D, par. 122.

1. Cost and carrying amount of leased property, and the amount of accumulated depreciation as of the balance sheet date
2. Minimum future rentals on noncancelable leases as of the balance sheet date, in the aggregate, and for each of the five succeeding fiscal years

All lessors must disclose a general description of their leasing transactions. Exhibit 6-7 illustrates how a lessor may satisfy disclosure requirements.

SUMMARY (EXHIBIT 6-8)

The critical decision regarding whether one should lease or purchase an asset is primarily a financial decision. In accounting for leases, the critical decision is the determination, at lease inception, of the appropriate lease classification (capital or operating), based on the criteria outlined in FASB Statement No. 13. Lease classification can have a significant impact on the reported accounting results of a lease arrangement.

The accounting rules treat lessors, under certain types of leases, as effectively selling the leased asset. Lessors under these types of leases

Exhibit 6-8
Summary of Key Leasing Concepts for Lessees and Lessors

ISSUE	LESSEE	LESSOR
1. DETERMINING THE CLASSIFICATION	- capital lease must meet at least one of the FASB 13 criteria	- capital lease meets the FASB 13 criteria
2. ACCOUNTING FOR CAPITAL LEASES	- records an asset and liability at lesser of present value of minimum lease payments or fair market value of the asset. - recognizes amortization expense * - each payment represents reduction of lease obligation and interest expense	- records a receivable at minimum lease payment - records unearned interest revenue
3. ACCOUNTING FOR SPECIFIC ISSUES: - unguaranteed residual values - guaranteed residual values - sales-type lease	- excluded in minimum lease payments - included in minimum lease payments - not applicable	- included in minimum lease payments - included in minimum lease payments - fair market value of asset exceeds lessor's cost - record sale = present value of minimum lease payments; cost of goods sold = asset's cost, less present value of unguaranteed residual value.

	Lessee	Lessor
- bargain purchase option	- present value of minimum lease payments includes present value of option price - computes depreciation over estimated useful life of asset*	
- lessor initial direct costs	- not applicable	- expense in year incurred for sales-type lease; add to investment in lease and amortize over lease term for direct-financing lease.
- sales-leaseback	- record sale equal to present value of minimum lease payments	- account for as purchase and either financing or operating lease
- leveraged lease	- account for as capital or operating lease	- record investment net of nonrecourse debt
- lease termination	- remove asset from books; may result in gain or loss	- remove net investment from accounts
- renewal, modifications	- if renewal or modification is capital in nature, adjust balances	- if renewal or modification is capital in nature, adjust balances
4. ACCOUNTING FOR OPERATING LEASES	- record rent expense	- record rent revenue and depreciation

* Amortize over lease term, or if lease transfers asset ownership or contains a bargain purchase option, over the estimated useful life of asset.

129

record a profit. On the other hand, no profit is recognized under operating leases, and lessors record depreciation. Lessees under operating leases deduct rent expense. Lessees under capital leases record an asset, incur a reportable obligation, and recognize periodic interest and depreciation expense.

Companies having lease transactions may consider these different consequences when determining whether to lease or buy an asset. The most important criterion determining the lease-versus-buy decision is whether the transaction makes overall business sense. Over the lease term, there is little impact of the different reporting standards on a company's overall financial position. While users of financial statements may make decisions based on the current impact of a lease classification, many sophisticated users refer to the required disclosures to determine overall claims on resources.

NOTES

1. Differences between accounting and tax treatment give rise to deferred-tax liability. A discussion of deferred taxes is beyond the scope of this book.

2. This chapter presents basic concepts central to understanding the effect of accounting on the lease–buy decision. Accounting for leases of real property, leases between related parties, and sub-leases is a complex area and, therefore, beyond the scope of this book.

3. See Exhibit 6-5.

4. An exception exists if an existing direct-financing lease is renewed or extended. In this case, the fact that the carrying amount of the property at the end of the original lease term differs from its fair market value does not preclude classification as direct-financing.

5. The lease term also includes all periods covered by ordinary renewal options if the lessee guarantees the lessor's debt related to the leased property, all periods covered by ordinary renewal options predating the date a bargain-purchase option is exercisable, and, all periods representing renewals or extensions of the lease at the lessor's option.

6. FASB Statement No. 13, par. 5(1).

7. Examples 1, 2, 4, 5, and 6 are adapted from FASB Statement No. 13, Appendix C, par. 121.

8. Accounting for sales-leaseback transactions is complex. This chapter presents basic accounting concepts pertaining to sales-leaseback transactions involving tangible personal property. The rules applicable to accounting for sales-leaseback transactions involving real property are somewhat different from the rules discussed here, and are more complicated if related parties are involved.

9. The sale must be made with full transfer of risk for profit to be recognized. If the sale is made to a related party, all the risks of ownership may not

have passed. Accounting for sales-leaseback transactions between related parties is beyond the scope of this book.

10. Accounting for changes due to refunding by the lessor of tax-exempt debt is beyond the scope of this book.

11. The straight-line method has more significance with respect to leases of real property.

12. If a direct-financing lease is renewed or extended during the lease term, and the fair market value of the asset at that date differs from its cost, the lease will, nevertheless, be classified as a direct-financing lease.

13. Another difference relates to the treatment of costs incurred in performing the lease and originating the lease. Lessors expense these costs when incurred if they arise in connection with a sales-type lease. Unless the costs are insignificant, lessors under financing leases capitalize and amortize these costs.

14. FASB Statement No. 13, Appendix B, par. 108.

15. This chapter presents only the theory behind accounting for leveraged leases. Accounting for leveraged leases can be complex and is beyond the scope of this chapter.

REFERENCES

Alderman, J., and C. Alderman. "Accounting for Leases." *The Journal of Accountancy* (June 1979): 74–79.

Blum, J. "Accounting and Reporting for Leases by Lessees: The Interest Rate Problems." *Management Accounting* (April 1987): 25–28.

Dieter, R. "Is Lessee Accounting Working?" *The CPA Journal* (August 1979): 13–19.

Ferrara, W. "The Case for Symmetry in Lease Reporting." *Management Accounting* (April 1978): 17–24.

Financial Accounting Standards Board. *Statement No. 13, Accounting for Leases*. Stamford, CT: FASB, 1976.

Kieso, D., and J. Weygandt. *Intermediate Accounting*. 6th ed. New York: Wiley, 1989.

IV

Evaluating Lease
Transactions

7

Introduction to Lease Valuation

In general, financial leases and corporate borrowing are very similar—both require that firms acquiring new assets make a contractual commitment to repay a fixed number of dollars over a long period of time. In the simplified and rarefied world of financial theory—where things like corporate taxes and business uncertainty do not exist to make life difficult—leasing and borrowing costs are identical to one another. In the real business world, however, leasing and borrowing costs can be quite dissimilar. Corporate tax rates are usually different across different businesses, firms in the market for new assets usually do not know with certainty the future salvage value of these assets, and the transaction costs associated with buying and selling assets are different for different firms. As a consequence, in the real world, leasing and borrowing costs usually differ.

At first glance, it might seem that this difference would present little difficulty in evaluating the lease-versus-borrow problem. Managers could simply decide on appropriate business projects, and then seek out the cheapest means to finance them. In the language of finance, picking the right projects is termed "the investment decision," while finding the best way to pay for these projects represents "the financing decision." In the case of borrowing, these two decisions are independent of one another. First the manager identifies the best projects, then the firm turns its attention to the optimal way to pay for them. Simply stated, the financing method does not affect the decision to select or reject a given project.

Leasing is somewhat more complicated because it combines certain aspects of investment and financing decisions. Rather than treating each step in the acquisition process separately and sequentially, leasing combines the decision to invest and the decision to lease into a single problem. Exhibit 7-1 provides a conceptual overview of the lease-

Exhibit 7-1
Evaluating the Leasing Alternative

136

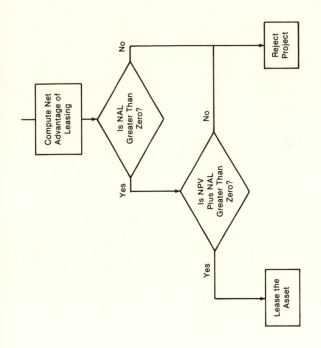

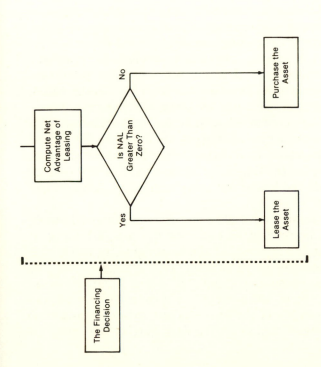

137

evaluation process. First, the net present value of the project is established using standard rules from capital budgeting.[1] In cases where this NPV is negative, the project is not automatically rejected because the financing advantages associated with leasing – known as the net advantage to leasing – can completely offset the negative NPV of the project. In this case, leasing can "rescue" an otherwise unprofitable project and lead the firm to accept it.

On the other hand, leasing can make good projects even better. In cases where a given project's NPV is greater than zero, a positive NAL can provide the firm with even larger cash flows by using the lease-financing option. In cases where the project NPV is positive but the NAL is negative, borrowing becomes the preferred way to acquire assets. In short, the important thing to remember is that evaluation of financial leases requires a joint, rather than independent analysis of the investment and financing decisions. This joint evaluation requires managers to calculate project NPVs and NALs. A number of reference books exist in the finance literature discussing business investment decisions and NPV analysis; the remainder of this chapter describes how to obtain the net advantage to leasing and evaluate the lease-versus-borrow dilemma.

THE NET ADVANTAGE TO LEASING

Calculating the net advantage of various leasing contracts represents a straightforward extension of corporate capital-budgeting concepts, recognizing that leasing and borrowing contain different financial consequences. In essence, the leasing transaction involves the purchase of necessary cash to acquire a particular asset, where the purchaser agrees to give up the asset's depreciation tax shields, salvage value, and investment tax credit in exchange for favorable financing terms. These financing terms are contained within the fixed series of cash lease payments that the lessee promises to pay the lessor. In the case of borrowing, the loan transaction involves the acquisition of cash to support asset purchases, where the financing transaction does not require the purchaser to provide the lender with any ownership rights in the acquired asset.

The net advantage to leasing recognizes the different financial consequences of leasing and borrowing, and adjusts the cost of leasing to reflect the loss of ownership rights that the lessee gives to the lessor. This adjustment process can be illustrated with a simple example. Consider the lease transaction in Exhibit 7-2, where a $50,000 asset can be leased for a series of six $10,500 payments. The first lease payment is due at the signing of the lease (today), with the remaining five payments due annually on the anniversary date of the lease. To

Exhibit 7-2
Leasing versus Borrowing: Sample Application for Business Assets (Base Case)

II. ASSET DEPRECIATION SCHEDULE (MACRS)

Depreciable Basis.................. $50,000

	YEAR 0 (1990)	YEAR 1 (1991)	YEAR 2 (1992)	YEAR 3 (1993)	YEAR 4 (1994)	YEAR 5 (1995)
	20.00%	32.00%	19.20%	11.52%	11.52%	5.76%
	$10,000	$16,000	$9,600	$5,760	$5,760	$2,880

I. INPUT DATA

Cost of Asset....................	$50,000.00
Modification/Delivery Costs....................	$0.00
Down Payment Required by Lease....................	$10,500.00
Lease Payment....................	$10,500.00
Term of Lease (Years)....................	5
Annual Maintenance Costs Paid by Lessor....................	$0.00
Corporate Tax Rate....................	34.00%
Asset Salvage Value....................	$0.00
Borrowing Cost (Before Tax)....................	11.00%
Weighted Average Cost of Capital....................	13.00%

LESSEE'S CAPITAL COSTS

After-Tax Cost of Debt....................	7.26%
Weighted Average Cost of Capital....................	13.00%

III. NET PRESENT VALUE OF LEASE CASH FLOWS

ITEM	YEAR 0 (1990)	YEAR 1 (1991)	YEAR 2 (1992)	YEAR 3 (1993)	YEAR 4 (1994)	YEAR 5 (1995)
Total Asset Cost (Including Modification & Delivery)....................	$50,000	$0	$0	$0	$0	$0
Lost Depreciation Tax Shield on Lease....................	($3,400)	($5,440)	($3,264)	($1,958)	($1,958)	($979)
Lease Payment....................	($10,500)	($10,500)	($10,500)	($10,500)	($10,500)	($10,500)
Tax Shield Provided by Lease Payment....................	$3,570	$3,570	$3,570	$3,570	$3,570	$3,570
Annual After-Tax Costs Paid by Lessor....................	$0	$0	$0	$0	$0	$0
After-Tax Salvage Value of Leased Asset....................	$0	$0	$0	$0	$0	$0
NET CASH FLOW OF LEASE....................	$39,670	($12,370)	($10,194)	($8,888)	($8,888)	($7,909)
PRESENT VALUE OF EACH NET CASH FLOW....................	$39,670	($11,533)	($8,861)	($7,203)	($6,715)	($5,571)
NET PRESENT VALUE OF LEASE FINANCING....................	($213)					

keep things simple, the 5-year duration of the lease corresponds to the asset's expected life, and the asset is depreciated on an accelerated basis toward a zero salvage value. The lessee's corporate tax rate is 34%, the before-tax cost of debt to this firm is 11%, and the corporate weighted-average cost of capital (WACC) is 13%.

These input data are summarized in Section I of Exhibit 7-2, and the annual depreciation charges for the asset and the prospective lessee's borrowing costs are shown in Section II. Computation of the NPV of the leasing alternative, which represents the net advantage to leasing, is provided in Section III of the exhibit. The relevant cash flows corresponding to the lease are recorded in the appropriate year; then these cash flows are discounted back to the present using the firm's appropriate cost of capital. For most cash flows in the lease evaluation, the lessee's after-tax cost of debt (7.26%) represents the proper discount rate. Lease payments, like debt payments, are contractual obligations of the lessee, and these payments take on the same default risk as the firm's other debts.

The annual cash flows associated with the lease transaction reflect the $50,000 cash inflow received by the lessee in the form of the asset acquisition, followed by a series of cash outflows corresponding to the costs of the lease. The depreciation tax shield foregone by the lessee represents the additional taxes that the lessee must pay in Years 0–6 because the depreciation expense from the $50,000 acquisition is lost to the lessor. The lease payment, adjusted downward for the tax savings it provides to the lessee, is shown next, followed by the after-tax salvage value of the leased asset at the conclusion of the lease. This value is shown as zero in Year 5, indicating that the leased asset will be worthless at the conclusion of the 5-year lease.

The annual net cash flows of the lease transaction are shown in Section III. Positive numbers represent net cash inflows to the lessee, while negative numbers capture the net cash costs of leasing. These cash flows are then discounted to the present (Year 0), using the 7.26% after-tax cost of debt as the relevant cost of capital. Adding the individual present values for Years 0–6 shows that the net advantage of this particular lease is negative $213. In this case, the net advantage of leasing is actually a disadvantage to the lessee, and the leasing option should be rejected by the firm.

In order to understand why the firm should reject the sample lease, it is necessary to explore the debt-displacement effect implied in the lease transaction. Because lease payments and debt are very similar, firms that lease assets find they are able to borrow less in debt markets. This occurs because the corporate cash flows used to make lease payments are not available to make loan payments, so the total debt burden of the firm must be adjusted downward to reflect the cash committed to leasing.

Exhibit 7-3 shows exactly how much debt is displaced, or given up, by the sample lease transaction shown in Exhibit 7-2. Looking first at Section II in Exhibit 7-3, we see the annual net cash flows associated with the lease transaction described in Exhibit 7-2. Section III of Exhibit 7-3 describes a borrowing transaction that requires exactly the same after-tax cash payments as the lease in Years 1–5. These debt-service payments support a loan of $39,883 in Year 0, while the very same after-tax lease cash flows provide only $39,670 in total financing under the lease option.

This shows that the cash outflows in Years 1–5 provide $213 more in debt capacity than the lease alternative offers the firm. In other words, the after-tax value received under the lease transaction in Year 0 ($39,670) displaces $39,883 worth of equivalent debt on the lessee's balance sheet. The negative $213 net advantage to leasing reflects that the firm actually gives up $213 in total financing by selecting the lease alternative.

Section I in Exhibit 7-3 shows that the net advantage to the lease, when subtracted from the after-tax cash inflow at the beginning of the lease, yields the total debt proceeds supported by the lease transaction's net cash outflows in Years 1–5. A negative NAL suggests that the prospective lessee will gain more borrowing capacity by using the net cash outflows from the lease transaction to borrow money and buy the asset. A positive NAL suggests the opposite – the net cash outflows from the lease provide greater borrowing capacity under the lease alternative. The same payments, when used to service debt, support a smaller loan balance than the original net cash inflow provided by the lease.

Unfortunately, realistic lease transactions are seldom as uncluttered as this example indicates, and subtle changes in the terms of the lease agreement can have a dramatic impact on the net advantage of leasing. The remainder of this section introduces a number of changes to the original lease contracts described in Exhibit 7-2 to make the illustration more realistic, and show how the terms of the lease influence the value of this financing option. First, consider a slight modification to the original lease where the lessee is able to negotiate a maintenance contract with the lessor. In this case, the lessor agrees to service the leased asset, saving the lessee $3000 in before-tax maintenance costs each year of the project's life. This before-tax reduction in maintenance costs translates into an annual $1980 after-tax gain to the lessee, and the net advantage to the lease rises to $9829.

Exhibit 7-4 illustrates how this modification to the original lease contracts yields substantial benefits to the lessee – the lease contract now provides $9829 more in total financing than the equivalent loan would offer. In other words, the after-tax net cash outflows in Years 1–5 shown in Section III provide the lessee the ability to borrow only

Exhibit 7-3
The Equivalent Loan Provided by the Net Cash Outflows of the Lease Transaction in Exhibit 7-2

I. LOAN TRANSACTION DETAILS

After-Tax Cash Inflow at Beginning of Lease	$39,670.00
- NPV of Lease	($213.00)
= Principal Balance	$39,883.00
Borrowing Cost (Before-Tax)	11.00%
Corporate Tax Rate	34.00%

II. THE LEASE TRANSACTION

	Year 0 (1990)	Year 1 (1991)	Year 2 (1992)	Year 3 (1993)	Year 4 (1994)	Year 5 (1995)
NET CASH OUTFLOWS FROM LEASE	$39,670.00	($12,370.00)	($10,194.00)	($8,888.00)	($8,888.00)	($7,909.00)

III. THE LOAN TRANSACTION

	Year 0 (1990)	Year 1 (1991)	Year 2 (1992)	Year 3 (1993)	Year 4 (1994)	Year 5 (1995)
Beginning Principal Balance	$39,883.00	$39,883.00	$30,408.51	$22,422.16	$15,162.01	$7,374.77
Before-Tax Interest Payment	---	$4,387.13	$3,344.94	$2,466.44	$1,667.82	$811.23
Interest Tax Shield	---	$1,491.62	$1,137.28	$838.59	$567.06	$275.82
After-Tax Interest Payment	---	$2,895.51	$2,207.66	$1,627.85	$1,100.76	$535.41
Principal Reduction	---	$9,474.49	$7,986.34	$7,260.15	$7,787.24	$7,373.59
Ending Principal Balance	---	$30,408.51	$22,422.16	$15,162.01	$7,374.77	$1.18
NET CASH OUTFLOWS FROM LOAN	$39,883.00	($12,370.00)	($10,194.00)	($8,888.00)	($8,888.00)	($7,909.00)

142

Exhibit 7-4

Leasing versus Borrowing: Sample Application for Business Assets
(Adding Maintenance Costs Borne by the Lessor to the Base Case)

I. INPUT DATA

Cost of Asset	$50,000.00
Modification/Delivery Costs	$0.00
Down Payment Required by Lease	$10,500.00
Lease Payment	$10,500.00
Term of Lease (Years)	5
Annual Maintenance Costs Paid by Lessor	$3,000.00
Corporate Tax Rate	34.00%
Asset Salvage Value	$0.00
Borrowing Cost (Before Tax)	11.00%
Weighted Average Cost of Capital	13.00%

II. ASSET DEPRECIATION SCHEDULE (MACRS)

Depreciable Basis........ $50,000

	YEAR 0 (1990)	YEAR 1 (1991)	YEAR 2 (1992)	YEAR 3 (1993)	YEAR 4 (1994)	YEAR 5 (1995)
	20.00%	32.00%	19.20%	11.52%	11.52%	5.76%
	$10,000	$16,000	$9,600	$5,760	$5,760	$2,880

LESSEE'S CAPITAL COSTS

After-Tax Cost of Debt	7.26%
Weighted Average Cost of Capital	13.00%

III. NET PRESENT VALUE OF LEASE CASH FLOWS

ITEM	YEAR 0 (1990)	YEAR 1 (1991)	YEAR 2 (1992)	YEAR 3 (1993)	YEAR 4 (1994)	YEAR 5 (1995)
Total Asset Cost (Including Modification & Delivery)	$50,000	$0	$0	$0	$0	$0
Lost Depreciation Tax Shield on Lease	($3,400)	($5,440)	($3,264)	($1,958)	($1,958)	($979)
Lease Payment	($10,500)	($10,500)	($10,500)	($10,500)	($10,500)	($10,500)
Tax Shield Provided by Lease Payment	$3,570	$3,570	$3,570	$3,570	$3,570	$3,570
Annual After-Tax Costs Paid by Lessor	$1,980	$1,980	$1,980	$1,980	$1,980	$1,980
After-Tax Salvage Value of Leased Asset	$0	$0	$0	$0	$0	$0
NET CASH FLOW OF LEASE	$41,650	($10,390)	($8,214)	($6,908)	($6,908)	($5,929)
PRESENT VALUE OF EACH NET CASH FLOW	$41,650	($9,687)	($7,140)	($5,598)	($5,219)	($4,176)
NET PRESENT VALUE OF LEASE FINANCING	$9,829					

$31,821 in Year 0. Under the lease alternative, these cash payments provide $41,650 in total financing to the firm.

Asset salvage values also have a significant impact on the net advantage of leasing. Higher salvage values translate into less attractive leasing terms from the perspective of the lessee because the lessee forfeits all disposal rights associated with leased assets. Returning to the original lease described in Exhibit 7-2, suppose the $50,000 leased asset retains 40% of its original value at the conclusion of the lease. Because the asset is fully depreciated at the end of Year 5, this $20,000 salvage value would represent a taxable gain to the firm, and the after-tax value of this gain becomes $13,200. Under the terms of the lease contract, however, the asset must be returned to the lessor at the end of the lease; the lessee gives up, rather than receives, the asset's $13,200 after-tax value.

Exhibit 7-5 modifies the original lease data to reflect the salvage value lost to the lessee. The problem is complicated somewhat by the addition of a second discount rate necessary to establish the present value of future cash flows. While the lease payments are still discounted at the after-tax cost of debt facing the lessee, the expected after-tax salvage value is discounted at the firm's 13% weighted-average cost of capital. In this case, the expected salvage value of the leased asset is known with far less certainty than the lessee's future lease payments; the added uncertainty regarding salvage value calls for the use of a higher discount rate. How much higher depends on the degree of uncertainty attached to the residual-value estimate. Since the leased asset is used in the lessee's normal business operations, the example requires a discount factor that, at minimum, captures the riskiness of the firm's operating cash flows. Hence, the lessee's weighted-average capital cost is used to discount the expected residual value.

Introducing a residual-value term within the original lease valuation problem causes the net advantage of the lease to decline from negative $213 to negative $7377, illustrating that forfeiture of disposal rights by the lessee can be extremely expensive. All other things being equal, the higher the expected residual value, the lower the net advantage to leasing, and the less attractive the leasing option from the lessee's perspective.

A final modification of the original lease data provided in Exhibit 7-2 concerns the introduction of different lessor–lessee tax rates. In many cases, prospective lessees in relatively low tax brackets can benefit from leasing because the value of depreciation tax shields given up in connection with the lease are more valuable to the lessor. This occurs when the lessor faces a higher tax rate than the lessee, so that the depreciation tax shield has a greater value in shielding the lessor's income from taxes. A portion of this value can be returned to the lessee,

Exhibit 7-5
Leasing versus Borrowing: Sample Application for Business Assets (Adding Asset Salvage Value to the Base Case)

I. INPUT DATA

Cost of Asset..	$50,000.00
Modification/Delivery Costs......................	$0.00
Down Payment Required by Lease..............	$10,500.00
Lease Payment...	$10,500.00
Term of Lease (Years)...............................	5
Annual Maintenance Costs Paid by Lessor...	$0.00
Corporate Tax Rate....................................	34.00%
Asset Salvage Value...................................	$20,000.00
Borrowing Cost (Before Tax).....................	11.00%
Weighted Average Cost of Capital..............	13.00%

II. ASSET DEPRECIATION SCHEDULE (MACRS)
Depreciable Basis........................ $50,000

	YEAR 0 (1990) 20.00%	YEAR 1 (1991) 32.00%	YEAR 2 (1992) 19.20%	YEAR 3 (1993) 11.52%	YEAR 4 (1994) 11.52%	YEAR 5 (1995) 5.76%
	$10,000	$16,000	$9,600	$5,760	$5,760	$2,880

LESSEE'S CAPITAL COSTS

After-Tax Cost of Debt...................	7.26%
Weighted Average Cost of Capital....	13.00%

III. NET PRESENT VALUE OF LEASE CASH FLOWS

ITEM	YEAR 0 (1990)	YEAR 1 (1991)	YEAR 2 (1992)	YEAR 3 (1993)	YEAR 4 (1994)	YEAR 5 (1995)
Total Asset Cost (Including Modification & Delivery)...	$50,000	$0	$0	$0	$0	$0
Lost Depreciation Tax Shield on Lease...................	($3,400)	($5,440)	($3,264)	($1,958)	($1,958)	($979)
Lease Payment...	($10,500)	($10,500)	($10,500)	($10,500)	($10,500)	($10,500)
Tax Shield Provided by Lease Payment..................	$3,570	$3,570	$3,570	$3,570	$3,570	$3,570
Annual After-Tax Costs Paid by Lessor.................	$0	$0	$0	$0	$0	$0
After-Tax Salvage Value of Leased Asset...............	$0	$0	$0	$0	$0	($13,200)
NET CASH FLOW OF LEASE.............................	$39,670	($12,370)	($10,194)	($8,888)	($8,888)	($21,109)
PRESENT VALUE OF EACH NET CASH FLOW.......	$39,670	($11,533)	($8,861)	($7,203)	($6,715)	($12,736)
NET PRESENT VALUE OF LEASE FINANCING........	($7,377)					

provided the lessor is willing to share the value of the depreciation tax shield by adjusting the lease payments downward.

Exhibit 7-6 illustrates how differential tax rates can influence the net advantage of the lease, even where the lease payment remains unchanged. In this illustration, the lessee's marginal tax rate is changed from the original 34% to 0%, holding all other data from the original example constant. This tax change would be appropriate when prospective lessees report little taxable income to the Internal Revenue Service due to operating losses or the availability of sufficient tax shields to offset positive operating income. The elimination of corporate taxes reduces the respective tax shields provided by asset depreciation and lease payments to zero; the net effect of these cash flow changes is to reduce the after-tax cost of the lease and increase the NPV of leasing to $693. In short, as the lessee's tax rate declines, the lease alternative becomes more and more attractive.

While the sample lease transactions described in this chapter present the net advantage to leasing from the perspective of the lessee, evaluating the lessor's financial gain or loss from leasing follows a similar structure. The lessor's financial consequences from the lease represent a mirror image of the lessee's position: the cash costs to the lessee represent cash receipts to the lessor, and the lessee's cash inflows become the lessor's cash costs. By inserting the relevant capital costs and tax rate for the lessor into the valuation framework shown in the illustrations, and reversing the direction of each cash flow in the analysis, the lease transactions presented in this section can be evaluated from the perspective of the lessor.

In this respect, notice that leasing represents a zero-sum activity as long as the lessor and lessee share similar tax rates and borrowing costs. A negative net advantage to leasing from the standpoint of the lessee becomes a positive lease advantage to the lessor, while a positive net advantage to the lessee represents a negative advantage for the lessor. The really interesting cases, where leases do not represent zero-sum transactions, occur when the lessee and lessor do not share the same tax rates and/or borrowing costs. In these cases, both lessors and lessees can realize a positive net advantage from a given lease contract, and share in the benefits of leasing.

THE EFFECTIVE COST OF LEASING

While the net advantage to leasing provides a clear indication regarding the value of different lease contracts, there may be circumstances in which it is difficult to use this valuation framework. Discounting future cash flows requires explicit specification of relevant capital costs to be effective. In some cases, the NAL valuation framework is compli-

Exhibit 7-6
Leasing versus Borrowing: Sample Application for Business Assets (Lessee's Marginal Tax Rate Changed from 34% to 0%)

I. INPUT DATA

Cost of Asset...	$50,000.00
Modification/Delivery Costs...	$0.00
Down Payment Required by Lease...	$10,500.00
Lease Payment...	$10,500.00
Term of Lease (Years)...	5
Annual Maintenance Costs Paid by Lessor...	$0.00
Corporate Tax Rate...	0.00%
Asset Salvage Value...	$0.00
Borrowing Cost (Before Tax)...	11.00%
Weighted Average Cost of Capital...	13.00%

II. ASSET DEPRECIATION SCHEDULE (MACRS)
Depreciable Basis... $50,000

	YEAR 0 (1990) 20.00%	YEAR 1 (1991) 32.00%	YEAR 2 (1992) 19.20%	YEAR 3 (1993) 11.52%	YEAR 4 (1994) 11.52%	YEAR 5 (1995) 5.76%
	$10,000	$16,000	$9,600	$5,760	$5,760	$2,880

LESSEE'S CAPITAL COSTS

After-Tax Cost of Debt...	11.00%
Weighted Average Cost of Capital...	13.00%

III. NET PRESENT VALUE OF LEASE CASH FLOWS

ITEM	YEAR 0 (1990)	YEAR 1 (1991)	YEAR 2 (1992)	YEAR 3 (1993)	YEAR 4 (1994)	YEAR 5 (1995)
Total Asset Cost (Including Modification & Delivery)...	$50,000	$0	$0	$0	$0	$0
Lost Depreciation Tax Shield on Lease...	$0	$0	$0	$0	$0	$0
Lease Payment...	($10,500)	($10,500)	($10,500)	($10,500)	($10,500)	($10,500)
Tax Shield Provided by Lease Payment...	$0	$0	$0	$0	$0	$0
Annual After-Tax Costs Paid by Lessor...	$0	$0	$0	$0	$0	$0
After-Tax Salvage Value of Leased Asset...	$0	$0	$0	$0	$0	$0
NET CASH FLOW OF LEASE...	$39,500	($10,500)	($10,500)	($10,500)	($10,500)	($10,500)
PRESENT VALUE OF EACH NET CASH FLOW...	$39,500	($9,459)	($8,522)	($7,678)	($6,917)	($6,231)
NET PRESENT VALUE OF LEASE FINANCING...	$693					

cated by the need to identify multiple discount rates, where each rate reflects a level of risk corresponding to the degree of uncertainty associated with various cash flow estimates. For example, Exhibit 7-5 discounts the certain lease payments at the lessee's after-tax cost of debt, and the more uncertain asset salvage value at the firm's weighted-average cost of capital.

As a practical matter, the NAL evaluation process described above may lead to difficulties in valuing lease transactions. In some cases, it may be difficult or impossible to relate the riskiness of various cash flows to an appropriate series of discount rates. In other cases, managers of smaller firms may be unable to specify accurately their firms' weighted-average capital cost for use as a benchmark in selecting appropriate discount rates. Finally, it may be desirable for managers to express the cost of lease financing in percentage terms, so that leasing costs, borrowing costs, and project returns can be directly compared to one another. In these cases, the lease valuation procedure contained within the NAL framework can be modified to report the effective percentage cost of leasing.

This modification follows the familiar style of the internal rate of return calculation used in capital budgeting.[2] To establish the effective percentage cost of leasing in the IRR framework, the future net cash outflows associated with the lease are discounted at various interest rates to determine the specific rate of discount at which the present value of these future outflows will equal the net cash receipt provided at the beginning of the lease.[3] This particular interest rate represents the effective annual cost of the lease, expressed in percentage terms.

Exhibit 7-7 provides the annual net cash flows associated with each of the lease transactions described in this chapter. The annual cash flows from Exhibit 7-2 are reported in the first line of the exhibit. The effective cost of this particular lease, 7.48%, represents the rate of discount at which the present value of the cash flows from Years 1–5 is equal to $39,670, which is the net after-tax receipt to the lessee in Year 0. In this particular case, the effective cost of leasing (7.48%) lies above the firm's after-tax cost of debt (7.26%), indicating that the lease option should be rejected in favor of borrowing. This result is consistent with the negative $213 net advantage to leasing obtained for this lease transaction in Exhibit 7-2.

Using a similar comparison between the effective lease cost and after-tax borrowing cost for the four different lease transactions shown in Exhibit 7-7, it is easy to verify that financing decisions based on the percentage cost of leasing are consistent with decisions reached using the NAL method. This consistency may not extend to all possible lease transactions, however, because the IRR method, which provides a framework for the effective cost of leasing, yields inaccurate results in

Exhibit 7-7
The Effective Cost of Leasing

Lease Example	YEAR 0 (1990)	YEAR 1 (1991)	YEAR 2 (1992)	NET CASH FLOWS FROM THE LEASING TRANSACTION YEAR 3 (1993)	YEAR 4 (1994)	YEAR 5 (1995)	EFFECTIVE COST OF THE LEASE
Exhibit 7-2	$39,670	($12,370)	($10,194)	($8,888)	($8,888)	($7,909)	7.48%
Exhibit 7-4	$41,650	($10,390)	($8,214)	($6,908)	($6,908)	($5,929)	-2.94%
Exhibit 7-5	$39,670	($12,370)	($10,194)	($8,888)	($8,888)	($21,109)	15.21%
Exhibit 7-6	$39,500	($10,500)	($10,500)	($10,500)	($10,500)	($10,500)	10.30%

certain cases.[4] In addition, the effective cost of the leasing procedure requires that the investment decision and the financing decision be treated separately. As described at the beginning of this chapter, separation of the investment and financing decisions violates the premise that lease financing joins these two decisions in a single, related framework. By using the effective cost of leasing as a basis for the selection of appropriate financing alternatives, managers give up the opportunity to rescue negative NPV projects with positive NAL lease financing. This leads to inappropriate financial decisions, and the rejection of value-creating projects within the firm.

VALUING VARIABLE-RATE LEASE CONTRACTS

While the evaluation of fixed-rate leases is relatively straightforward, variable-rate leases require a bit more effort to understand. However, the valuation principles presented above provide the basic foundation necessary to evaluate variable-rate lease agreements. In essence, the variable-rate lease represents a financing arrangement in which the lease payments may be adjusted during the term of the lease in response to a change in interest rates. These adjustments usually occur on a periodic basis by applying the change in interest rates to the amount of the lessor's investment in the lease.

The purpose of the variable-rate lease is to protect the lessor against changes in interest rates during the term of the lease. When interest rates rise, the lease payment also increases to provide the lessor with an additional return on capital invested in the lease. When interest rates fall, the lease payment is reduced to reflect the lower cost of funds prevailing in the capital market. Because variable-rate leases protect lessors from interest rate variations in much the same way that variable-rate loans protect commercial lenders, these financing arrangements are quite popular. Given this popularity, any discussion of lease valuation is not complete without an introduction to the essential elements of variable-rate leases.

The methods used to evaluate variable-rate leases are similar to the methods of fixed-rate lease analysis—with one major exception. Prior to computing the NAL, the variable-rate lease payment must be transformed into its fixed-rate equivalent in order to adjust the variable-lease payment for the possibility that it can increase and decrease over the term of the lease. Adjusting the variable-rate lease payment to its fixed-rate equivalent rests on the premise that fixed-rate financing options can be expressed as a combination of a variable-rate investment and a fixed-rate borrowing transaction. In the language of finance, this synthetic combination of securities—a loan and an investment— produces cash flows that are exactly the same as the cash flows in the variable-rate lease. Because these cash flows are the same, the value of the synthetic borrowing/lending combination and the variable-rate lease must also be the same. As such, the synthetic combination of securities is useful for deriving the value of the variable-rate lease.

A simple illustration, based on the original lease data presented in Exhibit 7-2, helps to demonstrate the variable-rate lease valuation process. First, it is important to understand how lessors "price" a particular lease, or develop a schedule of payments that lessees must pay. Exhibit 7-8 provides a pricing schedule for the original lease described in Exhibit 7-2. The second column in Exhibit 7-8 shows the after-tax lease cash flows from the perspective of the lessor. A net investment of $39,670 produces net returns of $12,370 in Year 1, $10,194 in Year 2, and so forth. In order to keep the illustration as simple as possible, the lessor's tax rate (34%) is the same as the lessee's tax rate, as shown in Exhibit 7-2.

Columns 3–5 show how the lessor's net investment in the lease changes over the life of this financing contract, where the lessor's after-tax cost of funds is 7.48%. As lease payments are received, the lessor first covers its financing costs, and then applies the balance of the net cash inflows to reduce the net principal balance invested in the lease. Viewed in this manner, Exhibit 7-8 represents a brief amortization schedule for the lease, where the lessor has priced the lease to yield an after-tax return of 7.48%.

The most important element in Exhibit 7-8, from the standpoint of the variable-rate lease, is Column 3, representing the lessor's periodic net investment in the lease. When interest rates rise or fall, this change in rates is applied to the lessor's current investment in the lease to obtain the revised variable-rate lease payment. This adjustment process is shown in Exhibit 7-9. For purposes of illustration, it is assumed that the lease payment is linked to the annual level of the prime lending rate. Column 2 in Exhibit 7-9 shows that, during the life of the lease, the prime rate rises from 10% in 1990 to a peak of 12% in 1992, and then falls to 9% by 1995. The variable-rate lease payment is established by taking the base lease payment of $10,500, shown in Column 4, and adding or subtracting an adjustment factor based on the change in interest rates. The specific annual-adjustment factors for Years 1–5, shown in Column 6, are obtained by multiplying the change in interest rates by the lessor's remaining net investment in the lease.

Given the variable-rate lease payments shown in Column 7 of Exhibit 7-9, it should be fairly easy to value the lease contract. Unfortunately, the variable-rate lease payments remain unknown until a change in interest rates occurs. The level of interest rates shown in Exhibit 7-9 is provided only for purposes of illustration. In 1990, lessees have no way of knowing what rate changes are in store over the 5-year term of the

Exhibit 7-8
Lessor's Net Investment in the Lease (Base Case)

(1) Date	(2) Lease Cash Flow	(3) Net Investment in Lease (Beginning of Period)	(4) (3) x 7.48% Lessor's Cost of Funds (7.48%)	(5) (3)+(4)-(2) Net Investment in Lease (End of Period)
1990	($39,670)	$0	$0	$39,670
1991	$12,370	$39,670	$2,966	$30,266
1992	$10,194	$30,266	$2,263	$22,335
1993	$8,888	$22,335	$1,670	$15,117
1994	$8,888	$15,117	$1,130	$7,359
1995	$7,909	$7,359	$550	$0

Exhibit 7-9
Variable Lease Payment Calculation

(1) Date	(2) Prime Lending Rate*	(3) Lessor's Investment Basis	(4) Base Lease Payment	(5) Variable Payment Adjustment Formula	(6) Variable Payment Adjustment Dollars	(7) (4)+(6) Total Lease Payment
1990	10% (r0)	$0	$10,500	N/A	$0	$10,500
1991	11% (r1)	$39,670	$10,500	$39,670 x (r1 - r0)	$397	$10,897
1992	12% (r2)	$30,266	$10,500	$30,266 x (r2 - r0)	$605	$11,105
1993	11% (r3)	$22,335	$10,500	$22,335 x (r3 - r0)	$223	$10,723
1994	10% (r4)	$15,117	$10,500	$15,117 x (r4 - r0)	$0	$10,500
1995	9% (r5)	$7,359	$10,500	$7363 x (r5 - r0)	($74)	$10,426

* r(n) represents the prime lending rate of interest in year n.

153

lease. By comparing the variable-rate lease to the synthetic invest-
ment/borrowing transaction described above, however, we see that it is
not necessary to know future interest rate changes throughout the
1991–1995 period in order to value the lease in 1990.

Exhibit 7-10 provides the data necessary to transform the variable-
rate lease payment into its fixed-rate equivalent. The prime lending
rates shown in Column 2 and the variable-rate lease payments in Column 3 are the original data shown in Exhibit 7-9. In order to transform
these lease payments into fixed-rate equivalents, notice that the lessee's exposure to changes in interest rates could be completely eliminated by borrowing on a fixed-rate basis, and simultaneously lending
on a variable-rate basis, an amount equal to the declining annual principal balance of the lease.

If interest rates rise during the course of the lease, the increase in the
lease payment will be offset by a similar increase in interest revenue
received from the variable-rate investment transaction, while the interest expense from the fixed-rate loan remains constant. If interest rates
decrease during the term of the lease, the reduction in the variable-rate
lease payment is offset by a reduction in interest revenue from the
variable-rate investment. In the language of finance, the lessee has
obtained a perfectly hedged position, where changes in interest rates no
longer change the firm's lease cash flows.

The trick to valuing variable-rate leases, however, is not for the lessee
actually to borrow on a fixed-rate basis, and lend on a variable-rate
basis, amounts equal to the principal balance of the lease. Rather,
the real idea here is to map out the cash flows from the synthetic-
investment strategy to see how they relate to the variable-rate lease
payments, and then use this relationship to transform the variable-rate
payments into their fixed-rate equivalents. This transformation is illustrated in Exhibit 7-10: Column 4 shows the principal balance of the
lease exposed to interest-rate risk in each year of the contract; Column
5 shows the variable rate at which the lessee can lend in the capital
market (assumed here to be 2% below the prime lending rate); and
Column 6 shows the lessee's current (1990) fixed-rate borrowing cost.
This borrowing cost is assumed to be 1% above the 10% prime lending
rate in 1990.

The bottom portion of Exhibit 7-10 details the lessee's hedged position in 1991 that results from these details. Notice that the firm's total, before-tax cash outflows include the variable-rate lease payment
and the 11% fixed borrowing cost on the $39,670 loan transaction.
These outflows are partially offset, however, by the interest revenue received from the one-year variable-rate loan made by the lessee at prime
minus 2% (10% − 2% = 8%). Combining these cash flows, the net effect is to increase the lessee's total lease expense from $10,500 (the base

Exhibit 7-10
Developing the Equivalent Fixed-Rate Lease Payment

(1)	(2)	(3)	(4)	(5)	(6)	(7) (4) x (5)	(8) (4) x (6)	(9) (3)−(7)+(8)	(10) $10,500 + (4) x (.03)
	Prime Lending Rate	Variable-Rate Lease Payment	Lease Balance Exposed to Interest Rate Risk	Lessee's Variable Lending Rate (Prime − 2%)	Lessee's Fixed Borrowing Cost (11%)	Interest Paid to Lessee from Variable-Rate Loan	Interest Paid by Lessee on Fixed-Rate Borrowing	Equivalent Fixed-Rate Lease Payment Method 1	Equivalent Fixed-Rate Lease Payment Method 2
Date									
1990	10%	$10,500	$0	8%	11%	$0	$0	$10,500	$10,500
1991	11%	$10,897	$39,670	9%	11%	$3,570	$4,364	$11,690	$11,690
1992	12%	$11,105	$30,226	10%	11%	$3,023	$3,325	$11,407	$11,407
1993	11%	$10,723	$22,335	9%	11%	$2,010	$2,457	$11,170	$11,170
1994	10%	$10,500	$15,117	8%	11%	$1,209	$1,663	$10,954	$10,954
1995	9%	$10,426	$7,363	7%	11%	$515	$810	$10,721	$10,721

Summarizing Lessee's Hedged Position in 1991:

Cash Outflows:

Variable-Rate Lease Payment* .... $10,500 + $39,670 x (r1 − 10%)

(Plus)   Interest Paid by Lessee on Fixed-Rate Borrowing .... $39,670 x (11%)

     ========= =========

TOTAL CASH OUTFLOWS .... $10,500 + $39,670 x (r1 − 10% + 11%)

Cash Inflows:

Interest Earned by Lessee on Variable-Rate Loan* .... $39,670 x (r1 − 2%)

Net Cash Outflow:

TOTAL CASH OUTFLOWS* .... $10,500 + $39,670 x (r1 + 1%)

(Minus)   TOTAL CASH INFLOWS* .... $39,670 x (r1 − 2%)

     ========= =========

NET CASH OUTFLOW* .... $10,500 + $39,670 x [(r1 + 1%) − (r1 − 2%)]

$10,500 + $39,670 x .03

*r(n) represents the prime lending rate of interest in year n.

variable-rate payment) to $10,500 plus 3% of the lessor's 1991 investment in the lease.

While the transaction details of the hedge are presented only for the 1991 position of the lease, the results from the synthetic lending/borrowing transaction are the same for each year of the lease. The net cash outflow paid by the lessee will always be the base variable-rate payment ($10,500) plus 3% of the lease's annual principal balance. Because this result occurs regardless of any change in the prime lending rate between 1990 and 1995, the lessee is completely protected from any variation in interest rates. This net cash outflow represents the fixed-rate equivalent for the original variable-rate lease payment.

Columns 7 through 10 in Exhibit 7-10 demonstrate this result for each year of the lease. Column 9 shows the equivalent fixed-rate lease payment in each year by adding the annual interest cost of the lessee's fixed-rate borrowing transaction (Column 8) to the variable-rate lease payment (Column 3), and then subtracting the interest received each year from the lessee's variable-rate loan (Column 7). This is the hard way to obtain equivalent fixed-rate lease payments. The easy way, shown in Column 10, simply adds 3% of the lease's annual principle balance to the original $10,500 lease payment. Notice that Columns 9 and 10 both produce the same schedule of equivalent fixed-rate lease payments for the sample transaction.

It is important to note that the 3% premium, paid by the lessee to avoid interest-rate risk, follows from the variable-lending return of two percentage points below the prevailing prime rate and the fixed-borrowing cost equal to 1% above the original prime lending rate. As these borrowing costs and lending returns differ across different lessees, the fixed-rate equivalent lease payment will also change. Once the borrowing cost and lending returns for a particular lessee are known, it becomes quite simple to calculate the fixed-rate equivalent lease payment. This is achieved by adding the lending deficit (in this illustration, the 2% difference between the original prime rate and the lessee's variable-rate return) and the borrowing premium (in this illustration, the 1% difference between the lessee's fixed-rate borrowing cost and the prime rate), and then multiplying this percentage figure by the annual principal balance of the lease. As a final step, this fixed-rate adjustment factor is added to the base variable-rate lease payment ($10,500) to obtain the fixed-rate equivalent lease payment.

Once the fixed-rate equivalent payments have been identified, valuing the variable-rate lease becomes easy. Exhibit 7-11 shows the details of this valuation, where the fixed-rate lease payments are inserted for the before-tax lease payments in each year of the contract. Notice that the payments shown in Exhibit 7-10 are presented in before-tax terms, so that the net impact of corporate taxes can be shown in Exhibit 7-11.

Exhibit 7-11
Valuing the Equivalent Fixed-Rate Lease

I. INPUT DATA

Cost of Asset...	$50,000.00
Modification/Delivery Costs..................	$0.00
Down Payment Required by Lease..........	$10,500.00
Lease Payment......................................	Variable
Term of Lease (Years)..........................	5
Annual Maintenance Costs Paid by Lessor.	$0.00
Corporate Tax Rate................................	34.00%
Asset Salvage Value..............................	$0.00
Borrowing Cost (Before Tax).................	11.00%
Weighted Average Cost of Capital..........	13.00%

II. ASSET DEPRECIATION SCHEDULE (MACRS)

Depreciable Basis.................. $50,000

	YEAR 0 (1990) 20.00%	YEAR 1 (1991) 32.00%	YEAR 2 (1992) 19.20%	YEAR 3 (1993) 11.52%	YEAR 4 (1994) 11.52%	YEAR 5 (1995) 5.76%
	$10,000	$16,000	$9,600	$5,760	$5,760	$2,880

LESSEE'S CAPITAL COSTS

After-Tax Cost of Debt..........................	7.26%
Weighted Average Cost of Capital..........	13.00%

III. NET PRESENT VALUE OF LEASE CASH FLOWS

ITEM	YEAR 0 (1990)	YEAR 1 (1991)	YEAR 2 (1992)	YEAR 3 (1993)	YEAR 4 (1994)	YEAR 5 (1995)
Total Asset Cost (Including Modification & Delivery)...	$50,000	$0	$0	$0	$0	$0
Lost Depreciation Tax Shield on Lease...	($3,400)	($5,440)	($3,264)	($1,958)	($1,958)	($979)
Lease Payment......................................	($10,500)	($11,690)	($11,407)	($11,170)	($10,954)	($10,721)
Tax Shield Provided by Lease Payment.	($3,570)	($3,975)	($3,878)	($3,798)	($3,724)	($3,645)
Annual After-Tax Costs Paid by Lessor.	$0	$0	$0	$0	$0	$0
After-Tax Salvage Value of Leased Asset.	$0	$0	$0	$0	$0	$0
NET CASH FLOW OF LEASE...............	$32,530	($21,105)	($18,549)	($16,926)	($16,637)	($15,345)
PRESENT VALUE OF EACH NET CASH FLOW...	$32,530	($19,676)	($16,123)	($13,717)	($12,569)	($10,809)
NET PRESENT VALUE OF LEASE FINANCING...	($40,365)					

As always, the net cash flows from the lease are discounted at the lessee's after-tax cost of debt, producing a net advantage to leasing equal to negative $40,365. This represents the lessee's reward for working through the details of variable-rate lease valuation. By correctly evaluating this particular lease and summarily rejecting it, the firm can save $40,365 in reserve borrowing capacity.

VALUING CONSUMER LEASE AGREEMENTS

The lease-versus-borrow dilemma is seldom confined to business transactions. It also invades consumer finance decisions, particularly in the acquisition of motor vehicles. Private new car leasing volume accelerated at an average annual rate of 24% between 1982 and 1987, reaching 750,000 leased vehicles in 1987. This total represented 7% of the new car sales market, and according to leasing industry sources, the growth in consumer vehicle leasing is expected to accelerate in the 1990s. Sooner or later, most new car buyers will confront the choice between leasing or borrowing to acquire personal transportation.

In many cases, consumers incorrectly select the leasing option because it offers lower monthly payments, a smaller down payment, or the opportunity to acquire a more expensive vehicle than the installment-purchase alternative. In other cases, consumers incorrectly select leasing to take advantage of the tax deductibility of lease payments. The Tax Reform Act of 1986 significantly restricts this tax benefit; most consumers can no longer deduct vehicle lease payments from taxable income. Specifically, individuals earning income as employees are not permitted to deduct any personal vehicle lease payments, even if the auto is used in connection with the taxpayer's employment — unless the vehicle is required as a condition of employment and used at the convenience of the employer.

Moreover, the 1986 tax law phases out the personal interest deduction associated with vehicle installment purchases. After 1990, the tax deduction for personal interest charges is completely eliminated. While business interest expenses remain tax deductible after 1990, individuals performing services as employees do not constitute a business for purposes of deducting installment interest payments. In short, neither installment interest charges nor vehicle lease payments paid by most consumers after 1990 will be tax deductible.

That is the bad news. But there is a small amount of good news associated with consumer finance and the 1986 tax law revisions. Because neither leasing nor borrowing costs are tax deductible, evaluating the lease–borrow dilemma is really quite simple. Unfortunately, new car buyers must do a bit of work to identify the best financing option because lease data and installment-borrowing costs are seldom presented to consumers in comparable terms. The Truth-In-Lending Act of 1969 requires installment lenders to express the effective cost of borrowing in the form of an annual percentage rate of interest, so that consumers can accurately and quickly compare the cost of different borrowing options. In contrast, the Consumer Leasing Act of 1976 does not require lessors to report the effective cost of leasing in a manner comparable with the APR. Therefore, a simple and direct comparison of the percentage costs of leasing and installment borrowing is impossible.

All is not lost, however, because the lease evaluation methods presented in this chapter can be adapted to address the consumer lease evaluation problem. In general, the valuation of consumer leases follows the effective cost of leasing methodology. Exhibit 7-12 summarizes the details from one particular lease–borrow alternative recently promoted in the new car sales literature. In this case, consumers could acquire a new General Motors automobile with a $12,000 purchase price by (1) leasing the vehicle for a 48-month period at $222.58 per month or (2) placing $2400 down against the vehicle's purchase and financing the $9600 balance for 48 months at $245.71 per month. The installment-borrowing option carried an APR of 11%, but the effective cost of the lease was not provided to potential customers.

Sections II–IV of Exhibit 7-12 summarize the cash flow differences between the leasing and borrowing options. At the signing of the financing contract, lessees were required to pay a refundable security deposit of $225 and the first month's $222.58 lease payment, for a total cash outflow of $447.58. Installment borrowers were required to provide a cash down payment of $2400 at the signing of the loan contract. Subtracting the initial lease expenses from the down payment required in the loan contract yields a $1952.42 net advantage to the lease transaction (see Section II).

In Months 1–47, the net advantage of the lease shrinks to $23.13, representing the difference between the monthly lease payment ($222.58) and the monthly loan payment ($245.71). In Month 48, the net payment advantage to the lease is $245.71, because the final lease payment occurs in Month 47, while the final installment loan payment is due in Month 48 (see Section III).

Section IV details the final cash costs associated with the leasing and borrowing alternatives. Lessees receive $225 in cash from the refund of the original lease security deposit, but they give up the $4884 residual value of the leased vehicle to the lessor. In this illustration, the vehicle retains 41% of its original value, obtained from the cost at which the lessee can buy the vehicle at the conclusion of the lease.

Exhibit 7-12
Leasing versus Borrowing for Personal Assets

I. DETAILS

A. Asset: 1990 GM
B. Cost: $12,000.00

II. INITIAL CASH COSTS (t=0)

A. Leasing
  1. Refundable Security Deposit $225.00
  2. First Lease Payment (Due in Advance) $222.58
     TOTAL $447.58

B. Installment Purchase
  1. Down Payment $2,400.00
     TOTAL $2,400.00

C. Net Advantage to Leasing (Initial) $1,952.42

IV. FINAL CASH COSTS (t=48)

A. Leasing
  1. Refund of Security Deposit $225.00
  2. Asset Value Returned to Lessor $4,884.00
     TOTAL .... ($4,659.00)

B. Installment Purchase $0.00

C. Net Advantage to Leasing (Final) .... ($4,659.00)

V. LEASE HURDLE RATE 11.75%

III. MONTHLY CASH COSTS

Month	0	1	2	3	4	5	6	7	8	9	10
Loan Payment	$2,400.00	$245.71	$245.71	$245.71	$245.71	$245.71	$245.71	$245.71	$245.71	$245.71	$245.71
Lease Payment	$447.58	$222.58	$222.58	$222.58	$222.58	$222.58	$222.58	$222.58	$222.58	$222.58	$222.58
Net Advantage to Leasing	$1,952.42	$23.13	$23.13	$23.13	$23.13	$23.13	$23.13	$23.13	$23.13	$23.13	$23.13

Month	11	12	13	14	15	16	17	18	19	20	21
Loan Payment	$245.71	$245.71	$245.71	$245.71	$245.71	$245.71	$245.71	$245.71	$245.71	$245.71	$245.71
Lease Payment	$222.58	$222.58	$222.58	$222.58	$222.58	$222.58	$222.58	$222.58	$222.58	$222.58	$222.58
Net Advantage to Leasing	$23.13	$23.13	$23.13	$23.13	$23.13	$23.13	$23.13	$23.13	$23.13	$23.13	$23.13

Month	22	23	24	25	26	27	28	29	30	31	32
Loan Payment	$245.71	$245.71	$245.71	$245.71	$245.71	$245.71	$245.71	$245.71	$245.71	$245.71	$245.71
Lease Payment	$222.58	$222.58	$222.58	$222.58	$222.58	$222.58	$222.58	$222.58	$222.58	$222.58	$222.58
Net Advantage to Leasing	$23.13	$23.13	$23.13	$23.13	$23.13	$23.13	$23.13	$23.13	$23.13	$23.13	$23.13

Month	33	34	35	36	37	38	39	40	41	42	43
Loan Payment	$245.71	$245.71	$245.71	$245.71	$245.71	$245.71	$245.71	$245.71	$245.71	$245.71	$245.71
Lease Payment	$222.58	$222.58	$222.58	$222.58	$222.58	$222.58	$222.58	$222.58	$222.58	$222.58	$222.58
Net Advantage to Leasing	$23.13	$23.13	$23.13	$23.13	$23.13	$23.13	$23.13	$23.13	$23.13	$23.13	$23.13

Month	44	45	46	47	48
Loan Payment	$245.71	$245.71	$245.71	$245.71	$245.71
Lease Payment	$222.58	$222.58	$222.58	$222.58	$0.00
Net Advantage to Leasing	$23.13	$23.13	$23.13	$23.13	$245.71

Because this purchase option price is clearly stated in the original lease contract, it is easy for lessees to identify the expected salvage value of a leased vehicle.

Finally, note that all cash flows shown in Exhibit 7-12 contain no adjustment for personal taxes because both lease payments and installment borrowing costs are assumed to be non-tax deductible. Armed with these data, it is a simple matter to identify the optimal financing alternative. The lease hurdle rate, reported in Section V, defines the after-tax rate of return necessary to transform the periodic cash savings from leasing during the term of the lease into the final net cash outflow incurred by lessees at the conclusion of the lease. In this illustration, lessees, who can earn an annual, after-tax return of 11.75% by investing the positive net cash advantage to the lease from Months 0 through 47, will have a cash balance equal to $4659 in Month 48. Thus, the savings generated from leasing exactly offsets the loss of the vehicle at the conclusion of the lease.

When lessees can earn an after-tax return on invested capital exceeding 11.75%, the leasing alternative provides greater total wealth than borrowing. By investing the net advantage to leasing over the term of the lease, the lessee's total invested cash balance at the maturity of the lease exceeds the net residual value of the leased asset returned to the lessor. If lessees face an after-tax return on invested capital below 11.75%, then installment purchase is the preferred financing alternative. In this case, the future value of invested cash flows from leasing falls short of the vehicle's market value at lease maturity, so that the wealth of the vehicle owner exceeds the value of the lessee's cash investment.

In cases where lessees earn exactly 11.75% on invested capital, leasing once again represents the best financing alternative. While this condition suggests that the future value of the lessee's invested capital will equal the market value of the borrower's asset at lease maturity, the lessee's financial investment provides greater liquidity than the owner's vehicle. It is easier to convert financial assets to cash at their fair market value than automobiles.

Of course, the validity of this analysis requires that consumers are able to invest periodic net cash flows at the 11.75% after-tax rate throughout the term of the lease contract. As market interest rates become increasingly volatile, the rates of return at which the incremental cash flows are invested will vary over time. In this situation, the appropriate investment return used to evaluate the lease hurdle rate should represent the average annual return consumers expect to earn on invested cash over the life of the lease.

As a final point, note that the lease hurdle rate shown in Exhibit 7-12 is particularly sensitive to the estimated residual value of the leased asset at the maturity of the lease. The higher this value, the less attractive the leasing option; higher salvage values correspond to larger cash outflows at the conclusion of the lease. As a consequence, vehicles that depreciate at rapid rates — such as autos used for business purposes, those subject to excessive mileage, or those operated in a hostile environment — are better candidates for leasing. Vehicles that depreciate more slowly, in contrast, represent stronger candidates for installment purchase.

SUMMARY

This chapter presents a variety of analytical tools useful in evaluating lease-versus-borrow decisions. These tools are derived from two basic lease valuation techniques: (1) the net advantage to leasing framework, which discounts the net after-tax cash flows associated with lease transactions to obtain the present value of leasing costs and (2) the effective cost of leasing methodology, which identifies the annual percentage cost of lease contracts. The chapter also provides a number of lease valuation illustrations, showing how the terms of the lease, the use of the leased asset, and the lessee's tax status influence the cost of leasing. Finally, the chapter treats the valuation of variable-rate leases and consumer motor vehicle leases.

In general terms, leasing and borrowing costs are quite similar in cases where lessors and lessees share the same marginal tax rate, the same expectations regarding the salvage value of leased assets, the same borrowing costs, and the same return on financial investments. In cases where lessors and lessees do not share these financial characteristics, it follows that leasing and borrowing costs will diverge from one another. Accordingly, leasing may provide reduced financing costs in cases where the lessee falls into a lower tax bracket than the lessor; the lessor maintains a lower cost of borrowing than the lessee, or the lessor has a comparative advantage over the lessee in estimating the salvage value of leased assets and disposing of these assets in secondary markets.

NOTES

1. The finance literature offers many sources of information concerning the capital budgeting process. These include H. Bierman, Jr. and S. Smidt, *The Capital Budgeting Decision*, 7th rev. ed. (New York: MacMillan, 1988); J. J. Clark, T. J. Hindelang, and R. E. Pritchard, *Capital Budgeting* (Englewood Cliffs, NJ: Prentice-Hall, 1989); and N. E. Seitz, *Capital Budgeting and Long-Term Financing Decisions* (Hinsdale, IL: Dryden Press, 1990).

2. An introduction to the internal rate of return calculation methodology is contained in R. Cissell, H. Cissell, and D. C. Flaspohler, *Mathematics of Finance*, 7th rev. ed. (Boston: Houghton Mifflin, 1986), pp. 379–82.

3. A mathematical presentation of the effective cost of leasing is provided in R. L. Roenfeldt, and J. S. Osteryoung, "Analysis of Financial Leases," *Financial Management* 2 (Spring 1973), pp. 74–87.

4. A review of the technical shortcomings associated with the internal rate of return methodology is contained in E. F. Brigham, and L. C. Gapenski, *Intermediate Financial Management* (Hinsdale, IL: Dryden Press, 1990), pp. 261–90.

REFERENCES

Brealey, R. A., and S. C. Myers. *Principles of Corporate Finance*. 3d rev. ed. New York: McGraw-Hill, 1988, 629–50.

Brealey, R. A., S. C. Myers, and C. M. Young. "Debt, Taxes, and Leasing – A Note." *Journal of Finance* 35 (December 1980): 1245–50.

Brigham, E. F., and L. C. Gapenski. *Intermediate Financial Management*. 3d rev. ed. Hinsdale, IL: Dryden Press, 1990, 547–76.

Copeland, T. E., and J. F. Weston. *Financial Theory and Corporate Policy*. 3d rev. ed. New York: Addison-Wesley Publishing, 1988, 614–37.

Franks, J. R., and S. D. Hodges. "Lease Valuation When Taxable Earnings Are a Scarce Resource." *Journal of Finance* 42 (September 1987): 987–1005.

Hodges, S. D. "The Valuation of Variable Rate Leases." *Financial Management* 14 (Spring 1985): 68–74.

Lerro, A. J., and J. G. Bond. "Financing Acquisitions: To Lease or To Borrow." *The National Public Accountant* 35 (January 1990): 42–45.

Levy, H., and M. Sarnat. "Leasing, Borrowing, and Financial Risk." *Financial Management* 8 (Winter 1979): 47–54.

Lewellen, W. G., M. S. Long, and J. J. McConnell. "Asset Leasing in Competitive Capital Markets." *Journal of Finance* 31 (June 1976): 787–98.

Loewenstein, M. A., and J. E. McClure. "Taxes and Financial Leasing." *Quarterly Review of Economics and Business* 28 (Spring 1988): 21–38.

Long, M. S. "Leasing and the Cost of Capital." *Journal of Financial and Quantitative Analysis* 12 (November 1977): 579–86.

McConnell, J. J., and J. S. Schallheim. "Valuation of Asset Leasing Contracts." *Journal of Financial Economics* 12 (1983): 237–61.

Martin, J. D., S. H. Cox, and R. D. MacMinn. *The Theory of Finance*. Hinsdale, IL: Dryden Press, 1988: 583–602.

Miller, M. H., and C. W. Upton. "Leasing, Buying, and the Cost of Capital Services." *Journal of Finance* 31 (June 1976): 761–86.

Myers, S. D., D. A. Dill, and A. J. Bautista. "Valuation of Financial Lease Contracts." *Journal of Finance* 31 (June 1976): 799–819.

Nunnally, B. H., Jr., and D. A. Plath. "Leasing versus Borrowing: Evaluating Alternative Forms of Consumer Credit." *The Journal of Consumer Affairs* 23 (Winter 1989): 383–92.

Roenfeldt, R. L., and J. S. Osteryoung. "Analysis of Financial Leases." *Financial Management* 2 (Spring 1973): 74–87.

Ross, S. A., R. W. Westerfield, and J. F. Jaffe. *Corporate Finance.* 2d rev. ed. Homewood, IL: Richard D. Irwin, 1988, 620–47.

Shall, L. D. "Analytic Issues in Lease versus Purchase Decisions." *Financial Management* 16 (Summer 1987): 12–20.

————. "The Evaluation of Lease Financing Opportunities." *Midland Corporate Finance Journal* (Spring 1985): 48–65.

————. "The Lease-or-Buy and Asset Acquisition Decisions." *Journal of Finance* 29 (June 1974): 1203–14.

Shapiro, A. C. *Modern Corporate Finance.* New York: MacMillan Publishing, 1989, 670–98.

8

Advanced Topics in
Lease Valuation

Given the basic valuation principles introduced in Chapter 7, it is now appropriate to examine some of the more complicated leasing arrangements commonly observed in business. These extensions of the basic lease contracts described in Chapter 7 contain many of the same attributes as simple financial leases, and the valuation of these contracts also follows the techniques introduced in Chapter 7. However, the leases introduced in this chapter take on an additional degree of complexity in order to exploit opportunities in the tax code, permit more flexible contract terms between lessors and lessees, and provide more attractive financing terms for corporate borrowers, as well as higher returns to corporate lenders.

This chapter begins by reviewing lease valuation techniques associated with leveraged leases, lease cancellation options, and options to purchase leased assets. Leveraged leases offer lessors the opportunity to increase returns associated with lease contracts by borrowing a portion of the funds necessary to sustain the lease investment; lease option clauses offer lessees the opportunity to terminate the lease and permanently acquire the leased asset before the contract's maturity date. In addition, this chapter reviews how federal tax laws influence the pricing of lease contracts written by asset manufacturers and third-party leasing firms, and shows how businesses that are asset-rich yet cash-poor can use a sale-and-leaseback transaction to generate both cash and financial flexibility for their operations. While each of these topics adds complexity to the basic lease contracts discussed in Chapter 7, this complexity brings added financial rewards to leasing firms, and increased financing flexibility to borrowers. Consequently, the transactions reviewed here are common landmarks on the leasing landscape.

LEVERAGED LEASES

The concept of a leveraged lease is quite simple, but the execution of the concept is complicated by the number of participants in the transaction. In essence, a leveraged lease represents a standard financial lease in which the lessor borrows a portion of the funds necessary to support the lease. From the lessee's perspective, there is no difference between leveraged and non-leveraged leases, just as most borrowers do not ask their bankers where the funds came from to support their commercial loans. From the standpoint of the lessor, however, the leveraged lease operates quite differently from its non-leveraged counterpart. Given this difference, the remainder of this section focuses on the evaluation of leveraged leases from the perspective of the lessor.

In general terms, a leveraged lease permits the lessor to enjoy 100% of the tax benefits associated with owning assets while incurring only a fraction of the costs associated with buying assets. The "leverage" comes from using borrowed capital—someone else's money—to purchase assets, while retaining all of the depreciation tax shields provided to asset owners. Quite naturally, the use of leverage magnifies the financial returns to lessors. In a competitive leasing market, this is good news for lessees as well as lessors. The enhanced returns associated with leveraged leases mean lessors can lower the lease payment charged to the lessee, and still earn a satisfactory rate of return on capital invested in the lease.

Gaining this financial advantage from a leveraged lease does require a bit of work, however. The contractual arrangements necessary to establish a levered lease are more complex than for a non-levered lease because more investors have a vested interest in the financial outcome of the transaction. Exhibit 8-1 provides an overview of the participants and cash flows encountered in a simple leveraged lease. In this case, the lessor contributes 20% of the funding required to purchase the leased asset (see Step 1a in Exhibit 8-1), while the lender contributes the remaining 80% (Step 1b). Rather than purchasing the asset directly from the manufacturer, the lessor and lender appoint an indenture trustee to represent and safeguard the interests of the lender throughout the term of the lease. This trustee records the receipt of funds from the lessor and lender, and then places the order for the leased asset with its manufacturer (Step 2).

In a typical leveraged lease transaction, the equipment order specifies that the asset be delivered to the lessee (Step 3b), while the asset's title is forwarded to the owner trustee (Step 3a). The owner trustee represents the interests of the lessor, or equity participant, in the lease transaction. The owner trustee holds the original lease agreement executed by the lessee (Step 3c), and insures that residual income generated by the lease is passed along to the lessor.

Exhibit 8-1
Anatomy of a Leveraged Lease

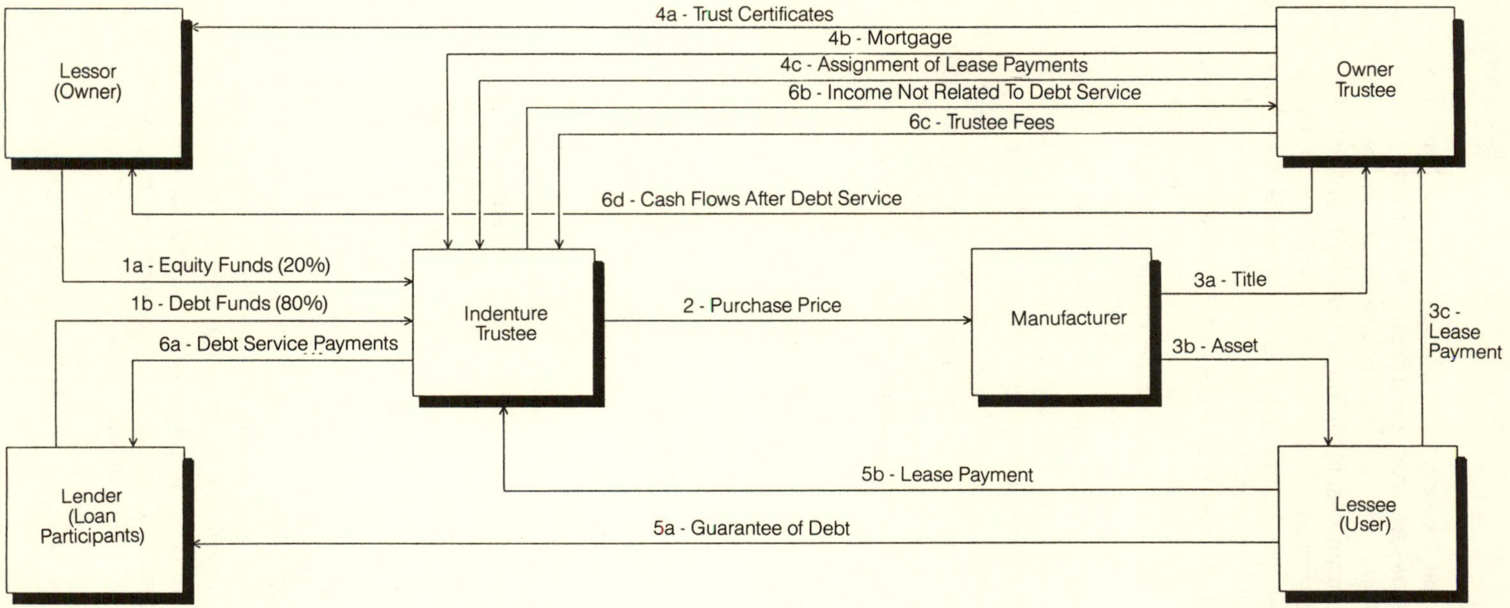

As the lessor's representative in the lease transaction, the owner trustee issues trust certificates evidencing claims to ownership in the lease (Step 4a). In addition, the owner trustee provides certain contractual guarantees, including a first lien on the leased asset (Step 4b) and an assignment of the lease payment stream (Step 4c) to the indenture trustee. The lender requires these guarantees because he or she issues non-recourse debt in connection with the lease. If the lessor is unable or unwilling to repay the debt used in the lease, the lender has no general claim against the assets or income of the lessee. The contractual guarantees offered by the owner trustee, as well as by the lessee (Step 5a), reduce the lender's risk in the transaction. In addition, these guarantees suggest that the credit quality of the levered lease rests on the financial strength of the lessee and the value of the leased assets — as well as on the credit worthiness of the lessor.

In keeping with the lease payment assignment, the lessee forwards lease payments directly to the indenture trustee (Step 5b). This trustee first applies the payments to the lender's debt-service requirements (Step 6a), and then forwards any remaining cash to the owner trustee (Step 6b). The owner trustee is responsible for the payment of administrative charges to the indenture trustee (Step 6c), and, finally, the remaining proceeds are distributed to holders of the trust certificates in the lease. Given the administrative complexity of the leveraged lease, the legal fees and transactions costs associated with this financing option are significant. Accordingly, leveraged leases are usually associated with large financing transactions (those exceeding $1 million) to provide sufficient revenues to offset the administrative cost burden of these transactions.

After all this paperwork, it might seem prudent to abandon the leveraged lease and return to a basic financing arrangement in which the lessor provides all the funds to support the lease. While this approach simplifies matters, it ignores the substantial returns that lessors can realize from leveraged leases. The net cash flows associated with a simple leveraged lease are provided in Exhibit 8-2. This transaction closely parallels the original lease described in Exhibit 7-2. In the case of the leveraged lease, however, slightly more than 75% ($38,000) of the original $50,000 purchase price for the leased asset is borrowed. The cash flows shown in Exhibit 8-2 record the depreciation and interest tax shields received by the lessor, along with the debt-service payments necessary to retire the $38,000 loan over the 5-year term of the lease. In order to preserve the details of the original lease transaction described in Chapter 7, the lessor's tax rate is 34% in this illustration, and the lessor's before-tax borrowing cost remains 11%.

Notice that the after-tax net cash flows associated with the leveraged lease are negative in Year 0, positive in Years 1 and 2, and then negative

Exhibit 8-2
Net Cash Flows for a Leveraged Lease

	YEAR 0 (1990)	YEAR 1 (1991)	YEAR 2 (1992)	YEAR 3 (1993)	YEAR 4 (1994)	YEAR 5 (1995)
Cost of Asset............	($50,000.00)					
Loan Proceeds..........	$38,000.00					
Lease Payment..........	$10,500.00	$10,500.00	$10,500.00	$10,500.00	$10,500.00	$10,500.00
Asset Salvage Value....						$0.00
	========	========	========	========	========	========
Before-Tax Cash Flow........	($1,500.00)	$10,500.00	$10,500.00	$10,500.00	$10,500.00	$10,500.00
Depreciation Expense........	$10,000.00	$16,000.00	$9,600.00	$5,760.00	$5,760.00	$2,880.00
Annual Loan Payment........		$10,281.67	$10,281.67	$10,281.67	$10,281.67	$10,281.67
Interest Payment (11%)........		$4,180.00	$3,508.82	$2,763.80	$1,936.84	$1,018.90
Principal Payment........		$6,101.67	$6,772.85	$7,517.87	$8,344.83	$9,262.77
	========	========	========	========	========	========
Taxable Income........	$500.00	($9,680.00)	($2,608.82)	$1,976.20	$2,803.16	$6,601.10
Income Taxes........	$170.00	($3,291.20)	($887.00)	$671.91	$953.07	$2,244.37
Net Cash Flow After Taxes........	($1,670.00)	$3,509.53	$1,105.33	($453.58)	($734.74)	($2,026.04)
Cumulative Cash Flow........	($1,670.00)	$1,839.53	$2,944.86	$2,491.28	$1,756.54	($269.51)

Net Present Value (discount rate = 11%)........... $370.84
Internal Rate of Return........ 3.54% and 125.64%

again in Years 3–5. This negative–positive–negative cash flow pattern is characteristic of most leveraged leases. While the negative net cash flow in Year 5 is attributable in part to the zero salvage value of the leased asset, the cash flows shown in Exhibit 8-2 follow the common practice of conservatively estimating the leveraged lease's cash flows. While the salvage value might indeed be greater than zero at the conclusion of the lease and, according to tax regulations, the asset *must* retain at least 20% of its original value to qualify as a true lease, recording a zero salvage value at the termination of the lease reduces the cash inflows from the transaction in Year 5. This, in turn, reduces the rate of return evidenced by the lease, and expresses the lease cash flows in the most conservative manner.

The negative–positive–negative net cash flow pattern suggests that leveraged leases first require funds, then generate funds, and finally require more funds toward the end of the lease. After the initial purchase of the asset by the lessor, the depreciation and interest tax shields dominate the annual lease cash flows, producing the positive returns shown in Years 2 and 3. Following these periods, however, the tax shields from accelerated depreciation and amortized repayment of debt grow smaller each successive year; the net cash flows associated with the lease once again become negative as the maturity date of the contract approaches. Conceptually, the positive cash flows in the early years of the leveraged lease contain two different components: one representing a cash return to the lessor and a second containing funds that must be invested during the term of the lease to offset the negative net cash flows that occur later in the lease.

While the negative–positive–negative cash flow pattern is characteristic of most leveraged leases, it produces a major problem in valuing the lease. Note that the annual net cash flows shown in Exhibit 8-2 produce two different internal rates of return: 3.54% and 125.64%. Multiple IRRs can occur whenever there is more than one sign change in the net cash flow pattern. In this case, there are two sign changes (negative to positive and positive to negative). Hence, this particular lease contains two different rates of return, and the lessor's effective return on the lease is ambiguous.

Exhibit 8-3 graphically illustrates the ambiguity regarding the effective return on the lease by showing how the net present value of the lease changes as the lessor's cost of capital changes. Where this capital cost lies within the interval of 3.54% to 125.64%, the NPV of the leveraged lease is positive, indicating that the lease should be accepted by the lessor. Note that where the cost of capital is exactly 3.54% and 125.64%, the NPV of the lease is zero, which defines the two internal rates of return for this transaction. Outside the interval of 3.54% to

Exhibit 8-3
Net Present Value Profile

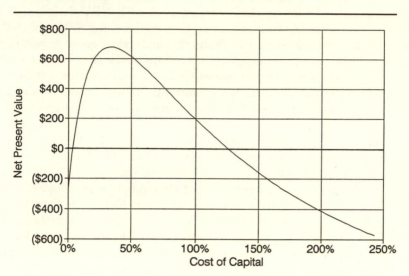

125.64%, the lease's NPV is negative, indicating that the lessor should reject the opportunity to enter into this credit transaction.

Given this visual profile of the NPVs for the leveraged lease, it becomes simple to reach an appropriate investment decision. Discounting the annual net cash flows in Exhibit 8-2 at the before-tax cost of debt (11%), the lease yields a positive NPV equal to $370.84. Since this value exceeds zero, the leveraged lease should be accepted by the lessor. Notice that this NPV calculation differs slightly from the illustrations provided in Chapter 7 because the interest tax shield associated with the leveraged lease is stated explicitly in the derivation of the annual net cash flows of the lease. As such, the before-tax cost of debt, rather than the after-tax cost of debt, represents the appropriate discount rate in the NPV framework. Using the after-tax debt cost here would "double count" the tax shield provided by the interest payments in the leveraged lease.

While the lease's NPV answers the lessor's question concerning the value of the lease, another question remains unanswered. What rate of return does the lessor earn from this investment? Since the IRR provides two possible answers to this question, a number of alternative techniques are found in the finance literature to provide a more definitive answer to the question. These techniques include the sinking-fund return method (SFR), and the return-on-invested-capital approach (RIC).

In general, both of these techniques yield the same answer to the question, and, more important, both techniques provide an accept/ reject signal to the lessor that is consistent with NPV decision. It is critical to emphasize, however, that this consistency with the NPV approach holds only in cases where the analyst discounts net cash flows from the lease *at the lessor's cost of capital*. In all other cases, the effective rate of return on the leveraged lease may provide a different accept/reject signal from the NPV method; in these cases, use of the SFR or RIC method to evaluate leveraged leases is dangerous and misleading.

To illustrate the calculation of effective returns on leveraged leases, first consider the sinking-fund approach. This method recognizes that positive net cash inflows in the early years of the lease contain both a return to the lessor and an endowment that must be invested to meet the cash needs of the lease in its waning years. Exhibit 8-4 illustrates the sinking-fund valuation technique. The sinking-fund balance required by the leveraged lease is established by discounting the lease's negative cash flows in Years 3–5 back to Year 3 at the lessor's appropriate cost of capital (in this case, the 11% before-tax cost of debt). Adding these discounted cash flows produces the $2759.89 sinking-fund balance required by the lease at the beginning of Year 3. This sum represents the total cash the lessor must have on hand in Year 3 to satisfy the net cash outflows required by the lease in Years 3–5.

Positive cash flows from the early years of the lease must be invested to satisfy this $2759.89 sinking-fund requirement in Year 3. This investment is funded from the $1105.33 positive cash flow in Year 2, while the remaining $1244.19 necessary to fund the sinking-fund requirement fully is drawn from the lease's $3509.53 net cash inflow from Year 1. Section 2 of Exhibit 8-4 shows that these annual investments in Years 1 and 2, earning a rate of return equal to the lessor's 11% after-tax cost of debt, will grow into the $2759.89 sinking-fund requirement by Year 3.

Now that we have provided for the repayment of the sinking-fund obligation, the remaining net cash inflows from the lease in Year 1 ($3509.53 − $1244.19 = $2265.34) contain the lessor's return. The particular discount rate that equates the present value of the $2265.34 cash return in Year 1 with the Year 0 net investment in the lease ($1670) represents the lessor's effective annual return on the lease. In this instance, Section 3 of Exhibit 8-4 shows that the lessor earns an after-tax return of 35.65% on the leveraged lease.

Notice the dramatic increase in the effective return on this sample lease made possible by the use of leverage. Exhibit 7-7 shows the lessor's return on the original, non-leveraged lease as 7.48%. By borrowing 76% of the asset's purchase price, however, the return on the lease rises

Exhibit 8-4
Determining the Rate of Return on the Leveraged Lease:
Sinking-Fund Method

1. Determine the Sinking Fund Balance Required by Leveraged Lease

(1)	(2)	(3)	(4)
			(2) x (3)
		Discount	
	Cash	Factor	Present
Year	Flow	11%	Value
1995	$2,026.04	0.81162	$1,644.38
1994	$734.74	0.90090	$661.93
1993	$453.58	1.00000	$453.58
			========
Sinking Fund Balance Required at beginning of 1993...............................			$2,759.89

2. Determine the Required Contribution to the Sinking Fund

(1)	(2)	(3)	(4)	(5)
		Interest	(2) x (3)	
	Cash	Factor	Annual	Cumulative
Year	Flow	11%	Contribution	Contribution
1992	$1,105.33	1.11000	$1,226.92	$1,226.92
1991	$1,244.19	1.23210	$1,532.97	$2,759.89

3. Identify Residual Cash Flows Generated by the Leveraged Lease

(1)	(2)	(3)	(4)
			(2) - (3)
		Cash Flow	
	Net Cash Flow	Committed to	Residual
Year	from Lease	Sinking Fund	Cash Flow
1990	($1,670.00)	N/A	($1,670.00)
1991	$3,509.53	$1,244.19	$2,265.34
1992	$1,105.33	$1,105.33	$0.00
Rate of Return on Leveraged Lease...........................			35.6489316%

to almost 36%. This demonstrates precisely how the use of debt attenuates the return to the lessor.

One advantage of the sinking-fund valuation method is that it produces a single, unambiguous rate of return for the leveraged lease. Moreover, the accept/reject decision associated with this method is consistent with the NPV decision framework, provided the discount and investment factors used to determine the sinking-fund balance and required contribution to the sinking fund, respectively, are the lessor's cost of capital. Notice that the discount and investment factors in Exhibit 8-4 represent the 11% before-tax cost of debt to the lessor. This rate corresponds to the rate of discount used to obtain the NPV of the lease in Exhibit 8-2.

Exhibit 8-5 demonstrates that the accept/reject decisions obtained from the sinking-fund method correspond to the NPV decisions shown in Exhibit 8-3, within the NPV framework, the lease yields a positive NPV where the lessor's cost of capital falls within the interval of 3.54% to 125.64%, signaling that the lease should be accepted. Exhibit 8-5 shows that the sinking-fund evaluation technique yields a similar region of acceptance. The 45-degree line in the exhibit defines the accept/reject conditions for the sinking-fund method by showing where the lessor's cost of capital (the before-tax cost of debt in this illustration) exactly equals the sinking-fund return on investment. In cases where this investment return exceeds the cost of capital, the sinking-fund return lies above the 45-degree line, and the lease should be accepted. Where the sinking fund falls below the lessor's cost of capital (below the 45-degree line), the lease should be rejected.

Note that for all cases between the 3.54% and 125.64% cost-of-capital endpoints, the sinking-fund return exceeds the lessor's cost of capital. In all other cases, the opposite is true. This result occurs because the discount and investment factors used in the sinking-fund

Exhibit 8-5
Sinking-Fund Return on Leveraged Lease

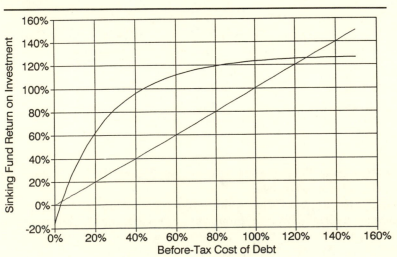

framework correspond with the lessor's cost of capital. As long as this condition is satisfied, the sinking-fund method and the NPV framework provide consistent accept/reject signals for leveraged leases.

A second evaluation technique used to examine leveraged leases, the return on invested capital, is demonstrated in Exhibit 8-6. This measure also provides the effective return on the lease; however, it obtains this result in a slightly different way. The RIC approach rests on the idea that the lessor has funds "invested" in the lease for part of the lease's duration; for the remainder of the lease term the lessor has a "loan" from the lease. The RIC represents the interest rate that gives a future value of zero to the cash balance of the lease, where the balance is compounded at the lessor's cost of capital when it is positive, and compounded at the RIC when it is negative.

As long as the lease balance remains negative, the lessor maintains a continuing investment in the lease. This investment is compounded at the RIC to provide the effective return on the lease. When the lease balance turns positive, however, the lessor is receiving a loan from the lease. This loan component is compounded at the lessor's cost of capital. These different compounding rules are demonstrated in Exhibit 8-6, where the lease balance turns from negative to positive in Year 1 (1991). According to the RIC procedure, the negative Year 0 (1990) lease balance is compounded at the RIC (35.65%), while in all remaining years of the lease, the positive balance is compounded at the les-

Exhibit 8-6
Determining the Rate of Return on the Leveraged Lease:
Return-on-Invested-Capital Method

(1)	(2)	(3)	(4)
Year	Annual Net Cash Flow	Reinvestment Rate (k)	Project Balance
1990	($1,670.00)	35.65%	($1,670.00)
1991	$3,509.53	11.00%	$1,244.19
1992	$1,105.33	11.00%	$2,486.38
1993	($453.58)	11.00%	$2,306.31
1994	($734.74)	11.00%	$1,825.26
1995	($2,026.04)	11.00%	$0.00

Return On Capital Invested in the Lease...................   35.65%
Lessor's Cost of Capital (Before-Tax Cost of Debt).......   11.00%

sor's relevant cost of capital (the before-tax cost of debt in this illustration). Establishing the RIC at 35.65% yields a terminal investment in the lease of $0, which defines the effective rate of return on the lease.

While leveraged leases provide attractive returns to lessors, these financing arrangements are not without risk. The transaction shown above uses the lessor's before-tax cost of debt as the appropriate cost of capital because the cash receipts from the lease assume the same risk level to the lessor as secured debt issued by the lessee. Returning to the transaction details originally presented in Chapter 7, notice that the lessee's before-tax cost of debt is 11%. This method for quantifying the riskiness of the leveraged lease simplifies the calculations demonstrated in this chapter, but overlooks some of the risks inherent in the leveraged lease.

While the receipt of lease payments by the lessor is assured by the contractual guarantees established within the leveraged lease, the lessor's return also depends on the ability of the lessor to use the depreciation and interest tax shields provided by the lease, and the expected residual value of the leased asset. This example avoids the question of residual-value risk by assuming the leased asset will be worthless at the maturity of the lease. While this conservative estimation of residual value is common practice by lessors, it is inaccurate. Adding a non-zero residual value to the SFR and RIC models significantly complicates the calculation of effective lease returns. Under these more realistic conditions, residual-value risk clearly exceeds the risk level of the lease-payment stream, and requires the use of a second discount rate to obtain the present value of the asset's residual value.

Finally, the lessor's ability to use the depreciation and interest tax shields requires that the firm have taxable income. In situations where this assumption is not realistic because the lessor's operating income exhibits significant variability through time, the use of the before-tax cost of debt as the appropriate cost of capital is invalid. In this case, the lessor's cost of capital should be revised upward to incorporate the additional riskiness associated with the firm's operating cash flows. This introduces still another discount rate within the evaluation of the leveraged lease, and, for practical purposes, renders the SFR and RIC evaluation frameworks intractable.

CANCELLATION OPTIONS AND PURCHASE OPTIONS

Another contractual feature that frequently complicates the valuation of lease contracts is the lessee's option to terminate the financing agreement. This option may take the form of a cancellation option, which gives the lessee the right to terminate the lease and return the leased asset to the lessor prior to the maturity of the contract, or a purchase option, which gives the lessee the right to purchase the leased asset on some specified date or dates before the maturity of the lease. In both cases, the lessee effectively terminates the lease agreement prior to the agreed-upon maturity date.

Pure financial leases contain no such option because these contracts are not cancelable at the discretion of the lessee. As a consequence, cancellation options are frequently associated with operating leases, or short-term lease agreements that do not bind the lessee to repay a debt-like obligation over a long period of time. In recent years, however, cancellation options have become popular additions to long-term leases that fully amortize the value of the leased asset over the life of the lease.

This creates some confusion regarding lease definitions. In effect, these newer lease agreements represent financial leases, but, in contrast with the traditional financial lease, they are cancelable financial leases. Given the contradiction between the non-cancelability of a traditional financial lease and the cancellation option provided by these long-term, debt-like leases, a third category of lease agreements has emerged: mixed leases. These newer contracts share common characteristics of financial leases, yet they are cancelable at the option of the lessee.

The potential for early termination of the financial lease creates value for the lessee because it provides an additional feature not contained in the non-cancelable lease. In addition, the cancellation option adds to the riskiness of the lessor's investment in the lease because the cash flows defined in the lease agreement are subject to an additional source of uncertainty. During the course of the lease, the lessee may decide to terminate the financing agreement and return the leased asset to the lessor (by exercising the cancellation option), or purchase the leased asset from the lessor (by exercising the purchase option). Accordingly, the lessor's expected rate of return on cancelable lease contracts should exceed the rate of return on pure financial leases in order to compensate for this additional risk.

The cancellation option adds two different types of risk to the lessor's financial position: replacement-cost risk and revenue risk. The former type of risk reflects changes in the value of the leased asset over time, due to both physical deterioration and obsolescence. The latter risk category considers the possibility that the lease will be terminated because the lessee's revenue derived from the use of the leased asset falls below the cost of the lease.

As long as the lessor constructs the lease so that the present value of the remaining lease payments is equal to the salvage value of the leased asset, revenue risk is immaterial to the lessor. If the lessee exercises the cancellation option due to poor operating performance, the value of the asset returned to the lessor compensates for the loss of the remaining lease payments. The only relevant risk added by the cancellation option is, therefore, replacement-cost risk. Because it is impossible for lessors to specify in advance the exact rate of deterioration in the value of leased assets, premature termination of the lease may find the lessor holding an asset the value of which is less than the present value of the lost lease payments.

Given this added source of risk, lessees can expect to pay a premium to obtain a lease-cancellation option. As an illustration, Exhibit 8-7 compares the cost of a cancelable and non-cancelable lease. In both cases, lessees can obtain a $50,000 asset; the pure financial lease (non-cancelable) requires an annual payment of $10,500, while the cancelable lease requires a $12,000 annual payment. The duration of both contracts is 5 years, and the lessee's marginal tax rate (34%) and after-tax borrowing costs (7.26%) are the same for both leases. Exhibit 8-7 shows that under these conditions, the net after-tax cost of the lease-cancellation option is $5021.09. This figure is established by comparing the NPV of the cancelable lease to the NPV of the non-cancelable lease (see Section III).

The really important question here concerns whether the flexibility provided by the cancellation option is worth an additional $5000 to the lessee. Unfortunately, there are no contemporary capital-budgeting rules to answer this question in a systematic manner. Recent advances in financial theory demonstrate that the lessee's cancellation option resembles a put option (or option to sell) held by the lessee against the leased asset. Accordingly, the value of the lessee's contract is similar to the value of a pure financial lease, enhanced by the value of owning a put on the leased asset.

While the mathematical models necessary to value this put option are beyond the scope of this text, viewing the lease-cancellation option as a put contract does provide insight into the lessee's decision to accept or reject the cancellation option. Because it resembles a put, the value of the cancellation option increases as (1) the initial cost of the leased asset increases; (2) the uncertainty regarding the leased asset's future residual value increases; (3) the length of time before the cancellation option expires increases; (4) the present value of the remaining lease payments increases; and (5) the expected life of the leased asset increases.

Following these fundamental determinants regarding the value of the put option, it is possible to offer a few general guidelines concerning the value of cancellation options in lease contracts. On balance, the cancellation option will be more valuable to lessees in cases where

1. the initial cost of the leased asset is relatively large

2. there is a great deal of uncertainty concerning the rate at which the leased asset will decline in value over time

3. the cancellation option extends over the life of the lease, rather than being limited to a finite period of time (e.g., the first two years) within the lease

4. the lease payments represent a major component of the lessee's total financing costs

5. the expected life of the leased asset is relatively long

In addition to lease-cancellation options, the opportunity to purchase leased assets at some point during the term of the financing contract also enhances the value of the lease contract to the lessee. This option might exist throughout the duration of the lease, or it might be limited to some specific time period within the lease. For example, many consumer lease agreements permit the lessee to buy leased automobiles at any point during the term of the lease, while others permit this purchase option only at the expiration of the lease. The price of the lessee's purchase option may be established as the leased asset's fair market value at the time of purchase, or specified in some other manner at the signing of the lease. Many leases contain a schedule of purchase-option prices covering the entire lease period, where the exercise price at which the lessee may acquire ownership of the asset decreases as the lease moves from period to period.

The purchase option provides the lessee with two courses of action that are not possible in the absence of this option: (1) the lessee can acquire ownership of the asset, terminate the lease contract, and continue to use the asset; or (2) the lessee can acquire the asset, cancel the lease obligation, and sell (or lease) the asset to a third party. Like the cancellation option, the purchase option exposes the lessor to added risk. If the purchase-option price is established in the lease agreement, then the lessor must correctly estimate the future salvage value of the leased asset to avoid replacement-cost risk. When accurate residual-value estimation is difficult or impossible, the lessor demands a higher rate of return on the lease to cover this risk.

Whether the added flexibility provided by the purchase option creates value for the lessee depends on the lessee's ability to recognize appropriate times to exercise, or not exercise, the purchase option. The optimal period in which to abandon the lease depends on the operating cash flows associated with the leasing project, the purchase-option price, the market value of the leased asset, and how each of the variables changes over the life of the lease. Fortunately, the analytical methods necessary to evaluate the purchase-option question are well established in the finance literature.

Exhibit 8-7

Valuing the Cancellation Option Contained in the Lease Contract

I. NET PRESENT VALUE OF LEASE CASH FLOWS - WITHOUT CANCELLATION OPTION

ITEM	YEAR 0 (1990)	YEAR 1 (1991)	YEAR 2 (1992)	YEAR 3 (1993)	YEAR 4 (1994)	YEAR 5 (1995)
Total Asset Cost (Including Modification & Delivery)......	$50,000	$0	$0	$0	$0	$0
Lost Depreciation Tax Shield on Lease......	($3,400)	($5,440)	($3,264)	($1,958)	($1,958)	($979)
Lease Payment......	($10,500)	($10,500)	($10,500)	($10,500)	($10,500)	($10,500)
Tax Shield Provided by Lease Payment......	$3,570	$3,570	$3,570	$3,570	$3,570	$3,570
Annual After-Tax Costs Paid by Lessor......	$0	$0	$0	$0	$0	$0
After-Tax Salvage Value of Leased Asset......	$0	$0	$0	$0	$0	$0
NET CASH FLOW OF LEASE......	$39,670	($12,370)	($10,194)	($8,888)	($8,888)	($7,909)
PRESENT VALUE OF EACH NET CASH FLOW......	$39,670	($11,533)	($8,861)	($7,203)	($6,715)	($5,571)
NET PRESENT VALUE OF LEASE FINANCING......	($212)					

180

II. NET PRESENT VALUE OF LEASE CASH FLOWS - WITH CANCELLATION OPTION

ITEM	YEAR 0 (1990)	YEAR 1 (1991)	YEAR 2 (1992)	YEAR 3 (1993)	YEAR 4 (1994)	YEAR 5 (1995)
Total Asset Cost (Including Modification & Delivery)	$50,000	$0	$0	$0	$0	$0
Lost Depreciation Tax Shield on Lease	($3,400)	($5,440)	($3,264)	($1,958)	($1,958)	($979)
Lease Payment	($12,000)	($12,000)	($12,000)	($12,000)	($12,000)	($12,000)
Tax Shield Provided by Lease Payment	$4,080	$4,080	$4,080	$4,080	$4,080	$4,080
Annual After-Tax Costs Paid by Lessor	$0	$0	$0	$0	$0	$0
After-Tax Salvage Value of Leased Asset	$0	$0	$0	$0	$0	$0
NET CASH FLOW OF LEASE	$38,680	($13,360)	($11,184)	($9,878)	($9,878)	($8,899)
PRESENT VALUE OF EACH NET CASH FLOW	$38,680	($12,456)	($9,721)	($8,005)	($7,463)	($6,268)
NET PRESENT VALUE OF LEASE FINANCING	($5,233)					

III. NET COST OF THE LEASE CANCELLATION OPTION

NPV of Lease with Cancellation Option	($5,233.26)
NPV of Lease without Cancellation Option	($212.17)
Net Cost of Cancellation Option	$5,021.09

181

Consider the lease transaction in Exhibit 8-8. In this illustration, a $50,000 asset can be leased over a five-year period for $10,000 annually, plus a $10,000 down payment required at the signing of the lease. Given the lessee's after-tax cost of debt (7.26%), the net financing advantage to this lease is $1461; the project for which the asset is acquired generates a positive NPV of $46,338 to the lessee. Notice that the financing cash flows are discounted at the after-tax cost of debt to produce the $1461 net advantage to leasing because these cash flows share the risk characteristics of the lessee's long-term debt. In contrast, the operating cash flows are discounted at the lessee's weighted-average cost of capital (13%) because the riskiness of this project is assumed to equal that of the firm's other (collective) projects. Together, the financing and operating cash flows generate $47,799 in new value for the lessee.

This particular lease also offers a limited purchase option to the lessee. The option is termed "limited" because the lessee can only acquire the leased asset in Years 2–4. The exercise price of the option declines in each successive year of the lease, where the values shown for this option correspond to the lessor's estimates of the asset's future salvage value in each year of the lease. The lessee seeks to answer two basic questions: Should the purchase option be exercised? When is the best year for exercise?

Exhibits 8-9 and 8-10 provide the answers to these questions under two different scenarios. In Exhibit 8-9, the lessor's estimates of the asset's future salvage value are exactly correct. The cost of the purchase option in Year 1 ($35,000) equals the asset's market value after one year of use. The cost of the purchase option in Year 2 ($25,000) equals the asset's market value after two years of use, and so forth. Exhibit 8-9 shows the value to the lessee from each of the five options provided by the lease. The lessee can (1) lease the asset for its full five-year term and never exercise the purchase option; (2) lease the asset for a four-year period, and exercise the purchase option in Year 4; (3) lease the asset for a three-year period and exercise the purchase option in Year 3; and so on.

Notice that in each case in which the lessee exercises the purchase option, the asset is sold, the project terminated, and the future cash flows associated with the project are foregone. Because the leasing alternative provides $1461 in additional value to the lessee (the net advantage to leasing), the lessee would never exercise the purchase option without also selling (or leasing) the asset. Exercising the option to continue operating the asset would deny the lessee a portion of the $1461 in benefits associated with the lease contract. As long as the operating cash flows from the lease project remain consistent with the original estimates shown in Exhibit 8-8, the lessee's decision involves either continuing the lease contract or, purchasing the asset, terminating the project and the lease, and selling (leasing) the asset.

Exhibit 8-9 shows that where the lessor accurately sets the schedule of purchase-option prices to correspond with the salvage value of the asset, the lessee will never exercise the purchase option. After exercise, the lessee's gain from selling the asset is completely offset by the cost of exercise, and the operating cash flows lost in the termination of the project render the NPV of the purchase option below the NPV of the continuing lease. Different levels of risk contained in the component cash flows shown in Exhibit 8-9 complicate the decision to abandon the lease. In particular, all cash flows associated with lease payments are discounted at the lessee's low-risk, after-tax cost of debt. Cash flows associated with the future residual value of the leased asset, as well as all future operating cash flows, are discounted at the firm's (higher) weighted-average cost of capital. The latter cash flows are known with far less certainty, hence the use of a higher risk-adjusted discount rate.

Exhibit 8-10 repeats the same abandonment analysis, only this time the salvage value of the leased asset deviates dramatically from the lessor's original estimates. For example, in Year 3 the asset's market value is $30,000, while the residual value estimated by the lessor for this period (which is used to establish the purchase-option price) is $15,000. In this case, it pays the lessee to abandon the project, exercise the purchase option, and sell the asset in Year 3. This transaction generates $2433 in value to the lessee, representing the NPV of the three-year lease, followed by exercise of the purchase option.

This illustration demonstrates the flexibility and opportunity provided by the purchase option. The lessee acquires the ability to capitalize on the lessor's mistake in estimating the future residual value of the leased asset. In addition, the abandonment framework shows when this pricing mistake provides the greatest value for the lessee. Similar analyses can (and should) be performed in each year of the lease transaction to revise the original operating cash flow estimates and market-value estimates for the leased asset as new information becomes available to the lessee.

The larger the deviation between the original and subsequent estimates of lease cash flows, the greater the chance that the added flexibility contained in the purchase-option lease will contain value for the lessee. In circumstances where the original lease cash-flow estimates are subject to considerable uncertainty, it is worthwhile for lessees to negotiate with lessors to provide a purchase option in the lease, even when this option effectively raises the cost of the lease.

(text continues on page 190)

Exhibit 8-8
Valuing the Purchase Option Contained in the Lease Contract

I. INPUT DATA

Cost of Asset	$50,000.00
Modification/Delivery Costs	$0.00
Down Payment Required by Lease	$10,500.00
Lease Payment	$10,500.00
Term of Lease (Years)	5
Annual Maintenance Costs Paid by Lessor	$3,000.00
Corporate Tax Rate	34.00%
Asset Salvage Value	$0.00
Borrowing Cost (Before Tax)	11.00%
Weighted Average Cost of Capital	13.00%

II. ASSET DEPRECIATION SCHEDULE (MACRS)

Depreciable Basis............ $50,000

	YEAR 0 (1990) 20.00%	YEAR 1 (1991) 32.00%	YEAR 2 (1992) 19.20%	YEAR 3 (1993) 11.52%	YEAR 4 (1994) 11.52%	YEAR 5 (1995) 5.76%
	$10,000	$16,000	$9,600	$5,760	$5,760	$2,880

LESSEE'S CAPITAL COSTS

After-Tax Cost of Debt............ 7.26%

Weighted Average Cost of Capital............ 13.00%

III. NET PRESENT VALUE OF LEASE CASH FLOWS

ITEM	YEAR 0 (1990)	YEAR 1 (1991)	YEAR 2 (1992)	YEAR 3 (1993)	YEAR 4 (1994)	YEAR 5 (1995)
Total Asset Cost (Including Modification & Delivery)	$50,000	$0	$0	$0	$0	$0
Lost Depreciation Tax Shield on Lease	($3,400)	($5,440)	($3,264)	($1,958)	($1,958)	($979)
Lease Payment	($10,500)	($10,500)	($10,500)	($10,500)	($10,500)	($10,500)
Tax Shield Provided by Lease Payment	$3,570	$3,570	$3,570	$3,570	$3,570	$3,570
Annual After-Tax Costs Paid by Lessor	$1,980	$1,980	$1,980	$1,980	$1,980	$1,980
After-Tax Salvage Value of Leased Asset	$0	$0	$0	$0	$0	$0
NET CASH FLOW OF LEASE	$41,650	($10,390)	($8,214)	($6,908)	($6,908)	($5,929)
PRESENT VALUE OF EACH NET CASH FLOW	$41,650	($9,687)	($7,140)	($5,598)	($5,219)	($4,176)
NET PRESENT VALUE OF LEASE FINANCING	$9,829					

185

Exhibit 8-9
Financial Alternatives Provided by the Lease: Scenario #1

OPTION	YEAR 0 (1990)	YEAR 1 (1991)	YEAR 2 (1992)	YEAR 3 (1993)	YEAR 4 (1994)	YEAR 5 (1995)
1. PURCHASE OPTION NEVER EXERCISED:						
Net Financing Cash Flows from Lease	$40,000	($12,040)	($9,864)	($8,558)	($8,558)	($7,579)
NET PRESENT VALUE OF FINANCING CASH FLOWS	$1,461					
2. FOUR-YEAR LEASE, WITH PURCHASE OPTION EXERCISED IN YEAR FOUR:						
Net Financing Cash Flows from Lease	$40,000	($12,040)	($9,864)	($8,558)	($8,558)	
Cost of Purchase Option					($10,000)	
Selling Price of Asset					$10,000	
Tax Consequences from Asset Sale					$0	
Net After-Tax Proceeds from Asset Sale					$0	
Operating Cash Flows Foregone						$10,000
ANNUAL NET CASH FLOW	$40,000	($12,040)	($9,864)	($8,558)	($8,558)	($10,000)
NET PRESENT VALUE	$1,372					
3. THREE-YEAR LEASE, WITH PURCHASE OPTION EXERCISED IN YEAR THREE:						
Net Financing Cash Flows from Lease	$40,000	($12,040)	($9,864)	($8,558)		
Cost of Purchase Option				($15,000)		
Selling Price of Asset				$15,000		
Tax Consequences from Asset Sale				$0		
Net After-Tax Proceeds from Asset Sale				$0		
Operating Cash Flows Foregone					$20,000	$10,000
ANNUAL NET CASH FLOW	$40,000	($12,040)	($9,864)	($8,558)	($20,000)	($10,000)
NET PRESENT VALUE	($4,428)					

4. TWO-YEAR LEASE, WITH PURCHASE OPTION EXERCISED IN YEAR TWO:

Net Financing Cash Flows from Lease...........	$40,000	($12,040)	($9,864)			
Cost of Purchase Option...........			($25,000)			
Selling Price of Asset...........			$25,000			
Tax Consequences from Asset Sale...........			$0			
Net After-Tax Proceeds from Asset Sale...........			$0			
Operating Cash Flows Foregone...........				$30,000	$20,000	$10,000
ANNUAL NET CASH FLOW...........	$40,000	($12,040)	($9,864)	($30,000)	($20,000)	($10,000)
NET PRESENT VALUE...........	($18,286)					

5. ONE-YEAR LEASE, WITH PURCHASE OPTION EXERCISED IN YEAR ONE:

Net Financing Cash Flows from Lease...........	$40,000	($12,040)				
Cost of Purchase Option...........		($35,000)				
Selling Price of Asset...........		$35,000				
Tax Consequences from Asset Sale...........		$0				
Net After-Tax Proceeds from Asset Sale...........		$0	$25,000			
Operating Cash Flows Foregone...........				$30,000	$20,000	$10,000
ANNUAL NET CASH FLOW...........	$40,000	($12,040)	($25,000)	($30,000)	($20,000)	($10,000)
NET PRESENT VALUE...........	($29,290)					

187

Exhibit 8-10
Financial Alternatives Provided by the Lease: Scenario #2

OPTION	YEAR 0 (1990)	YEAR 1 (1991)	YEAR 2 (1992)	YEAR 3 (1993)	YEAR 4 (1994)	YEAR 5 (1995)
1. PURCHASE OPTION NEVER EXERCISED:						
Net Financing Cash Flows from Lease	$40,000	($12,040)	($9,864)	($8,558)	($8,558)	($7,579)
NET PRESENT VALUE OF FINANCING CASH FLOWS	$1,461					
2. FOUR-YEAR LEASE, WITH PURCHASE OPTION EXERCISED IN YEAR FOUR:						
Net Financing Cash Flows from Lease	$40,000	($12,040)	($9,864)	($8,558)	($8,558)	
Cost of Purchase Option					($10,000)	
Selling Price of Asset					$12,000	
Tax Consequences from Asset Sale					$680	
Net After-Tax Proceeds from Asset Sale					$1,320	
Operating Cash Flows Foregone						$10,000
ANNUAL NET CASH FLOW	$40,000	($12,040)	($9,864)	($8,558)	($7,238)	($10,000)
NET PRESENT VALUE	$2,182					
3. THREE-YEAR LEASE, WITH PURCHASE OPTION EXERCISED IN YEAR THREE:						
Net Financing Cash Flows from Lease	$40,000	($12,040)	($9,864)	($8,558)		
Cost of Purchase Option				($15,000)		
Selling Price of Asset				$30,000		
Tax Consequences from Asset Sale				$5,100		
Net After-Tax Proceeds from Asset Sale				$9,900		
Operating Cash Flows Foregone					$20,000	$10,000
ANNUAL NET CASH FLOW	$40,000	($12,040)	($9,864)	$1,342	($20,000)	($10,000)
NET PRESENT VALUE	$2,433					

4. TWO-YEAR LEASE, WITH PURCHASE OPTION EXERCISED IN YEAR TWO:

Net Financing Cash Flows from Lease	$40,000	($12,040)	($9,864)			
Cost of Purchase Option			($25,000)			
Selling Price of Asset			$35,000			
Tax Consequences from Asset Sale			$3,400			
Net After-Tax Proceeds from Asset Sale			$6,600			
Operating Cash Flows Foregone				$30,000	$20,000	$10,000
ANNUAL NET CASH FLOW	$40,000	($12,040)	($3,264)	($30,000)	($20,000)	($10,000)
NET PRESENT VALUE	($13,117)					

5. ONE-YEAR LEASE, WITH PURCHASE OPTION EXERCISED IN YEAR ONE:

Net Financing Cash Flows from Lease	$40,000	($12,040)				
Cost of Purchase Option		($35,000)				
Selling Price of Asset		$40,000				
Tax Consequences from Asset Sale		$1,700				
Net After-Tax Proceeds from Asset Sale		$3,300				
Operating Cash Flows Foregone			$25,000	$30,000	$20,000	$10,000
ANNUAL NET CASH FLOW	$40,000	($8,740)	($25,000)	($30,000)	($20,000)	($10,000)
NET PRESENT VALUE	($15,144)					

MANUFACTURERS' LEASES VERSUS LEASE INTERMEDIARIES

The lease valuation issues introduced in previous sections of this volume assume that all lessors are part of a single homogeneous group with no distinguishing characteristics to differentiate one particular lessor from another. This blanket treatment of leasing firms oversimplifies the nature of leasing, because significant differences *do* exist across different lessors, and these differences can influence the cost and value of lease financing.

In general terms, there are two different classes of leasing firms: manufacturers' lessors and financial intermediaries. Manufacturing firms that produce a given product and directly offer to lease this product or offer a lease-financing option through a subsidiary corporation represent manufacturers' lessors. For example, IBM offers its mainframe computer products for sale or lease to potential customers, and General Motors offers leasing and installment borrowing alternatives to its customers through its financing subsidiary, General Motors Acceptance Corporation.

In contrast, lease intermediaries represent financing firms with no ownership connection to a given manufacturer. These intermediaries purchase assets from a manufacturer at the request of a prospective lessee, and then make these assets available to the lessee. Given the similarity between leasing and corporate borrowing, many commercial banks offer leasing as well as debt-financing options to their business customers. In this respect, commercial banks represent lease intermediaries.

In a world without taxes and transaction costs, there would be no difference between the leases offered by manufacturers and financial intermediaries. With corporate taxes, and different tax treatment for different firms' operating revenue, lease contracts offered by different kinds of lessors are not necessarily the same. The key to these leasing differences is found in the manner in which manufacturers' lessors and lease intermediaries recognize revenue from the leasing transaction and obtain depreciation tax shields from leased assets.

When a manufacturer leases a particular asset, the firm recognizes production revenue over the life of the lease. The lease transaction spreads the tax burden associated with operating profits over the life of the lease. In contrast to this tax deferral, outright sale of the asset requires the manufacturer to recognize immediately the revenue associated with the sale; this recognition produces a current tax liability against the full value of the sale. In other words, the lease transaction gives manufacturers a distinct tax advantage by postponing the recognition of taxable income.

Federal income tax regulations also penalize manufacturers' lessors because the manner in which manufacturers must depreciate leased assets differs from the depreciation standards governing lease intermediaries. The depreciable basis used by manufacturers' lessors is limited to production costs associated with a given asset; lease intermediaries depreciate leased assets at their full market value. Because the market value depreciable basis exceeds the production cost basis, lease intermediaries reap a greater depreciation tax shield from lease transactions.

These differences in the tax treatment of manufacturers' lessors and lease intermediaries translate into significant lease pricing advantages at different points in time. For example, the federal government might change the tax code in order to stimulate business investment. To make investment less costly and therefore more attractive, Congress can implement an investment tax credit to reduce the tax burden placed on firms that acquire capital assets. The value of this tax credit depends on the acquisition cost of any asset acquired. Because acquisition costs for lease intermediaries represent the fair market value of purchased assets, while manufacturers can only claim production costs as the basis for the ITC, this tax shield provides a competitive advantage for lease intermediaries.

At first glance, it would appear that the more tax shields allowed by the tax code, the greater the lease intermediary's advantage in offering lease contracts. While this is indeed correct, it overlooks another important determinant of the lease pricing advantage. The depreciation tax shield created by the lease transaction is not recognized immediately by the lessor; it extends across the depreciable life of the leased asset. Any pricing advantage that arises from the depreciation and ITC tax shields depends on the present discounted value of the tax shields, and the present value depends on the interest rate used to discount future cash flows back to the present. The higher the discount rate, the lower the present value of the tax shields, and the less significant the lease pricing advantage enjoyed by the lease intermediary.

In short, lease intermediaries obtain a lease price advantage whenever the present value associated with deferral of taxable income enjoyed by manufacturers' lessors is more than offset by greater depreciation and ITC tax advantages held by lease intermediaries. The more tax shields permitted by the government in support of capital acquisition, the stronger the advantage for lease intermediaries. In addition, the lower the level of market interest rates, the larger the present value of intermediaries' tax shields, and the stronger the pricing advantage maintained by these third-party lessors.

Exhibit 8-11 summarizes the different relationships that lead to a competitive advantage in lease pricing. When market interest rates are

Exhibit 8-11
Manufacturers' Leases versus Lease Intermediaries:
Potential Pricing Advantages

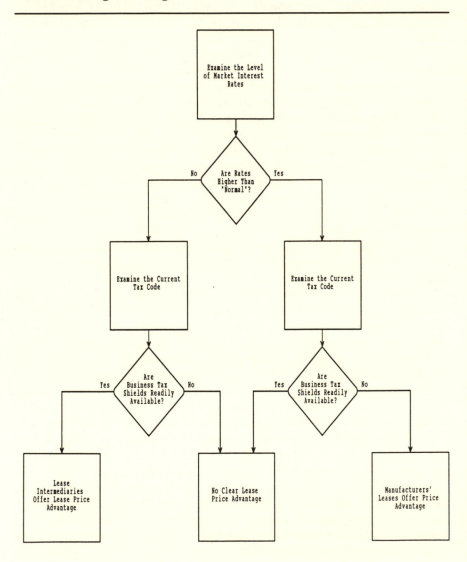

higher than normal, a lease pricing advantage exists for manufacturers' lessors. This advantage may be completely eradicated by the presence of extensive tax shields (such as a short depreciation period, cou-
pled with an accelerated depreciation schedule and a liberal ITC) that
favor lease intermediaries. As long as above-average market interest
rates combine with a tax code containing few tax shields for asset
purchasers, manufacturers' lessors enjoy a lease pricing advantage.
When high interest rates combine with liberal tax shields, however,
there is no clear pricing advantage for either manufacturers' lessors or
lease intermediaries.

In contrast to these cases, when market interest rates are relatively
low, lease intermediaries typically enjoy a lease pricing advantage. This
advantage is enhanced by a tax policy containing liberal depreciation
and ITC tax shields, so that the lease intermediary obtains a clear
lease-pricing advantage when interest rates are relatively low and tax
statutes permit liberal deductions for asset purchasers. The intermediary's competitive advantage is diminished, however, when low market
interest rates combine with a tax policy that permits fewer tax shields
associated with asset acquisition – in this case neither lease intermediaries nor manufacturers' lessors enjoy a clear pricing advantage on
leases.

The message for lessees is simple: environmental conditions influence lease pricing, giving certain kinds of lessors a competitive advantage in the delivery of low-cost lease agreements. When interest rates
are particularly high, and the tax code is relatively restrictive, manufacturers' lease contracts dominate the leasing landscape. Alternatively, when interest rates are particularly low and current tax regulations
actively encourage business investment with liberal tax shields given
to buyers of capital assets, lease intermediaries can offer more attractive leasing terms than manufacturers' lessors. In all other cases, there
is no clear pricing advantage associated with either type of lessor (see
Exhibit 8-11), and prospective lessees should investigate lease terms
offered by intermediaries as well as manufacturers' lessors to obtain
the most reasonably priced lease contract.

LEASING AND THE ALTERNATIVE MINIMUM TAX

As the preceding section demonstrates, environmental conditions ex-
ert an important influence on the cost of leasing. In particular, the
nature of corporate income tax regulations has a significant impact on
leasing costs, so that changes in tax law contain important implications for leasing decisions. One recent change in tax law, the extension
of the corporate Alternative Minimum Tax (AMT) in the 1986 Tax

Reform Act, significantly enhances the benefit of the lease alternative for firms in low tax brackets.

Chapter 5 provides a general introduction to leasing under the new AMT rules. To review this material briefly, the 1986 Tax Reform Act requires a separate calculation of taxable income (known as the alternative minimum taxable income) that adjusts ordinary taxable income by adding to it certain tax preferences (such as MACRS depreciation) and tax adjustments (such as the ACE adjustment). This alternative minimum tax income, less a $40,000 exemption, is multiplied by 20% to produce the tentative minimum tax for a given firm. In cases where the tentative minimum tax exceeds the firm's regular tax liability, the alternative minimum tax represents the difference between the tentative minimum tax and the regular tax liability. The AMT is then added to the firm's regular tax liability to produce the total taxes due to the government.

Firms that reside in low tax brackets are particularly susceptible to the AMT liability, especially when such firms obtain a low tax rate by using extensive tax preferences to minimize ordinary taxable income. When firms purchase assets, they often create both tax preferences and tax adjustments. Tax preference items originate as firms use an accelerated method to depreciate the value of newly acquired assets. Tax adjustments occur when firms use accelerated depreciation to calculate taxable income, and straight-line depreciation to report income to shareholders. In the years immediately following asset purchase, this causes income reported to shareholders to exceed taxable income reported to the government, and 75% of the difference in these figures must be treated as a tax adjustment by most corporations. As a consequence, purchasing assets increases the probability that the purchaser will be required to pay the AMT because asset purchases increase the difference between regular taxable income and alternative minimum tax income.

Lease acquisitions, however, create neither tax preferences nor tax adjustments for the lessee. Because the lessee does not acquire any depreciation tax shields in connection with leasing, this transaction permits asset acquisition without increasing the difference between ordinary taxable income and alternative minimum tax income. The extension of the AMT regulation in 1986 enhanced the value of leasing to corporate taxpayers who are in relatively modest income tax brackets.

The AMT introduces still another complication to the evaluation of lease contracts, because this tax regulation has the potential to alter the after-tax cost of debt used to discount lease cash flows. In cases where the AMT yields a non-zero tax liability, the corporate taxpayer's marginal tax rate must be revised to include the AMT liability. This changes the firm's after-tax cost of debt, and the change must be reflected in the evaluation of lease cash flows.

Returning to Exhibit 7-2, note that the lessee's marginal tax rate affects the value of the tax shield provided by the lease payment, the depreciation and interest tax shields foregone in the lease, the after-tax salvage value of the leased asset, and the after-tax cost of debt used to discount the annual net cash flows associated with the lease. When the AMT creates a positive tax liability for the lessee, the lease valuation framework must be completely revised to incorporate this additional tax obligation.

SALE-AND-LEASEBACK TRANSACTIONS

Sale-and-leaseback transactions provide a final example to illustrate how corporate tax regulations and financial accounting standards combine to create innovative financing opportunities. In its simplest form, a sale-and-leaseback transaction actually involves two separate financial events: first, the sale of an owned asset that is used in a given firm's operations, followed by an agreement to lease the asset from the buyer once the sale is complete. The lease agreement follows the asset's sale, however the sales contract requires the leaseback agreement as a condition for the sale.

More complicated variations on the sale-and-leaseback theme can involve the use of a third party to supply financing for the buyer–lessor in the lease agreement, and, in this instance, the leaseback transaction resembles the leveraged lease described above in this chapter. In most cases, lessees in the sale-and-leaseback transaction represent nonfinancial firms seeking to obtain greater liquidity from owned assets, while lessors represent traditional financial institutions, pension funds, insurance companies, and private trust or endowment funds.

The basic impetus behind the sale-and-leaseback transaction is the desire on the part of seller–lessees to obtain cash from existing assets without losing control of these assets. In most cases, the assets subject to sale-and-leaseback display a market value exceeding their book value, so that converting them to cash via the sales transaction produces an after-tax gain as well as an infusion of cash for the seller. This cash can be used for a variety of purposes, including the retirement of debt, investment in new corporate projects, or simply disbursement to shareholders.

In all cases, however, the sale-and-leaseback transaction provides the selling firm with the appearance of improved financial strength. Unrecognized value on the firm's balance sheet becomes recognized. When invested in new projects earning high rates of return, this cash can be used to boost the seller's corporate earnings. When used to retire existing liabilities, it can boost the proportion of the firm's assets supported by shareholder equity. When used to provide a cash distribution in the form of a special dividend to shareholders, this cash can boost the market value of equity. If used to repurchase shares of stock, it can increase the firm's return on equity by reducing the number of shares outstanding.

In addition, the sale-and-leaseback transaction can provide cash to fund mergers and acquisitions, as well as cash to reduce the debt burden of firms acquired in leveraged-buyout transactions. The cash created by the sale-and-leaseback can also be used to defend the firm against hostile acquisition. By transforming undervalued capital assets into cash, the selling firm renders its balance sheet less attractive to unwelcome suitors. At the same time, cash generated from the sale of undervalued assets can be used to defend against the hostile takeover attempt.

Sale-and-leaseback transactions bear a striking resemblance to secured debt, yet they provide more flexible financing terms than debt. In the case of both sale-and-leasebacks and debt financing, failure by the lessee/borrower to meet debt service payments results in loss of the asset's use. In the sale-and-leaseback, however, the buyer–lessor acquires ownership rights associated with the asset, and provides the seller–lessee with 100% of the asset's market value. Secured creditors rarely advance more than 80% of an asset's market value against a secured loan.

Also, the lender establishes the strength of the secured loan primarily from the borrower's ability to meet debt service payments from operating cash flows. While the leaseback transaction also hinges upon the lessee's credit strength, the buyer–lessor considers the future residual value of the leased asset in establishing the firm's required rate of return. As a consequence, lease payments are frequently lower than loan payments for a similar principal balance.

The similarity between sale-and-leaseback transactions and secured debt creates some drawbacks for the lease transaction. In cases where the lease clearly represents a disguised borrowing transaction, the Internal Revenue Service may recharacterize the lease contract as a secured loan. Under this condition, the buyer–lessor must surrender the depreciation tax shield provided with the sales agreement, effectively eliminating the primary tax benefit associated with asset ownership. In order for the lease transaction to represent a true lease, the IRS requires that (1) the economic life of the leased asset exceeds the term of the lease; (2) the buyer–lessor assumes economic risk associated with the leased asset's uncertain future value; and (3) the leased asset has an expected non-zero residual value at the maturity of the lease. Because reclassification of the leaseback transaction as secured debt destroys the lessor's tax advantage from the lease, most lessors require an indemnification agreement from lessees to protect them from loss if the IRS disallows the lease.

The sale-and-leaseback transaction contains other potential disadvantages for the seller–lessee. For one, converting capital assets into cash at the fair market value often results in a taxable gain, and the tax liability from this gain must be recognized when the sale-and-leaseback occurs. Secured debt financing produces no such tax obligation. Also, the asset sale preceding the leaseback transaction can trigger the recapture of all or part of the investment tax credit originally associated with asset purchase. Under the sale-and-leaseback arrangement, ITC recapture occurs when the seller–lessee later assigns or terminates the leaseback agreement. No similar provision in the tax code affects the early termination or assignment of debt contracts. In addition, transfer of ownership rights under the sale-and-leaseback precludes the seller from obtaining any additional capital gains from future price appreciation of the asset. Under secured debt contracts, future price appreciation remains the property of the borrower. Finally, at maturity of the leaseback contract, the seller–lessee must renegotiate the terms of the lease or lose the use of the leased asset. Secured debt requires neither of these actions at the conclusion of the loan.

Given the advantages and disadvantages associated with sale-and-leaseback transactions, do these financing arrangements provide additional value for lessees? In general, the answer appears to be yes. Recent empirical evidence reported in the finance literature suggests that corporate announcements of sale-and-leaseback transactions produce positive gains for shareholders of lessee firms. These gains stem from the positive tax consequences associated with leaseback arrangements. The seller–lessee benefits by recognizing the full deductibility of lease payments, while the depreciation tax shields available to the lessor reflect the revised market value of the leased asset. This translates into a transfer of wealth from the government, in the form of reduced tax collections, to the shareholders of the lessee firm. In short, lessees gain a financial advantage from sale-and-leasebacks, lessors break even on these transactions, and the government suffers a reduction in tax collections from both the lessor and lessee firms.

SUMMARY

This chapter extends the basic lease valuation framework presented in Chapter 7 to accommodate a number of more complicated lease transactions. In particular, this chapter shows how to evaluate leveraged leases, cancellation options embedded in capital leases, and purchase options offered in connection with various types of leases. Chapter 8 also explores how environmental conditions – especially tax regulations – can shape business decisions to lease assets.

The chapter reviews the impact of recent changes in the Alternative Minimum Tax rule on leasing activity, shows how different tax regulations can provide a competitive pricing advantage to certain types of lessors, and explains how the corporate tax code and financial accounting standards combine to create innovative financing opportunities, such as the sale-and-leaseback agreement. Each of these topics demonstrates how creative uses of lease financing can provide additional financial flexibility to corporate borrowers and lenders, providing higher returns to lessors and more reasonable financing terms to lessees.

REFERENCES

Athanasopoulos, P. J., and P. W. Bacon. "The Evaluation of Leveraged Leases." *Financial Management* (Spring 1980): 76–80.

Bierman, H., Jr. "Buy Versus Lease with an Alternative Minimum Tax." *Financial Management* (Winter 1988): 87–91.

Brick, I. E., W. Fung, and M. Subrahmanyam. "Leasing and Financial Intermediation: Comparative Tax Advantages." *Financial Management* (Spring 1987): 55–59.

Castle, D. E. "Sale/Leasebacks: Taking Advantage of Hidden Value." *Management Review* (November 1987): 39–43.

Copeland, T. E., and J. F. Weston. "A Note on the Evaluation of Cancellable Operating Leases." *Financial Management* (Summer 1982): 60–67.

Dyl, E. A., and S. A. Martin, Jr. "Setting Terms for Leveraged Leases." *Financial Management* (Winter 1977): 20–27.

Grimlund, R. A., and R. Capettini. "A Note on the Evaluation of Leveraged Leases and Other Investments." *Financial Management* (Summer 1982): 68–71.

Kim, E. H., W. G. Lewellen, and J. J. McConnell. "Sale-and-Leaseback Agreements and Enterprise Valuation." *Journal of Financial and Quantitative Analysis* (December 1978): 871–83.

McGrath, W. T. "Unwrapping Leasehold Equity: An Introduction to the 'Wraparound Lease.'" *Real Estate Review* (Winter 1990): 23–30.

Schall, L. D. "The Evaluation of Lease Financing Opportunities." *Midland Corporate Finance Journal* (Spring 1985): 48–65.

Slovin, M. B., M. D. Sushka, and J. A. Polonchek. "Corporate Sale-and-Leasebacks and Shareholder Wealth." *Journal of Finance* (March 1990): 289–99.

Smith, B. D. "Accelerated Debt Repayment in Leveraged Leases." *Financial Management* (Summer 1982): 73–80.

Sponseller, D. "Lease Financing: Sale and Leaseback Options." *Public Utilities Fortnightly* (March 19, 1987): 40–43.

Ryan, R. J., Jr. "Leveraged Leasing." *Management Accounting* (April 1977): 45–50.

V

The Role of Leasing in Modern Financial Management

9

Contemporary Leasing Practice

The finance literature has sought to maintain an ongoing dialogue concerning leasing. The focus of the published material has been divided between the theoretical and the practical. The benefits of such research accrue to the practitioner. The primary justification for any research in the area of finance is to improve the decision-making ability of financial managers.

What follows is a brief review of the literature that has addressed financial lease analysis. The articles are not a representative sample but a selection that highlights the key issues in the lease-versus-buy analysis elaborated in this book. The articles cited, and those in the bibliography at the end of this book, illustrate the wide range of approaches taken by researchers on the subject of leasing. Again, the focus is upon the financial lease.

The goal of making lease analysis clear and accessible to every finance decision-maker continues. Such an effort is necessary because of the importance of financial leases in the operation of the modern firm. Despite leasing's massive dollar volume, there is still a need to update and revise certain issues relative to the tax laws, LBOs, overseas operations, and other components of leasing analysis. This chapter illustrates the usefulness and importance of the existing literature.

THE COST OF LEASING

Leasing has been discussed and analyzed to a significant extent in the literature of academic finance. Several aspects of the financing alternative have been examined by scholars; the extensive study is justified. Leasing is important, complex, and a permanent part of the financial considerations of U.S. firms. Financial managers are interested in the cost of leasing. If leasing offers benefits to firms, what are its costs? If leasing is a substitute for debt financing, what is the cost of leasing compared to the cost (after-tax interest) of debt?

In a 1984 paper, Ang and Peterson[1] draw the conclusion that debt and lease financing are not substitutes for each other. The study shows that firms with high levels of debt also had high levels of leased assets, and that the two types of financing were increased together, not as substitutes for each other. In other studies, the cost of leasing has been addressed directly. Exhibit 9-1 highlights characteristics of certain borrowing rates versus lease rates. These data do not conform to the idea of a financial advantage to leasing. The apparent cost of the leases is higher than that of borrowed funds. The suspected reasons for the disparity between the two lending sources involves "capital market theory"; that is, the perception of the risk level of all lessees (from the viewpoint of the lessor) is greater than that perceived by users of regular debt. This idea seems to verify the research subsequent to 1981, which indicates that debt and leasing may be complementary instead of being substitutes for each other.

If debt and leasing are complementary forms of financing (if firms are inclined to add leased assets to their balance sheets as the debt level increases), how are the leases priced? What risk considerations can be attributed to the lessee that are different from those attributed to the same firm when it borrows? Crawford et al.[2] believe that several

Exhibit 9-1
Comparison of Lease Yields with Government and Corporate Bond Yields*

	Average Government Bond Yield	Average BBB Corporate Bond Yield	Average Calculated Purchase Price less than $1,000,000	Yield on Leases Purchase Price $1,000,000 or more
1975	7.65%	10.61%	22.77%	18.57%
1976	6.81%	9.75%	14.64%	18.39%
1977	7.07%	8.97%	31.09%	16.49%
1978	8.34%	9.49%	22.65%	15.23%
1979	9.94%	10.69%	30.09%	16.97%
1980	11.37%	13.42%	34.34%	27.71%

Source: Reprinted by permission from Note 2.

*The years 1973 and 1974 are omitted because in our sample no leases were made in those years on assets with a purchase price of more than $1 million.

explanations are plausible. One explanation is the idea that lessees are generally more prone to bankruptcy than are other borrowers. Also, there are inefficiencies in the leasing of assets not evident in the market for other borrowed funds. Concerning the first of the possible explanations, it is very unlikely that lessee firms are more prone to bankruptcy than are other borrowers. What could possibly account for such a phenomenon, given FASB 13? Moreover, are lessors somehow unable to recognize an unusual debt burden in potential lessees prior to providing the needed assets? The same questions could be asked by potential lenders in a non-leasing situation.

The question of inefficiencies in the market for leases attempts to address the larger question of lessees, lessors, and the market mechanisms that bring them together. The cost-versus-benefit of the arrangement for both parties is the "test" of the efficiency of the market mechanisms. One way to describe, or perhaps assess, the efficiency of the market for leases is to use the specialized lessor function as "proof" of efficiency. The specialized lessor exists because service can be rendered better through such an intermediary than if each potential lessee dealt with each individual manufacturer. Therefore, it is likely that some of the cost differential between leasing and borrowing is compensation for the intermediary function of the lessor. It is the job of further research (some of which is presently underway) to determine the symmetry of cost and pricing in the market for leases.

LEASING AND DEBT DISPLACEMENT

In a 1986 study, Bayless and Diltz[3] examine the "debt displacement effects of leasing." Their objective was to operationalize the question of how much debt is displaced by the lease contract. The authors' purpose was to "empirically estimate a measure of debt displacement" that conformed to theoretical models developed previously in the literature. The author's first task, after addressing the previous research, was to define unused debt capacity. Debt displacement refers to the amount of unused debt capacity taken up or used by future financing. Such unused debt capacity is defined as the "maximum additional amount of a firm's debt that lenders are willing to assume." The test performed by the authors was designed to determine which form of financing uses more of the unused debt capacity—leasing or borrowing. The importance of that question for the practitioner is clear. In planning financing sources for a growing firm, the ability to secure and afford suitable financing is of the highest importance.

In attempting fully to assess the debt displacement question, the authors surveyed bank lending officers. The purpose of the survey was to have 1500 commercial loan officers evaluate several firms' present and historical financial statements, and recommend a line of credit with appropriate terms for the loan. The surveyors varied the mixture of lease and debt financing for each firm, with the sum of the two held constant for all firms. The results of the study were based on 133 usable responses. The authors considered the response rate acceptable, given the complexity of the survey instrument. The statistical techniques used to interpret the response data indicate that a capital lease displaces approximately 10 to 26% more unused debt capacity than does debt financing.

The reasons for the difference in debt displacement between lease financing and debt financing have strong implications for the practitioner. The difference in tax shield value between the two financing sources, the senior status of the capital lease in the event of liquidation, and the loan cost all affect the willingness of the lender to provide debt financing. The authors also found a strong relationship between debt-capacity estimates and the firm's cost-of-capital estimates. In other words, the level of debt capacity can be known with increasing certainty as the accuracy of the cost of capital increases.

Financial management of a firm must understand and assess the following:

1. The level and type of tax shields that accompany each financing source
2. The loan cost as a major component of the firm's cost of capital and as a primary tax shield
3. The firm's overall cost of capital – the weighted average of the costs of long-term financing components (this number is also known as the "hurdle rate" or the "discount rate" in internal investment analysis)

It is only after these items are known with as much certainty as possible that optimum financing decisions can be made. Moreover, those items must be adequately assessed in light of the overall financial health of the firm; that is, a ratio analysis should be the first step in the examination of the debt capacity/lease-versus-borrow question. As an example, the earnings-before-interest-and-taxes (EBIT) level must be at a level sufficient to support the interest payments if debt is the resulting financing option. The fixed-charges-coverage ratio includes the lease payments in that particular assessment of the firm's financial strength.

Within the context of a comprehensive financial analysis, the empirical findings of Bayless and Diltz can have practical use for the firm. It is clear from the study that the opinion of the lender is a major determinant of unused debt capacity. That opinion is influenced by the manner in which the firm's financial statements have been managed up to that point. It is the responsibility of the firm's financial management to insure that all financial decisions are based on conformity to the economic realities, as seen through existing theory.

DETERMINANTS OF LEASE YIELDS

Schallheim and colleagues tested the hypothesis that lease yields are related to the yields of treasury bonds and the systematic risk of the asset's residual value.[4] It is necessary to know what lease yields are related to so that they may be better forecast. Moreover, the value of a financial contract (a lease, in this case) can be determined only if the "return" is known. Their methodology included examining the files of seven non-bank leasing companies. The examination provided 453 lease contracts that showed geographic location, type and cost of leased asset and its maturity, the amount of rental payments, and the status of the investment tax credit.

Multiple regression analysis was used as a framework for analysis of the determinant of lease yields. The yields on lease contracts were regressed against the yields of treasury bonds, the variance of returns, the inverse of the asset's purchase price, profitability of the firm, the financial ratios' total debt divided by total assets, and the current ratio. The regression analysis provided the following results. Lease yields are influenced (at a level that is statistically significant) by the yield on treasury bonds of the same maturity as the lease, and by the discounted value of the leased asset's residual-value covariance risk. Residual-value covariance risk is the manner in which the residual value of the asset varies, relative to its original estimate, in comparison to an average price for the asset at original purchase.

The authors' findings confirmed the working hypothesis that yields on capital leases are related to the yields on treasury bonds and the forecasted value of the asset at the end of the asset's life. The authors also report a relationship between the level of lease yields and the probability of default of the lessee – a predictable relationship that points to the need for a carefully managed balance sheet if the cost of financing is to be kept as low as possible.

In addition to these findings, the authors provide examples of the difference between debt and lease yields (costs). In their description, the average before-tax yield on a lease is 18.63% compared to a range of 7.15% to 15.49% for Aa corporate bonds. The question arises as to why firms (the 363 usable contracts in this sample), chose costly leases over less costly debt? The authors conclude that the answer is associated with the size of the borrowing firm. Small firms understand and seek the flexibility of leasing and may be unable to issue publicly traded, hence lower cost, debt. They are left then with only the leasing option with which to secure assets. Further, their smaller size provides no opportunity for "quantity discounts" in the transaction. Higher-cost financing results for these firms.

The implications for the financial manager are less clear due to the theoretical nature of the research. It does, however, provide important guidelines for more efficient use of fixed-cost financing, including the following:

1. The relationship of lease yields to treasury-bond yields provides an improved means of forecasting yields.
2. The residual value of the asset as a contributor to yields means that more attention should be given to improving the forecasting of that value.
3. An improved comparison of the two financing sources may reduce capital costs by employing the "yield curve" concept when comparing borrowing costs to leasing costs.

LEASE VALUATION

Theoretical Issues

In a 1987 paper, Franks and Hodges examine leasing as a "tax-arbitrage instrument."[5] The purpose of the paper was to explain why lessors earn large positive net present values (NPVs) on the assets they own. The authors contend that the tax positions between lessors and lessees are asymmetrical; that is, there is an advantage, relative to tax effects, available to either the lessor or lessee. The paper is theoretical, and seeks to develop a model to explain the positive NPVs "in terms of a market price for a scarce resource," which is identified as scarce taxable earnings. The purpose of the model was to determine whether the profitability of lease contracts could be improved by structuring the contracts to make better use of the lessors' taxable earnings. The contention was that profit improvement is possible because leasing markets are inefficient, or because the leasing market is segmented by "clienteles."

The conclusions drawn by the authors are as follows: lessors earn positive NPVs when taxable earnings are scarce in an economy; scarcity of taxable earnings gives them value; and the value of the earnings is the extent to which the available taxable earnings enable a present value savings to be made in future tax liabilities.

The Empirical Findings

The importance of theoretical leasing issues is grounded in the experience of business finance practitioners. There are several research efforts noteworthy for their attempt to highlight the concerns of the practicing financial manager about leasing. This empirical research has

focused on the analysis necessary to determine the incremental benefits of lease financing versus financing with borrowed funds.

In a 1977 paper, Anderson and Martin sought to determine the major issues faced by practitioners in the lease-versus-buy analysis.[6] The
authors determined that the question of whether or not a lease financing option served as an alternative capital budgeting project was on
the minds of financial managers. It is now known, after 20 years of
hindsight, that leasing and capital budgeting are not alternatives.
Leasing is a method of financing, and capital budgeting is an analytical
procedure for determining the level of dollar value added to the firm as
an internal investment. Lease financing may be a beneficial component
of that value. The view of leasing as a financial tool was in its infancy
during the period of the 1977 study. Many questions had to be formu-
lated and asked before progress could be made. What were the relevant
questions, and what contribution were textbooks and other published
sources making toward their formulation and resolution?

In a 1983 article, O'Brien and Nunnally sought to update the 1977
study.[7] The purpose was to determine what progress, if any, had been
made by practitioners in the lease-versus-buy analysis. The authors'
objectives were as follows:

The questions attempted to discover whether in 1982 changes had been made
by practitioners relating to the three potential problems perceived by [the
authors of the 1977 study and other researchers] (1) The use of the cost of
capital instead of cost of debt in certain portions of the NAL analysis; (2) the
failure to permit a positive NAL to salvage a project on a lease basis that was
rejected on a purchase basis, if the NAL was greater than the absolute value of
the negative NPV; and (3) the carrying out of the analysis as though the lease
and purchase decisions were two investment alternatives (the capital budgeting approach). (p. 33)

These questions were and are important because they relate directly
to the manner in which value is added to the firm. In terms of using the
cost of debt as the discount rate in the lease-versus-buy analysis, the
lease and loan cash flows are of sufficient certainty to warrant a relatively low discount rate. The lease payments and debt service payments are legal obligations; as a result, the providers of either form of
financing have the legal assurance of payment. The cash flows so discounted will reflect the economic reality of the transaction. When the
lease-versus-buy analysis is conducted so as to reflect financing
choices, an internal investment project that is not acceptable because
of a negative NPV or an IRR below the cost of financing may be
acceptable if leasing is the financing method chosen.

The material presented in finance textbooks and academic journals
is, in most cases, meant to guide the practitioner. The 1982 study also
meant to determine how efficient that guidance had been. The results

of the study, as reported by the authors, revealed that from 1977 to the time of the 1982 study "many practitioners appear to have switched from favoring the cost of capital to favoring the cost of debt in NAL analysis." The authors further conclude that "However, many practitioners still incorrectly believe that a lease analysis should be conducted if and only if a project has been approved on a purchase basis."

It is difficult to determine why the choice between leasing and borrowing to purchase an asset was not seen as financing by practitioners, because it is only within that context that the full advantage of leasing capital assets can accrue to a firm. Again, the purpose of capital budgeting (internal-investment analysis) is to determine under what conditions value is added to the firm. A clear understanding of all available financing choices and their relationship to the capital-budgeting process assures a decision based on correct analysis and assumptions.

The 1983 article concluded with a summary of issues in the lease-versus-buy analysis that are difficult for practitioners to quantify and resolve: the investment tax credit (severely restricted with 1986 TRA); lease duration; inflation; technological forecasting; and the level and rate of obsolescence. The issues bear directly on the lease-versus-buy analysis; however, their correct inclusion in a quantitative way is not well understood. The quantification of such factors as these is not clearly laid out in the literature, and represents very fertile ground for empirical research in leasing.

A 1984 article that addressed the terms (yields, etc.) of financial leases serves to illustrate the potential inaccuracy or confusion in the lease-versus-buy analysis.[1] The authors state at the outset: "The bad news is that we too are unable to explain the peculiarly high yields on lease contracts when compared with those on what generally are thought to be approximately equivalent debt securities." The authors obtained data from 50 financial leases issued from April 1973 through June 1980. The leases were issued by three commercial banks in Houston, Texas. The analytical technique used by the authors consisted of multivariate regression analysis. The lease yield was the dependent variable; asset cost, length of the lease period, down payment, ITC, and the bank's cost of funds constituted the independent variable. The results obtained by the authors are clear. "In particular, the average before-tax yield of the sample of 20.7% is significantly above the yield of 8.1% on government securities and 10.5% on BBB bonds issued during the same period and with the same maturity as the leases."

The relationship between lease yield and bond yield is described by the authors as a "puzzle." It is axiomatic in finance that higher risk warrants a higher yield, and the higher yield should be related to the incremental difference in risk. Thus, the disparity between the lease and bond yields seems to defy conventional wisdom. For the practicing financial manager, the disparity may indicate an "inefficiency" in the leasing market, based to a large extent upon the lack of widespread skill in comparing lease/borrow alternatives.

Certain research has indicated and highlighted more oblique "financial incentives of leases." The distinction is made between *user characteristics affecting the leasing decision* and *lessor characteristics affecting the leasing decision*. Among the user characteristics are financial incentives, compensation-related incentives, sensitivity to use and maintenance, and firm-specific assets. Taking these characteristics in turn further illustrates advantages and characteristics of leasing directly relevant in the post-TRA era.

Financial incentives refer to the interplay between lease and debt commitments on the firm's balance sheet. Two actions come about as a result of the interplay. First, non-cancelable leases have senior status over unsecured debt; therefore, the use of other fixed-payment funds sources is limited. It is not possible, in the coverage sense, to lower imprudently the firm's ability to meet its fixed obligations. Second, leasing may permit an otherwise unacceptable capital-budgeting expenditure to be acceptable – solely as a result of the financing choice.

Compensation-related incentives refer to the use of leases as a means of increasing the return on assets of a firm. The use of operating leases helps to keep the denominator, total assets, low in the return-on-assets calculation (net income after tax is the numerator in that equation). Adherence to FASB 13, however, would limit the influence of such off-balance-sheet financing, since the discounted lease payments would have to be included on the balance sheet as an offset to the asset's value.

Sensitivity to use and maintenance refers to the experience that a lessee has with the asset. The lessor is responsible for determining the level of use and abuse the asset will be subject to, and prices should be set accordingly. In attempting to understand the disparity between the cost of leasing (the implicit interest rate of a lease) versus the cost of borrowing, the likelihood of use or abuse may figure in. Among lessors, the two characteristics, use and abuse, may be assigned in the pricing process to type of asset and type of user. Given the specialized nature of some lessees, that pricing mechanism may be very well developed among lessors, and may explain a significant portion of the pricing differential.

Firm-specific assets are a major advantage to the lease-financing alternative in terms of the utility value of the asset. The sale–leaseback arrangement has remained popular, in part because in some instances it allows a custom-made asset to be acquired by the user firm without the commitment of a permanent large cash outlay. On the cost side, however, the acquisition of firm-specific assets may require more lengthy negotiation and more costly administration in order to bring about a contract suitable to both parties. This aspect may also help to explain some of the previously mentioned cost differential between lease financing and debt financing.

From the preceding discussion, it can be seen that leasing has advantages that are deeply related to the characteristics of the user. It is also clear that economic advantages have costs, and, in keeping with economic theory, the advantages may be transitory. The transitory nature of economic advantages adheres, of course, to the idea of perfect financial markets.

In addition to the user influences on the decision to have a specific leasing policy, the lessor also influences leasing policy. There are price discrimination opportunities available to the lessor in some instances. These may be in the form of an advantage held in the market for a certain asset. "Then becoming a lessor can provide additional opportunities to extract rents by circumventing those provisions of the Robinson-Patman Act. . . . "[8] Cason further states that the advantage, as always, should be directly related to supply and demand conditions for that asset. Lessors may also employ price discrimination when the lessee's demands are more closely related to certain lease characteristics, such as the maintenance provisions or the term of the lease.

Another manner in which the lessor may influence lessee policies toward leasing is through a comparative advantage in disposing of the asset. Such an advantage may be translated into lowered lease rates for the lessee (the rates would have to be communicated to the lessee, or, as indicated below, there may be serious problems in that undertaking). Any advantage or incentive to leasing must not be available to the lessee through a purchase. Again, the primary item in the lessor/lessee relationship appears to be information. It remains to be seen, as research continues, exactly how information is transmitted, the nature and type of that information, and its effect upon leasing costs and activity.

UPDATE ON LEASE-VERSUS-LOAN COSTS

The research cited in this chapter indicates a disparity between what lessors demand as a return for leased assets versus what is demanded for loans. A fundamental principle of modern business finance is that risk and return have a positive relationship: the required return increases as the risk increases. Data now being collected and analyzed do not indicate any discernible relationship between the rates offered through a loan and those offered through the lease alternative. These data indicate relatively minor differences in loan rates among lenders in a wide cross-section of geographical areas and lender categories. Yet, when data from the same geographic areas are analyzed for lessors, the resulting implicit lease rates appear random. No pattern emerges among the lease rates for lessor category or geographic region. The question clearly becomes, on what basis are lease rates set? Moreover, the customer's (lessee's) view of the rates would be interesting to assess. These data refer to a narrow segment of the leasing activity in the United States (automobiles for personal use), therefore care must be taken in generalizing from the early results. The results do indicate, however, that the lessee and lessor may be alternatively disadvantaged by the apparent lack of attention to proper pricing of available financing alternatives.

SUMMARY

The issues that remain as a hindrance to a clear exposition of the lease-versus-buy-analysis are as follows: the cost disparity between leasing and straight debt; how to forecast residual value with improved accuracy; and the relationship between leasing and a firm's debt capacity.

The finance researcher must continue to provide clarity and guidance to the practicing manager. This can only be done through a rigorous analysis of all relevant issues related to the evaluation and assessment of financial lease analysis. Practitioners must assist in that effort by reading the published material and offering comments tempered by the cold reality of experience.

NOTES

1. J. Ang, and P. Peterson, "The Leasing Puzzle," *Journal of Finance* (September 1984), pp. 1055–66.

2. P. J. Crawford et al. "Further Evidence on the Terms of Financial Leases," *Financial Management* (Autumn 1981), pp. 7–14.

3. M. E. Bayless, and J. D. Diltz, "An Empirical Study of the Debt Displacement Effects of Leasing," *Financial Management* (Winter 1986), pp. 53–60.

4. J. S. Schallheim, R. E. Johnson, R. C. Lease, and J. J. McConnell, "The Determinants of Yields on Financial Leasing Contracts," *Journal of Financial Economics* (March 1987), pp. 45–67.

5. J. R. Franks, and S. D. Hodges, "Valuation of Financial Lease Contracts," *Journal of Finance* (May 1978), pp. 657–72.

6. P. Anderson, and J. Martin, "Lease vs. Purchase Decisions: A Survey of Current Practice," *Financial Management* (Spring 1977), pp. 41–47.

7. T. J. O'Brien, and B. H. Nunnally, Jr., "A 1982 Survey of Corporate Leasing Analysis," *Financial Management* (Summer 1983), pp. 30–36.

8. R. L. Cason, "Leasing, Asset Lives and Uncertainty: Guides to Decision Making," *Financial Management* (Summer 1987), pp. 13–16.

10

Leasing Wisdom and Leasing Folly

THE WRONG REASONS TO LEASE

In the preceding chapters, the focus has been on the advantages, disadvantages, and analytical techniques of leasing. Financial leases have received the primary emphasis. It may be useful at this point to re-emphasize, as a means of summarizing the material, certain highlights of the lease-versus-buy conundrum. A list of some misconceptions concerning the favorability of leasing, or the lack thereof, include the following:

1. *Off-balance-sheet financing.* FASB 13, enacted in 1976, outlines the conditions under which a lease must be capitalized. As a result of such specific guidelines, lease obligations become a part of the firm's "fixed-charge" responsibility in a manner easily discernible by the analyst. Therefore, the distinction between "straight-debt" service and lease payments becomes less meaningful, and the firm's total-coverage ratio can be more accurately assessed.

2. *All rental payments are lease obligations.* It is up to the tax authorities to determine what constitutes a lease. The arrangement that involves payments to an asset provider may be, in actuality, an installment loan. The criteria for whether such an arrangement is a lease or a loan must be gathered from the prevailing tax rules.

3. *Any item subject to rapid obsolescence should be leased.* Flexibility has been cited as a primary motivation for the leasing of assets. Business finance decisions should be dictated by risk-and-return considerations. As a result, the need to remain flexible is directly related to the level of predictability of an asset's obsolescence. If the obsolescence can be forecast within a narrow range, then the need for flexibility may

be reduced accordingly, in which case leasing and borrowing should be compared as alternative *financing* arrangements instead of the asset disposal or replacement mechanism.

4. *The discount rate.* The risk/return considerations in business finance are, to a certain extent, captured in the discount rate (often referred to as a hurdle rate or opportunity cost) used to place cash flows on a present-value basis. In short, the discount rate used should reflect the level of uncertainty of the cash flows. In the lease-versus-buy (borrow) analysis, the loan-and-lease cash flows are relatively certain, and the analyst should be aware of the need to apply the appropriate discount rate. The firm's average cost of capital is generally not the rate by which the more certain cash flows should be discounted. The asset's residual value will usually demand a separate consideration of the appropriate discount rate.

5. *The asset's residual value.* There is considerable interest in the residual value of the asset on the part of the practicing manager. That interest is due, in large part, to the relationship between the residual value and the "cost" of the lease. The role of the lessor is to dispose of the asset at the end of its economic life. When the level of the asset's value is relatively certain, the certainty (lack of risk) of the lessor's total cash flows is increased, which should warrant a lower implicit interest rate for the leased asset. There is now increased cooperation between the lessee and the lessor to "manage" the obsolescence of the asset (relative to improved maintenance, for example) so that the cost of the lease financing can be more effectively managed for the benefit of both parties.

THE RIGHT REASONS TO LEASE

There are real and tangible benefits to leasing productive assets. These advantages exist even amid the misconceptions mentioned above and other misconceptions concerning leasing. The advantages to leasing may be most readily found in the following areas:

1. *Tax effects.* Tax benefits accrue to the lease arrangement because of the tax deductibility of the lease payments. The 1986 Tax Reform Act was looked upon as a potential impediment to strong volume increases in leased assets. After nearly four years, these forecasts have not borne fruit. The alternative minimum tax and the Modified Accelerated Cost Recovery System have changed certain approaches to lease-deal structuring and the accompanying accounting, but lease-volume increases are quite strong.

2. *Asset obsolescence.* The decrease in an asset's usefulness, due to technological changes or other causes, is a primary reason for financing

via the lease. When the asset's rate or period of obsolescence is uncertain, leasing is all the more important as a financing choice. The inability to forecast the asset's useful life may better be left to asset suppliers than asset users. As has been pointed out, such a benefit is not without cost. The lessor will need compensation in order to bear the risk of obsolescence.

3. *Flexibility*. It is precisely because technological change and other use-related factors bear much more heavily on some assets than others that leasing is an important financing alternative. In order to maintain an uninterrupted work flow, the firm relies upon the most efficient productive assets to which it has access. In the face of rapid asset deterioration, or equally rapid changes in technology, leasing may provide the firm with an ongoing access to the most efficient assets.

4. *Disposal of assets*. A part of the cost of leasing is the disposal of assets the economic life of which has ended. Leasing places the burden of disposal upon the lessor. Again, this advantage is not without cost. The lessor contributes efficiency to the market for used assets. The experience from such activities, which includes various types of assets, is reflective of that efficiency.

5. *Analysis of cash flows*. Based upon textbook expositions and other published materials, the advantages of leasing are best seen in a correct analytical framework. Financial managers must use an economic analysis that will expose all relevant cash flows and permit their proper treatment. That treatment revolves around present-value analysis. Present-value analysis, therefore, involves discounting cash flows relative to their tax consequences, if any, and places leasing and borrowing on a comparable footing. The net advantage to leasing exposition provides for that essential analysis. The NAL is described and discussed in this text not only for its conformity to modern finance principles, but also because of its ease of use, its compatibility with computer software, and its illustrative advantages.

In summary, the advantages of leasing are much more easily determined within the correct analytical framework. In addition, those advantages are likely to be much more widely available based on conformity to that analytical device.

OTHER FINAL CONSIDERATIONS

Evidence has been cited in this text that shows leasing as a considerably more expensive form of financing than debt. This is distressing because there is little or no apparent reason for such a cost differential. The differential exists, however, and financial managers must be aware of its effects upon their decisions. Leasing is shown to have costs different from borrowing in two important ways: (1) leasing is generally more expensive than borrowing and (2) the "relationship" between leasing costs and borrowing costs is random – there is no relationship. The phenomenon occurs without apparent reason.

It therefore behooves the financial manager to understand thoroughly the analytical technique referred to as NAL. It is also equally important to understand the lessor's analytical perspective and technique. The trend is toward increased cooperation and negotiation between the parties to a lease. As a result, the opportunity for sharing and therefore modifying the analytical process is greatly increased. The purpose of this cooperation is to remove randomness from the pricing of leases. Leasing has relatively few disadvantages; those cited here are primary. Again, the benefit of leasing may be readily seen through the NAL analysis.

Leasing and Taxes

The role of taxes in the decision to lease assets has been fully set out in Chapter 3. This section reiterates the most prominent aspects of that role and the relationship between leasing and taxes. A major distinction is that of the tax-oriented lease versus the non–tax-oriented lease. The tax-oriented lease allows the lessor to use the benefits related to taxes – depreciation and the investment-tax credit, if applicable. In a non–tax-oriented lease, the lessee is considered the owner of the asset relative to taxation. In this case, the lessee depreciates the asset and claims any tax credits. The following questions are pertinent to the lease-or-buy decision relative to taxes: Does the company pay minimum taxes? What is the relationship between avoidance of the minimum tax and the purchase price of the asset – do they provide a beneficial offset? When equipment is purchased, the difference between book income and tax income may be increased. The influence of depreciation causes that phenomenon, and, as a result, the purchase of an asset could mean a heavier tax burden for the company.

The alternative minimum tax imposes a 20% tax on one-half the difference between book income (income reported to stockholders) and income reported to tax authorities. The tax shields, previously used to reduce the level of taxes paid, are considered income under the AMT. The tax benefit items are added to normal taxable income to determine the alternate minimum taxable income. A 20% rate is applied against the AMTI to complete the *tentative minimum tax*. If the tentative minimum tax exceeds the taxpayer's normal taxable income, the difference is owed as AMT. The taxpayer must pay the AMT in addition to the normal tax. Based on the possible difference in depreciation between book accounting and tax accounting (book depreciation being the slower method, usually), the owning of assets may increase book income, and the AMT will take effect, raising the level of taxes owed.

The Valuation of Leases

The comparison between a financial lease and a purchase is critical to the financial manager. It permits a determination of which source of financing will add more value to the firm. The objective of increasing shareholder, or owner, wealth is the primary one for the financial decision-maker. The idea of lease valuation and lease-versus-borrow (buy) is at the center of that objective.

The most efficient means of lease-versus-buy comparison is the NAL analysis. This method of analysis permits a clear delineation of the relevant cash flows for either method of financing. The valuation of financial leases is directly related to their comparison with the purchase alternative from the standpoint of the lessee.

The cost of a lease, as noted above, cannot be directly determined through the comparison with the borrow alternative. The NAL permits a comparison of the present-value aspects of the lease alternative. The return to the lessor will likely not be readily apparent to the lessee. Data indicate an unclear relationship between the cost of borrowing and the cost of the lease as it relates to the providing of funds.

Operating leases may be valued through a method similar to that for the pricing of options. The residual value or resale value of the item is of primary consideration in the case of the operating lease. The financial lease is valued based upon changes in the borrowing patterns of the firm, the asset's use value, and the residual value of the asset. These items have to be considered in the context of the risk-and-return aspects of the firm's capital-budgeting practices, and then placed within the NAL framework.

Hybrid Leasing Arrangements

The two major variants to the "straight" two-party lease are the leveraged lease and the sale-and-leaseback arrangement. These are discussed in detail in Chapter 8. Summary comments are offered here.

Leveraged Leasing

The volume of leveraged leasing is now approximately $22 billion, or nearly 17% of U.S. leasing volume. The volume decreased somewhat, to about 12%, after 1986 TRA. It is now back to its pre-1986 level. One reason is the high cost of needed assets. Individual lessors may not have access to the level of funds necessary for asset purchase. The second reason is that specialized-nature equipment negotiations with the equipment manufacturer may necessitate progress payments or other advances. These may be burdensome for a single lessor.

The type of assets that may be acquired under a leveraged lease are varied. In today's financial environment, the needs of the lease dictate the type of equipment placed under the lease arrangement – including the leveraged lease. Actually, the means of financing employed by the lessor are irrelevant to the lessee. The aspects of lease valuation do not change with the leveraged lease from the standpoint of the lessee. The cost of the item, the relevant discount rate, and the asset's residual value are the primary components of the valuation process. That is, the use-value of the asset appraised against alternative financing methods is the manner in which the decision-maker will assess the lease. Again, the lease-versus-buy (borrow) decision provides the framework for the choice of financing. Those financing choices may then be analyzed through the NAL.

Sale-and-Leaseback Arrangements

The sale-and-leaseback arrangement is a method used by lessees to accomplish two objectives: to acquire an asset (often a building) with the specifications essential for a particular line and business, and to avoid a large investment (downpayment plus any other initial costs) in the asset. The lessor purchases the asset from the original owner, who then becomes the lessee. The grocery industry has used the sale-and-leaseback arrangement for many years. Again, in terms of valuation and the lease-versus-buy (borrow) decision, the relevant variables are the same as a more conventional financial-lease arrangement.

UNRESOLVED ISSUES IN LEASE FINANCING

The preceding chapters identify a series of factors that affect the lease-versus-borrow decision. These include the tax benefits provided by leasing, the impact of accounting and tax reporting requirements on a firm's financial position, the expected residual value of capital assets, and differences in corporate borrowing costs across different firms. At the risk of oversimplification, these factors can be distilled into a valuation framework that answers the lease–borrow question: a firm should lease an asset if the acquisition cost of the asset – less the present value of the depreciation tax shield, interest tax shield, residual value, and depreciation-recapture adjustments – exceeds present value of the after-tax lease payments. While this prescription is analytically simple, it is often difficult to apply because certain questions in lease valuation have not been answered in a definitive way.

These questions relate to uncertainties encountered in contemporary lease agreements. First, there is a question concerning the level of uncertainty contained in the lease cash flow estimates, and the selection of an appropriate discount factor that captures this risk. Second, the valuation of capital-budgeting projects that contain several different component lease transactions presents a problem, especially when the life of the project extends beyond the original maturity of the component leasing contracts used to finance the project. Third, there is some controversy surrounding the amount of debt displaced by leasing. Because leasing and debt are commonly viewed as complementary financing transactions, increasing a firm's lease obligations by a given amount should decrease the firm's reserve borrowing capacity by a similar magnitude. Recent evidence indicates, however, that this is not the case, suggesting that there is more to the lease-versus-borrow question than a simple tradeoff between comparative financing arrangements.

The Lease Discount Rate

The finance literature offers several different discount rate choices for valuing lease cash flows: the before-tax cost of debt, the after-tax cost of debt, and the corporate weighted-average cost of capital. The key in selecting an appropriate discount factor from this list is to associate the risk or uncertainty contained in the lease cash flow estimates with the degree of risk implied by a given interest rate. Higher risks demand higher returns – the greater the uncertainty attached to the lease cash flows, the larger the discount rate used to evaluate these cash flows.

The cash flows associated with debt financing are relatively low in risk because the borrower is under contractual obligation to meet his or her debt-service payments. In contrast, the cash flows promised to stockholders are subject to greater uncertainty because these payments are not required by contract. Hence, the firm's cost of equity necessarily exceeds its cost of debt. The firm's weighted-average cost of capital, which includes the cost of equity capital, must also exceed its cost of debt financing.

In valuing leases, the difficult task is to specify the degree of uncertainty attached to various estimates of lease cash flows. On one hand, this uncertainty reflects the general variability in the firm's operating cash flows because the productive use of the leased asset occurs in the context of the firm's normal business operations. As a consequence, the depreciation and tax shields provided by the lease – and the ability of the leased asset to generate operating revenue for the firm – depend on the firm's overall business risk characteristics. The aggregate-risk level of the firm's operating cash flows is reflected in its corporate weighted-average capital cost, hence this reasoning leads to the selection of the WACC as the appropriate discount rate for evaluating lease transactions.

In contrast to this logic, leasing gives rise to a financial obligation that is similar in risk to secured debt. Both financing options create a certain payment obligation for the firm. Unlike the risks associated with future operating cash flow estimates, both lease and debt payments can be estimated with a high degree of accuracy. Moreover, leasing and borrowing are complementary transactions because both create a claim against a specific portion of the firm's operating cash flows before any distributions can occur to equity holders.

So which particular discount rate – the cost of debt, or the WACC – more accurately captures the uncertainty contained in the lease obligation? While both arguments reviewed here have merit, the most common (and the most logical) answer to the question is the cost of debt. Lease cash flows share more in common with debt cash flows than with the firm's operating cash flows, hence the selection of the firm's debt cost to value the lease. In cases where the interest tax shield foregone under leasing is included in calculating the annual net cash flows of the lease, the before-tax cost of debt represents the appropriate discount rate. The tax deductibility of interest expense here is reflected in the numerator of the present-value equation. In cases where the interest tax shield foregone under leasing is not recorded within the annual cash flow estimates for the lease, the after-tax cost of debt represents the appropriate discount rate. In the latter instance, the tax deductibility of interest charges is noted in the denominator rather than the numerator of the present-value calculation.

The Multiple-Lease Project

The choice of an appropriate risk-adjusted discount rate for use in evaluating the lease transaction becomes more difficult when the term of the lease does not agree with the life of the project. Consider, for example, a 20-year investment project financed by a 5-year lease. In order to evaluate the total cash flows associated with this project, it is necessary to assume that a series of four consecutive lease transactions sustain the lessee's total capital investment. Unfortunately, however, the lease payment obligation within this arrangement is subject to periodic renegotiation at the maturity of each component lease contract, introducing additional uncertainty within the lease cash flows. In this circumstance, discounting the annual lease cash flows at the lessee's cost of debt is unwise. After the first 5-year lease contract expires, the degree of uncertainty surrounding future lease payments increases because the renegotiated payments cannot be specified explicitly at the beginning of the project. As such, these future lease payments no longer maintain a risk profile similar to the firm's debt-service payments.

Exhibit 10-1 provides an illustration of the multiple-lease project, and shows how the valuation difficulties associated with this project might be overcome. In this example, a hypothetical firm faces the choice of purchasing a $1,000,000 asset, or leasing it for a period of 5 years at $70,000 per year. Notice that the life of the project is 20 years, while the original lease is renegotiated on three separate occasions (Years 5, 10, and 15) to provide financing for the entire project life. Column 4 shows the net cash flows associated with buying the asset, while Column 5 provides the after-tax cash flows for the leasing option.

There are three possible ways to approach this lease-versus-buy problem. First, the firm considering the project might simply discount the net cash flows from leasing and buying that asset at the firm's WACC (13%). This approach assumes that all cash flows carry an average level of business risk for the firm. Notice that the net present value of the purchase alternative is negative $781,200 under this option, while the NPV of leasing is negative $602,200. At this point, although the project appears hopelessly unprofitable, the leasing option appears much more attractive than purchasing the asset.

A second approach to the valuation problem is to discount all of the net cash flows in Exhibit 10-1 at the lessee's after-tax cost of debt (7.26%). This recognizes that the lease payments share the risk characteristics of the firm's secured debt, and adjusts the discount rate downward to reflect this fact. Notice that the relative attractiveness of the leasing option deteriorates significantly under this valuation procedure. The net present value of the lease falls to negative $947,700, while the NPV of the purchase transaction actually improves when its cash flows are discounted at the after-tax cost of debt.

A third and final alternative method for valuing the lease recognizes that the relative uncertainty of the lease cash flows differs over the 20-year life of the project. For the first 5 years, the lease payments are known with certainty, so the after-tax cost of debt provides the appropriate risk-adjusted discount factor for these payments. The lease payments beyond the fifth year of the project are not known with certainty because these payments will be renegotiated with the lessor at the maturity of the first 5-year lease. Accordingly, the lease payments in Years 6–20 contain substantially more uncertainty, which means that the lessee's weighted-average cost of capital represents the appropriate risk-adjusted discount factor for these years.

Using this mixed-rate approach to lease valuation—7.26% for the first 5 years and 13% thereafter—the net present value of the lease is negative $640,800. This provides the most accurate estimate of the project's

Exhibit 10-1
Cash Flow Comparison in the Multiple-Lease Project

Assumptions

1. The asset can be purchased for $1,000,000.
2. All figures are shown in thousands of after-tax dollars.
3. The firm's marginal tax rate is 34 percent.
4. The long-term, after-tax borrowing rate is 7.26 percent.
5. The weighted average cost of capital is 13 percent.
6. The asset has no salvage value after 20 years.
7. Maintenance and operating costs under the lease and purchase are equal, and not shown below.
8. Tax and depreciation rates are based on forecasts of provisions under the current (1990) tax law.

			----------Purchase Transaction----------	Lease ---Transaction---
(1)	(2)	(3)	(4)	(5)
		Depreciation		
	Purchase	Tax	Net Cash	Lease
Year	Price	Shield	Flow	Payments
0	-$1000	$34.0	-$966.0	-----
1		61.2	61.2	-$70.0
2		49.0	49.0	-70.0
3		39.2	39.2	-70.0
4		31.3	31.3	-70.0
5		25.1	25.1	-70.0
6		22.3	22.3	-88.0
7		22.3	22.3	-88.0
8		22.3	22.3	-88.0
9		22.3	22.3	-88.0
10		11.2	11.2	-88.0
11		0	0	-108.0
12		0	0	-108.0
13		0	0	-108.0
14		0	0	-108.0
15		0	0	-108.0
16		0	0	-135.0
17		0	0	-135.0
18		0	0	-135.0
19		0	0	-135.0
20		0	0	-135.0
TOTAL	-$1000	$340.2	-$659.8	-$2005.0

Net Present Value

at 7.26%:			-$746.3	-$947.7
at 13.00%:			-$781.2	-$602.2
Using Mixed Rate:				-$640.8

value because it incorporates a more precise treatment of the uncertainty present in each period of the project. While this complicates the evaluation of the lease, it provides a better indicator of the value the firm gains (or loses) from the leasing transaction.

Leasing and Debt Displacement

The preceding sections demonstrate that debt and lease obligations share a similar risk profile. This similarity, however, does not necessarily imply that these financing options are conceptually the same, nor that they have a common impact on corporate financial condition. Rather, leasing seems to displace a greater quantity of debt capacity on the lessee's balance sheet than it provides. At fist glance, the debt-displacement effect associated with lease financing seems paradoxical. Why would a given firm lose more than one dollar in borrowing capacity simply because it assumes a single dollar in lease obligations?

The answer is quite simple: leasing and debt may look similar to one another, but they are not completely alike. In particular, lessees lose the tax shields provided by depreciation and interest expense. Because these tax shields have value to firms reporting taxable income, the lease displaces somewhat more financing capacity than it provides. In addition, lease payments represent a liability senior to the claim of debt holders, which reduces the value of existing debt within firms that lease a significant portion of their capital assets. This means that the cost of debt for these firms increases so that a given principal balance requires larger debt-service payments. Together, these important differences between leasing and borrowing explain why a single dollar's lease obligation displaces about $1.25 in excess borrowing capacity.

REFERENCES

Bayless, M. E., and J. D. Diltz. "An Empirical Study of the Debt Displacement Effects of Leasing." *Financial Management* (Winter 1986): 53–60.

Cason, R. L. "Leasing, Asset Lives and Uncertainty: A Practitioner's Comments." *Financial Management* (Summer 1987): 13–16.

Schall, L. D. "Analytic Issues in Lease vs. Purchase Decisions." *Financial Management* (Summer 1987): 17–20.

Weingartner, M. H. "Leasing, Asset Lives and Uncertainty: Guides to Decision Making." *Financial Management* (Summer 1987): 5–12.

_____. "The Lease-Analysis Problem: Response to Cason and Schall." *Financial Management* (Summer 1987): 21–23.

11

Leasing Bibliography

The subject of leasing has generated a tremendous amount of interest among financial researchers and business managers over the last 30 years, leading to a large body of published literature concerning the topic. Quite naturally, a great deal of this literature focuses on the lease-versus-borrow question, while other popular topics include the impact of tax regulations on leasing costs and accounting for lease transactions. In general, the results of academic research projects and practitioner commentary concerning leasing appear in the finance and accounting literature. The journals *Financial Management, Management Accounting*, and *Accounting Review* represent three particular sources containing a wealth of information concerning leasing practice and the analytical evaluation of lease transactions.

The references that follow identify a significant portion of the literature devoted to leasing. While this listing is by no means comprehensive, it does contain all of the sources of leasing information in print over the past three decades that have helped to advance our knowledge of leasing. As such, these works comprise the contemporary body of knowledge concerning lease financing.

This knowledge base will certainly expand and change in coming years as more researchers focus their efforts on the unanswered questions provided by leasing, as new methods of inquiry uncover additional information regarding lease transactions, and as more refined analytical techniques become available to evaluate practical leasing problems. In keeping with these trends, the American Association of Equipment Lessors sponsors a journal devoted entirely to reporting the latest practical developments concerning leasing research, *The Journal of Equipment Lease Financing*. Published semiannually since 1983, this source provides an excellent way for business managers to gain additional information about the latest developments in leasing practice and modern analytical tools available for lease evaluation.

Abdel-khalick, A., R. Thompson, and R. Taylor. "The Impact of Reporting Leases Off the Balance Sheet on Bond Risk Premiums: Two Exploratory Studies." In *Economic Consequences of Accounting Standards: Selected Papers*. Stamford, CT: Financial Accounting Standards Board, 1978.

———. *The Economic Effects on Leases of FASB Statement No. 13, Accounting for Leases*. Stamford, CT: Financial Accounting Standards Board, 1981.

Alderman, J., and C. Alderman. "Accounting for Leases." *The Journal of Accountancy* (June 1979): 74–79.

Altman, E. "Capitalization of Leases and the Predictability of Financial Ratios: A Comment." *The Accounting Review* (April 1976): 408–12.

Anderson, P., and J. Martin. "Lease vs. Purchase Decisions: A Survey of Current Practice." *Financial Management* (Spring 1977): 41–47.

Ang, J., and P. Peterson. "The Leasing Puzzle." *Journal of Finance* (September 1984): 1055–65.

Arcady, A., R. Herdman, and M. Stianese. "Real Estate Sale-Leasebacks Under FASB 98." *The Journal of Accountancy* (June 1989): 101–10.

Ashton, D. "The Reasons for Leasing – A Mathematical Programming Framework." *Journal of Business, Finance, and Accounting* (Summer 1978): 233–52.

Ashton, R. "Accounting for Finance Leases – A Field Test." *Accounting and Business Research* (Summer 1985): 233–38.

Athanasopoulos, P., and P. Bacon. "The Evaluation of Leveraged Leases." *Financial Management* (Spring 1980): 76–80.

Backer, C. "Leasing and the Setting of Accounting Standards: Mapping the Labyrinth." *Journal of Accounting, Auditing, and Finance* (Spring 1980): 197–206.

Barr, L. "Accounting Problems of Long-Term Leases." *The National Public Accountant* (August 1964): 8–12.

Batkin, A. "Leasing vs. Buying . . . Guide for the Perplexed." *Financial Executive* (June 1973): 62–68.

Bayless, M., and J. Diltz. "An Empirical Study of the Debt Displacement Effects of Leasing." *Financial Management* (Winter 1986): 53–60.

Beechy, T. H. "The Cost of Leasing: Comment and Correction." *Accounting Review* (October 1970): 769–73.

———. "Quasi-Debt Analysis of Financial Leases." *Accounting Review* (April 1969): 375–81.

Benton, I. "Surprise Loophole, Firms Expect Leasing to Save Them Millions Under New Law." *The Wall Street Journal* (March 11, 1987): 1, 33.

———. "Buy Versus Lease with an Alternative Minimum Tax." *Financial Management* (Winter 1988): 87–91.

———. *The Lease Versus Buy Decision*. Englewood Cliffs, NJ: Prentice-Hall, 1982.

Bierman, H., Jr. "Leveraged Leasing: An Alternative Analysis." *The Bankers' Magazine* (Winter 1973): 53–61.

Blum, J. "Accounting and Reporting for Leases by Lessees: The Interest Rate Problems." *Management Accounting* (April 1978): 25–28.

Bower, R. "Issues in Lease Financing." *Financial Management* (Winter 1973): 25–34.

Bower, R., F. Herringer, and J. Williamson. "Lease Evaluation." *Accounting Review* (April 1966): 257–65.

Bowman, R. "The Debt Equivalence of Leases: An Empirical Investigation." *Accounting Review* (April 1980): 237–53.

Brealey, R., and S. Myers. *Principles of Corporate Finance.* 3d rev. ed. New York: McGraw Hill, 1988, 629–50.

Brealey, R., and C. Young. "Debt, Taxes and Leasing – A Note." *Journal of Finance* (December 1980): 1245–50.

Brick, I., W. Fung, and M. Subrahmanyam. "Leasing and Financial Intermediation: Comparative Tax Advantages." *Financial Management* (Spring 1987): 55–59.

Brigham, E. "Equipment Lease Financing: A Bank Management Imperative." *The Bankers' Magazine* (Winter 1966): 65–75.

_____. "The Impact of Bank Entry on Market Conditions in the Equipment Leasing Industry." *National Banking Review* (September 1974): 11–26.

Brigham, E., and L. Gapenski. *Intermediate Financial Management.* 3d rev. ed. Hinsdale, IL: Dryden Press, 1990, 547–76.

Burns, J., K. Hreha, and S. Luttman. "Corporate Leasing Versus Property Ownership Under the Tax Reform Act of 1986." *Journal of the American Taxation Association* (Fall 1989): 105–13.

Burrows, C. "Some Questionable Advantages to Leasing." *The Chartered Accountant in Australia* (September 1969): 10–14.

Capettini, R., and H. Toole. "Designing Leveraged Leases: A Mixed Integer Linear Programming Approach." *Financial Management* (Autumn 1981): 15–22.

Carlson, C., and D. Wort. "A New Look at the Lease-vs-Purchase Decision." *Journal of Economics and Business* (Spring 1974): 199–202.

Cason, R. "Leasing, Asset Lives, and Uncertainty: A Practitioner's Comments." *Financial Management* (Summer 1987): 13–16.

Castle, D. "Sale/Leasebacks: Taking Advantage of Hidden Value." *Management Review* (November 1987): 39–43.

Chamberlain, D. "Capitalization of Lease Obligations." *Management Accounting* (December 1975): 37–38.

Childs, C., Jr., and W. Gridley, Jr. "Leveraged Leasing and the Reinvestment Rate Fallacy." *The Bankers' Magazine* (Winter 1973): 53–61.

Chueng, J. "The Association Between Lease Disclosure and the Lessee's Systematic Risk." *Journal of Business, Finance, and Accounting* (Autumn 1982): 297–306.

Clark, R., J. Jantorni, and R. Gann. "Analysis of the Lease-or-Buy Decision: Comment." *Journal of Finance* (September 1973): 1015–16.

Cohen, A. *Long Term Leases – Problems of Taxation, Finance, and Account-ing*. Ann Arbor: University of Michigan Press, 1954.

Cook, D. "The Case Against Capitalizing Leases." *Harvard Business Review* (January–February 1963): 145–62.

Cooper, K., and R. Strawser. "Evaluation of Capital Investment Projects In-volving Asset Leases." *Financial Management* (Spring 1975): 44–49.

Copeland, T., and J. Weston. "A Note on the Evaluation of Cancellable Operat-ing Leases." *Financial Management* (Summer 1982): 60–67.

————. *Financial Theory and Corporate Policy*. 3d rev. ed. New York: Addison-Wesley, 1988, 614–37.

Crawford, P., C. Harper, and J. McConnell. "Further Evidence on the Terms of Financial Leases." *Financial Management* (Autumn 1981): 7–14.

Cudworth, E. "Equipment Leasing, Hidden Benefits." *Financial Planning* (June 1987): 198–200.

Del Coto, L. "Sale-and-Leaseback: A Hollow Sound When Tapped?" *Tax Law Review* 37 (1981): 1–50.

Dieter, R. "Is Lessee Accounting Working?" *CPA Journal* (August 1979): 13–19.

Dillon, G. "The Discount Rate and Lease-Related Expense." *The CPA Journal* (November 1979): 37.

Doenges, R. "The Cost of Leasing." *Engineering Economist* (Fall 1974): 31–44.

Duty, G. "A Leasing Guide to Taxes." *Management Accounting* (August 1980): 45–51.

Dyl, E., and S. Martin, Jr. "Setting Terms for Leveraged Leases." *Financial Management* (Winter 1977): 20–27.

Elam, R. "The Effect of Lease Data on the Predictive Ability of Financial Ratios." *The Accounting Review* (January 1975): 25–43.

Elliot, G. "Leasing of Capital Equipment." *Management Accounting* (Decem-ber 1975): 39–42.

Endres, J. "Leasing After the Tax Reform Act of 1986." *The Tax Advisor* (August 1988): 537–50.

"Equipment Leasing." *U.S. Industrial Outlook*. U.S. Department of Commerce (January 1987): 53-1–53-4.

Fawthrop, R. "The Evaluation of an Integrated Investment and Lease-Financ-ing Decision: A Reply." *Journal of Business, Finance, and Accounting* (Spring 1979): 89–94.

Ferrara, W. "The Case for Symmetry in Lease Reporting." *Management Ac-counting* (April 1978): 17–28.

Ferrara, W., J. Thies, and M. Dirsmith. "The Lease-Purchase Decision." *Man-agement Accounting* (May 1980): 57–59.

Financial Accounting Standards Board. *Statement of Financial Accounting Standards No. 13: Accounting for Leases*. Stamford, CT: November 1976.

Findlay, M., III. "Financial Lease Evaluation: Survey and Synthesis." *Finan-cial Review* (September 1974): 1–15.

Finnerty, J., R. Fitzsimmons, and T. Oliver. "Lease Capitalization and System-atic Risk." *Accounting Review* (October 1980): 631–39.

Flath, D. "The Economics of Short-Term Leasing." *Economic Inquiry* (April 1980): 242–59.

Franks, J., and S. Hodges. "Lease Valuation When Taxable Earnings Are a Scarce Resource." *Journal of Finance* (September 1987): 987–1005.

Fritch, B., and A. Reisman, eds. *Equipment Leasing: Leveraged Leasing.* New York: Practicing Law Institute, 1977.

Gaumnitz, J., and A. Ford. "The Lease or Sell Decision." *Financial Management* (Winter 1978): 69–74.

General Electric Credit Corporation. *Leasing and Tax Reform: A Guide Through the Maze.* Stamford, CT: General Electric Credit Corporation, 1987.

———. *The New Corporate Alternative Minimum Tax: Why Equipment Leasing Makes Even More Sense.* Stamford, CT: General Electric Credit Corporation, 1987.

Gordon, M. "A General Solution to the Buy or Lease Decision: A Pedagogical Note." *Journal of Finance* (March 1974): 245–50.

Green, D. "The Evaluation of an Integrated Investment and Lease-Financing Decision: Comment." *Journal of Business, Finance, and Accounting* (Spring 1979): 71–88.

Grimlund, R., and R. Capettini. "A Note on the Evaluation of Leveraged Leases and Other Investments." *Financial Management* (Summer 1982): 68–71.

Gritta, R. "Capitalizing Net Lease Rentals: A Comment." *Management Accounting* (November 1974): 37–39.

Grossman, K. "RRA '89 Eases Corporate Alternative Minimum Tax Somewhat." *The Journal of Taxation* (March 1990): 140–45.

Haight, T., and K. Smith. "Equipment Leasing: Residual Values and Investor Returns." *Tax Notes* (December 4, 1989): 1233–37.

Hannon, J. "Lease Accounting: A Current Controversy." *Management Accounting* (September 1976): 25–28.

Harmelink, P., and R. Capettini. "Income Tax Consequences in Leasing." *The CPA Journal* (November 1979): 29–34.

Hartman, B., and H. Sami. "The Impact of the Accounting of Leasing Contracts on User Decision Making: A Field Experiment." *Advances in Accounting* (1989): 23–27.

Henderson, G. "A General Solution to the Buy or Lease Decision: A Pedagogical Note – Comment." *Journal of Finance* (March 1976): 147–51.

Henry, J. "Leasing: Cost Measurement and Disclosure." *Management Accounting* (May 1974): 42–48.

Hodges, S. "The Valuation of Variable Rate Leases." *Financial Management* (Spring 1985): 68–74.

Honig, L., and S. Coley. "An After-Tax Equivalent Payment Approach to Conventional Lease Analysis." *Financial Management* (Winter 1975): 28–35.

Houlihan, W. "De Facto Capitalization of Operating Leases: The Effect on Debt Capacity." *Corporate Accounting* (Summer 1984): 3–13.

Hull, J. "The Bargaining Positions of the Parties to a Lease Agreement." *Financial Management* (Autumn 1982): 71–79.

Idol, C. "A Note on Specifying Debt Displacement and Tax Shield Borrowing Opportunities in Financial Lease Valuation Models." *Financial Management* (Summer 1980): 24–29.

Imhoff, E., and J. Thomas. "Economic Consequences of Accounting Standards: The Lease Disclosure Rule Change." *Journal of Accounting and Economics* (December 1988): 277–310.

Johnson, R., and W. Lewellen. "Analysis of the Lease-or-Buy Decision." *Journal of Finance* (September 1972): 815–23.

――――. "Reply." *Journal of Finance* (September 1973): 1024–28.

Johnson, S., and T. Porcano. "The Safe Harbor Lease – Tax Implications." *The CPA Journal* (September 1893): 20–29.

Kendall, D. "How to Evaluate a Lease." *Corporate Accounting* (Fall 1983): 32–45.

Kieso, D., and J. Weygandt. "Accounting for Leases." In *Intermediate Accounting* 6th rev. ed., edited by D. Kieso and J. Weygandt, 1035–92. New York: Wiley, 1989.

Kim, E., W. Lewellen, and J. McConnell. "Sale-and-Leaseback Agreements and Enterprise Valuation." *Journal of Financial and Quantitative Analysis* (December 1978): 871–83.

Knight, R., and L. Knight. "True Leases Versus Disguised Installment Sale/Purchase: Factors the Court Use to Distinguish." *The Tax Advisor* (March 1987): 185–91.

Lawrence, D., and R. Bear. "Corporate Bankruptcy Prediction and the Impact of Leases." *Journal of Business, Finance and Accounting* (Winter 1986): 571–87.

Lee, W., J. Martin, and A. Senchack. "The Case for Using Options to Evaluate Salvage Value in Financial Leases." *Financial Management* (Autumn 1982): 33–40.

Lerro, A., and J. Bond. "Financing Acquisitions: To Lease or to Borrow?" *The National Public Accountant* (January 1990): 42–45.

Lev, B., and Y. Orgler. "Analysis of the Lease-or-Buy Decision: Comment." *Journal of Finance* (September 1973): 1022–23.

Levy, H., and M. Sarnat. "Leasing, Borrowing, and Financial Risk." *Financial Management* (Winter 1979): 47–54.

Lewellen, W., M. Long, and J. McConnell. "Asset Leasing in Competitive Markets." *Journal of Finance* (June 1976): 787–98.

Long, M. "Leasing and the Cost of Capital." *Journal of Financial and Quantitative Analysis* (November 1977): 579–86.

Lowenstein, M., and J. McClure. "Taxes and Financial Leasing." *Quarterly Review of Economics and Business* (Spring 1988): 21–38.

――――. "Managing the Lease-Sell Decision to Reduce Agency Costs." *The Sloan Management Review* (Spring 1986): 77–82.

Lusztig, P. "Analysis of the Lease-or-Buy Decision: Comment." *Journal of Finance* (September 1973): 1017–18.

McAdam, M. B. "Equipment Leasing." *U.S. Industrial Outlook 1988*. U.S. Department of Commerce (January 1988): 57-1–57-4.

McConnell, J., and J. Schallheim. "Valuation of Asset Leasing Contracts." *Journal of Financial Economics* 12 (1983): 761–86.

McGrath, W. "Unwrapping Leasehold Equity: An Introduction to the 'Wraparound Lease.'" *Real Estate Review* (Winter 1990): 23–30.

McGugan, V., and R. Caves. "Integration and Competition in the Equipment Leasing Industry." *Journal of Business* (July 1974): 382–96.

Malernee, J., Jr., and S. Senchack, Jr. "Secured Residual Values in Bank Leasing Arrangements." *Journal of Commercial Bank Lending* (September 1975): 56–61.

Marston, F., and R. Harris. "Substitutability of Leases and Debt in Corporate Capital Structures." *Journal of Accounting, Auditing and Finance* (Spring 1988): 165–70.

Martin, J., P. Anderson, and A. Keown. "Lease Capitalization and Stock Price Stability: Implications for Accounting." *Journal of Accounting, Auditing and Finance* (Winter 1979): 151–64.

Martin, J., S. Cox, and R. MacMinn. *The Theory of Finance*. Hinsdale, IL: Dryden Press, 1988, 583–602.

―――. "Equipment Leasing: Before the Cash Flow Analysis, What Else?" *Journal of Purchasing* (February 1974): 5–11.

Miller, M., and C. Upton. "Leasing, Buying, and the Cost of Capital Services." *Journal of Finance* (June 1976): 761–819.

Mitchell, G. "After-Tax Cost of Leasing." *Accounting Review* (April 1970): 308–14.

Moses, J. "Leasing Boosts Credit Capacity." *Financial Manager* (July–August 1989): 66–69.

Moyer, R. "Lease Evaluation and the Investment Tax Credit: A Framework for Analysis." *Financial Management* (Summer 1975): 39–42.

Munter, P., and T. Ratcliffe. "An Assessment of User Reactions to Lease Accounting Disclosures." *Journal of Accounting, Auditing and Finance* (Winter 1983): 108–14.

Murray, D. "The Irrelevance of Lease Capitalizations." *Journal of Accounting, Auditing and Finance* (Winter 1982): 154–59.

Myers, S., D. Dill, and A. Bautista. "Valuation of Financial Lease Contracts." *Journal of Finance* (June 1976): 786–99.

Nantel, T. "Equivalence of Lease vs. Buy Analyses." *Financial Management* (Autumn 1973): 61–65.

Nelson, A. "Capitalizing Leases – The Effect on Financial Ratios." *Journal of Accountancy* (July 1963): 49–58.

Nevitt, P., and F. Fabozzi. *Equipment Leasing*. 3d rev. ed. Homewood, IL: Dow Jones-Irwin, 1988.

Nunnally, B., Jr., and D. Plath. "Leasing Versus Borrowing: Evaluating Alternative Forms of Consumer Credit." *Journal of Consumer Affairs* (Winter 1989): 383–92.

O'Brien, T., and B. Nunnally, Jr. "A 1982 Survey of Corporate Leasing Practice." *Financial Management* (Summer 1983): 30–36.

Ofer, A. "The Evaluation of Lease Versus Purchase Alternatives." *Financial Management* (Summer 1976): 67–74.

Olsen, R. "Lease vs. Purchase or Lease vs. Borrow: Comment: *Financial Management* (Summer 1978): 82–83.

Ozark, T. "Leasing Strategies After Tax Reform." *Cashflow* (October 1987): 47–49.

Packman, E. "An Analysis of the Risks of Leveraged Leasing." *Journal of Commercial Bank Lending* (March 1975): 2-21.

Palmon, D., and M. Kwatinetz. "The Significant Role Interpretation Plays in the Implementation of SFAS No. 13." *Journal of Accounting, Auditing and Finance* (Spring 1980): 207-26.

Perg, W. "Leveraged Leasing: The Problem of Changing Leverage." *Financial Management* (Autumn 1978): 47-51.

Pettway, R. "Interest Rates on Direct Leases and Secured Term Loans." *National Banking Review* (June 1966): 533-37.

Pierce, H. "Leasing and the Lessee." *Management Accounting* (December 1975): 33-36.

Regan, W. "The Dual Aspect of Leveraged Leasing." *The Banker's Magazine* (Autumn 1976): 75-77.

Reilly, R. "Leasing: An Attractive Alternative Method of Asset Financing for Small Firms." *The National Public Accountant* (November 1982): 30-37.

Richardson, A. "The Measurement of the Current Portion of Long-Term Lease Obligation – Some Evidence from Practice." *Accounting Review* (October 1985): 744-52.

Ro, B. "The Disclosure of Capitalized Lease Information and Stock Prices." *Journal of Accounting Research* (Autumn 1978): 315-40.

Roberts, G., and A. Gudikunst. "Equipment Financial Leasing Practices and Costs: A Comment." *Financial Management* (Summer 1978): 79-81.

Roenfeldt, R., and J. Osteryoung. "An Analysis of Financial Leases." *Financial Management* (Spring 1973): 74-87.

Ross, S., R. Westerfield, and J. Jaffe. *Corporate Finance.* 2d rev. ed. Homewood, IL: Richard D. Irwin, 1988, 620-47.

Russo, F. "Escalations in Commercial Leases." *The CPA Journal* (April 1985): 28-35.

Ryan, R., Jr. "Leveraged Leasing." *Management Accounting* (April 1977): 45-50.

Sartoris, W., and R. Paul. "Lease Evaluation – Another Capital Budgeting Decision." *Financial Management* (Summer 1973): 46-52.

Saunders, G., and R. Saunders. "Template Solves Lease or Buy Dilemma." *Financial Manager* (November–December 1988): 52-57.

Schall, L. "The Lease-or-Buy and Asset Acquisition Decisions." *Journal of Finance* (September 1974): 1203-14.

_____. "The Evaluation of Lease Financing Opportunities." *Midland Corporate Finance Journal* (Spring 1985): 48-65.

_____. "Analytic Issues in Lease vs. Purchase Decisions." *Financial Management* (Summer 1987): 17-21.

Schall, L., R. Johnson, R. Lease, and J. McConnell. "The Determinants of Yields on Financial Leasing Contracts." *Journal of Financial Economics* 19 (1987): 45-67.

Schall, L., and G. Sundem. "The Investment Tax Credit and the Leasing Industry." *Journal of Accounting and Public Policy* (Winter 1982): 83-94.

Schallheim, J., J. McConnell, and R. Lease. "What Determines Yields on Financial Lease Contracts?" *Journal of Equipment Lease Financing* (Spring 1990): 9-14.

Schmidt, H. Jr., and M. Raddel. "The Implications of the Supreme Court's Decision in *Frank Lyon*." *The Tax Advisor* (September 1979): 516–21.

Shapiro, A. *Modern Corporate Finance*. New York: MacMillan, 1986, 670–98.

Shaw, W. "Measuring the Impact of the Safe Harbor Lease Law on Security Prices." *Journal of Accounting Research* (Spring 1988): 60–81.

Shevlin, T. "Taxes and Off-Balance Sheet Financing: Research and Development Limited Partnerships." *The Accounting Review* (July 1987): 480–509.

Slovin, M., M. Sushka, and J. Polonchek. "Corporate Sale-and-Leasebacks and Shareholder Wealth." *Journal of Finance* (March 1990): 289–99.

Smith, B. "Accelerated Debt Repayment in Leveraged Leases." *Financial Management* (Summer 1982): 73–80.

Smith, C., and L. Wakeman. "Determinants of Corporate Leasing Policy." *Journal of Finance* (July 1985): 895–910.

Smith, P. "A Straightforward Approach to Leveraged Leasing." *Journal of Commercial Bank Lending* (July 1973): 40–47.

Smith, W. "Equipment Leasing: A Clear Winner in the Post-Tax Reform Era." *Financial Strategies* (Spring 1987): 55–56.

Solomon, L., and W. Fones, Jr. "Sale-Leasebacks and the Shelter-Oriented Investor: An Analysis of *Frank Lyon Co.* and *Est. of Franklin*." *Taxes* (October 1978): 618–28.

Sorensen, I., and R. Johnson. "Equipment Financial Leasing Practices and Costs: An Empirical Study." *Financial Management* (Spring 1977): 33–40.

Sponseller, D. "Lease Financing: Sale and Leaseback Options." *Public Utilities Fortnightly* (March 19, 1987): 40–43.

Stickney, C., R. Weil, and M. Wolfson. "Income Taxes and Tax-Transfer Leases." *Accounting Review* (April 1983): 439–59.

Stiles, N., and M. Walker. "Leveraged Lease Financing of Equipment." *Journal of Commercial Bank Lending* (July 1973): 19–39.

Taylor, P., and S. Turley. "The Views of Management on Accounting for Leases." *Accounting and Business Research* (Winter 1985): 59–68.

Thompson, K. "Business Rentals Can Provide Hefty Deductions if the Deal is Structured Well." *Taxation for Accountants* (February 1988): 114–18.

Towles, M. "Leases and the Relevant APB Opinions." *Management Accounting* (May 1974): 37–41.

Upton, C. "Leasing as a Financial Instrument." In *Handbook of Financial Economics*, edited by J. Bicksler, 293–306. Amsterdam: North-Holland, 1979.

Vancil, R. "Lease or Borrow – New Method of Analysis." *Harvard Business Review* (September 1961): 122–36.

Volpi, J., and P. DeAngelis. "Using E&P to Compute AMT." *The Tax Advisor* (July 1989): 441–52.

Walthall, T. M., 12-6th, "Equipment Leasing." *1989 Tax Management Inc.*

Ward, C. "Property Lease-or-Buy Decisions." *Accounting and Business Research* (Spring 1983): 143–50.

Weingartner, H. "Leasing, Asset Lives, and Uncertainty: A Guide to Decision Making." *Financial Management* (Summer 1987): 5–12.

Weiss, G. "Equipment Leasing Faces Trial by Tax Reform" *Business Week* (January 12, 1987): 114–15.

Wiar, R. "Economic Implications of Multiple Rates of Return in the Leveraged Lease Context." *Journal of Finance* (December 1973): 1275–86.

Wilkins, T. "A Behavioural Investigation of Alternative Methods of Financing Capital Acquisitions and Lease Capitalization." *Accounting and Business Research* (Autumn 1984): 359–66.

Wilkins, T., and I. Zimmer. "The Effect of Leasing and Different Methods of Accounting for Leases on Credit Evaluations." *Accounting Review* (October 1983): 749–64.

Willis, M. "Leasing: A Financial Option for States and Localities." *Quarterly Review*, Federal Reserve Bank of New York (Winter 1981–82): 42–46.

Wyman, H. "Financial Lease Evaluation Under Conditions of Uncertainty." *Accounting Review* (July 1973): 489–93.

Zises, A. "Disclosure of Long-Term Leases." *Journal of Accountancy* (February 1961): 37–47.

Appendix

Table A-1
Future-Value Interest Factors (FVIF)

Period	1%	2%	3%	4%	5%	6%	7%	Rate 8%	9%	10%	12%	14%	16%	18%	20%
1	1.0100	1.0200	1.0300	1.0400	1.0500	1.0600	1.0700	1.0800	1.0900	1.1000	1.1200	1.1400	1.1600	1.1800	1.2000
2	1.0201	1.0404	1.0609	1.0816	1.1025	1.1236	1.1449	1.1664	1.1881	1.2100	1.2544	1.2996	1.3456	1.3924	1.4400
3	1.0303	1.0612	1.0927	1.1249	1.1576	1.1910	1.2250	1.2597	1.2950	1.3310	1.4049	1.4815	1.5609	1.6430	1.7280
4	1.0406	1.0824	1.1255	1.1699	1.2155	1.2625	1.3108	1.3605	1.4116	1.4641	1.5735	1.6890	1.8106	1.9388	2.0736
5	1.0510	1.1041	1.1593	1.2167	1.2763	1.3382	1.4026	1.4693	1.5386	1.6105	1.7623	1.9254	2.1003	2.2878	2.4883
6	1.0615	1.1262	1.1941	1.2653	1.3401	1.4185	1.5007	1.5869	1.6771	1.7716	1.9738	2.1950	2.4364	2.6996	2.9860
7	1.0721	1.1487	1.2299	1.3159	1.4071	1.5036	1.6058	1.7138	1.8280	1.9487	2.2107	2.5023	2.8262	3.1855	3.5832
8	1.0829	1.1717	1.2668	1.3686	1.4775	1.5938	1.7182	1.8509	1.9926	2.1436	2.4760	2.8526	3.2784	3.7589	4.2998
9	1.0937	1.1951	1.3048	1.4233	1.5513	1.6895	1.8385	1.9990	2.1719	2.3579	2.7731	3.2519	3.8030	4.4355	5.1598
10	1.1046	1.2190	1.3439	1.4802	1.6289	1.7908	1.9672	2.1589	2.3674	2.5937	3.1058	3.7072	4.4114	5.2338	6.1917
11	1.1157	1.2434	1.3842	1.5395	1.7103	1.8983	2.1049	2.3316	2.5804	2.8531	3.4785	4.2262	5.1173	6.1759	7.4301
12	1.1268	1.2682	1.4258	1.6010	1.7959	2.0122	2.2522	2.5182	2.8127	3.1384	3.8960	4.8179	5.9360	7.2876	8.9161
13	1.1381	1.2936	1.4685	1.6651	1.8856	2.1329	2.4098	2.7196	3.0658	3.4523	4.3635	5.4924	6.8858	8.5994	10.6993
14	1.1495	1.3195	1.5126	1.7317	1.9799	2.2609	2.5785	2.9372	3.3417	3.7975	4.8871	6.2613	7.9875	10.1472	12.8392
15	1.1610	1.3459	1.5580	1.8009	2.0789	2.3966	2.7590	3.1722	3.6425	4.1772	5.4736	7.1379	9.2655	11.9737	15.4070
16	1.1726	1.3728	1.6047	1.8730	2.1829	2.5404	2.9522	3.4259	3.9703	4.5950	6.1304	8.1372	10.7480	14.1290	18.4884
17	1.1843	1.4002	1.6528	1.9479	2.2920	2.6928	3.1588	3.7000	4.3276	5.0545	6.8660	9.2765	12.4677	16.6722	22.1861
18	1.1961	1.4282	1.7024	2.0258	2.4066	2.8543	3.3799	3.9960	4.7171	5.5599	7.6900	10.5752	14.4625	19.6733	26.6233
19	1.2081	1.4568	1.7535	2.1068	2.5270	3.0256	3.6165	4.3157	5.1417	6.1159	8.6128	12.0557	16.7765	23.2144	31.9480
20	1.2202	1.4859	1.8061	2.1911	2.6533	3.2071	3.8697	4.6610	5.6044	6.7275	9.6463	13.7435	19.4608	27.3930	38.3376
21	1.2324	1.5157	1.8603	2.2788	2.7860	3.3996	4.1406	5.0338	6.1088	7.4002	10.8038	15.6676	22.5745	32.3238	46.0051
22	1.2447	1.5460	1.9161	2.3699	2.9253	3.6035	4.4304	5.4365	6.6586	8.1403	12.1003	17.8610	26.1864	38.1421	55.2061
23	1.2572	1.5769	1.9736	2.4647	3.0715	3.8197	4.7405	5.8715	7.2579	8.9543	13.5523	20.3616	30.3762	45.0076	66.2474
24	1.2697	1.6084	2.0328	2.5633	3.2251	4.0489	5.0724	6.3412	7.9111	9.8497	15.1786	23.2122	35.2364	53.1090	79.4968
25	1.2824	1.6406	2.0938	2.6658	3.3864	4.2919	5.4274	6.8485	8.6231	10.8347	17.0001	26.4619	40.8742	62.6686	95.3962
26	1.2953	1.6734	2.1566	2.7725	3.5557	4.5494	5.8074	7.3964	9.3992	11.9182	19.0401	30.1666	47.4141	73.9490	114.4755
27	1.3082	1.7069	2.2213	2.8834	3.7335	4.8223	6.2139	7.9881	10.2451	13.1100	21.3249	34.3899	55.0004	87.2598	137.3706
28	1.3213	1.7410	2.2879	2.9987	3.9201	5.1117	6.6488	8.6271	11.1671	14.4210	23.8839	39.2045	63.8004	102.9666	164.8447
29	1.3345	1.7758	2.3566	3.1187	4.1161	5.4184	7.1143	9.3173	12.1722	15.8631	26.7499	44.6931	74.0085	121.5005	197.8136
30	1.3478	1.8114	2.4273	3.2434	4.3219	5.7435	7.6123	10.0627	13.2677	17.4494	29.9599	50.9502	85.8499	143.3706	237.3763

Table A-2
Present-Value Interest Factors (PVIF)

Period	1%	2%	3%	4%	5%	6%	7%	8%	9%	10%	12%	14%	16%	18%	20%
									Rate						
1	0.9901	0.9804	0.9709	0.9615	0.9524	0.9434	0.9346	0.9259	0.9174	0.9091	0.8929	0.8772	0.8621	0.8475	0.8333
2	0.9803	0.9612	0.9426	0.9246	0.9070	0.8900	0.8734	0.8573	0.8417	0.8264	0.7972	0.7695	0.7432	0.7182	0.6944
3	0.9706	0.9423	0.9151	0.8890	0.8638	0.8396	0.8163	0.7938	0.7722	0.7513	0.7118	0.6750	0.6407	0.6086	0.5787
4	0.9610	0.9238	0.8885	0.8548	0.8227	0.7921	0.7629	0.7350	0.7084	0.6830	0.6355	0.5921	0.5523	0.5158	0.4823
5	0.9515	0.9057	0.8626	0.8219	0.7835	0.7473	0.7130	0.6806	0.6499	0.6209	0.5674	0.5194	0.4761	0.4371	0.4019
6	0.9420	0.8880	0.8375	0.7903	0.7462	0.7050	0.6663	0.6302	0.5963	0.5645	0.5066	0.4556	0.4104	0.3704	0.3349
7	0.9327	0.8706	0.8131	0.7599	0.7107	0.6651	0.6227	0.5835	0.5470	0.5132	0.4523	0.3996	0.3538	0.3139	0.2791
8	0.9235	0.8535	0.7894	0.7307	0.6768	0.6274	0.5820	0.5403	0.5019	0.4665	0.4039	0.3506	0.3050	0.2660	0.2326
9	0.9143	0.8368	0.7664	0.7026	0.6446	0.5919	0.5439	0.5002	0.4604	0.4241	0.3606	0.3075	0.2630	0.2255	0.1938
10	0.9053	0.8203	0.7441	0.6756	0.6139	0.5584	0.5083	0.4632	0.4224	0.3855	0.3220	0.2697	0.2267	0.1911	0.1615
11	0.8963	0.8043	0.7224	0.6496	0.5847	0.5268	0.4751	0.4289	0.3875	0.3505	0.2875	0.2366	0.1954	0.1619	0.1346
12	0.8874	0.7885	0.7014	0.6246	0.5568	0.4970	0.4440	0.3971	0.3555	0.3186	0.2567	0.2076	0.1685	0.1372	0.1122
13	0.8787	0.7730	0.6810	0.6006	0.5303	0.4688	0.4150	0.3677	0.3262	0.2897	0.2292	0.1821	0.1452	0.1163	0.0935
14	0.8700	0.7579	0.6611	0.5775	0.5051	0.4423	0.3878	0.3405	0.2992	0.2633	0.2046	0.1597	0.1252	0.0985	0.0779
15	0.8613	0.7430	0.6419	0.5553	0.4810	0.4173	0.3624	0.3152	0.2745	0.2394	0.1827	0.1401	0.1079	0.0835	0.0649
16	0.8528	0.7284	0.6232	0.5339	0.4581	0.3936	0.3387	0.2919	0.2519	0.2176	0.1631	0.1229	0.0930	0.0708	0.0541
17	0.8444	0.7142	0.6050	0.5134	0.4363	0.3714	0.3166	0.2703	0.2311	0.1978	0.1456	0.1078	0.0802	0.0600	0.0451
18	0.8360	0.7002	0.5874	0.4936	0.4155	0.3503	0.2959	0.2502	0.2120	0.1799	0.1300	0.0946	0.0691	0.0508	0.0376
19	0.8277	0.6864	0.5703	0.4746	0.3957	0.3305	0.2765	0.2317	0.1945	0.1635	0.1161	0.0829	0.0596	0.0431	0.0313
20	0.8195	0.6730	0.5537	0.4564	0.3769	0.3118	0.2584	0.2145	0.1784	0.1486	0.1037	0.0728	0.0514	0.0365	0.0261
21	0.8114	0.6598	0.5375	0.4388	0.3589	0.2942	0.2415	0.1987	0.1637	0.1351	0.0926	0.0638	0.0443	0.0309	0.0217
22	0.8034	0.6468	0.5219	0.4220	0.3418	0.2775	0.2257	0.1839	0.1502	0.1228	0.0826	0.0560	0.0382	0.0262	0.0181
23	0.7954	0.6342	0.5067	0.4057	0.3256	0.2618	0.2109	0.1703	0.1378	0.1117	0.0738	0.0491	0.0329	0.0222	0.0151
24	0.7876	0.6217	0.4919	0.3901	0.3101	0.2470	0.1971	0.1577	0.1264	0.1015	0.0659	0.0431	0.0284	0.0188	0.0126
25	0.7798	0.6095	0.4776	0.3751	0.2953	0.2330	0.1842	0.1460	0.1160	0.0923	0.0588	0.0378	0.0245	0.0160	0.0105
26	0.7720	0.5976	0.4637	0.3607	0.2812	0.2198	0.1722	0.1352	0.1064	0.0839	0.0525	0.0331	0.0211	0.0135	0.0087
27	0.7644	0.5859	0.4502	0.3468	0.2678	0.2074	0.1609	0.1252	0.0976	0.0763	0.0469	0.0291	0.0182	0.0115	0.0073
28	0.7568	0.5744	0.4371	0.3335	0.2551	0.1956	0.1504	0.1159	0.0895	0.0693	0.0419	0.0255	0.0157	0.0097	0.0061
29	0.7493	0.5631	0.4243	0.3207	0.2429	0.1846	0.1406	0.1073	0.0822	0.0630	0.0374	0.0224	0.0135	0.0082	0.0051
30	0.7419	0.5521	0.4120	0.3083	0.2314	0.1741	0.1314	0.0994	0.0754	0.0573	0.0334	0.0196	0.0116	0.0070	0.0042

Table A-3
Future-Value Interest Factors (FVIFA)—Ordinary Annuity

Period	1%	2%	3%	4%	5%	6%	7%	8%	9%	10%	12%	14%	16%	18%	20%
1	1.0000	1.0000	1.0000	1.0000	1.0000	1.0000	1.0000	1.0000	1.0000	1.0000	1.0000	1.0000	1.0000	1.0000	1.0000
2	2.0100	2.0200	2.0300	2.0400	2.0500	2.0600	2.0700	2.0800	2.0900	2.1000	2.1200	2.1400	2.1600	2.1800	2.2000
3	3.0301	3.0604	3.0909	3.1216	3.1525	3.1836	3.2149	3.2464	3.2781	3.3100	3.3744	3.4396	3.5056	3.5724	3.6400
4	4.0604	4.1216	4.1836	4.2465	4.3101	4.3746	4.4399	4.5061	4.5731	4.6410	4.7793	4.9211	5.0665	5.2154	5.3680
5	5.1010	5.2040	5.3091	5.4163	5.5256	5.6371	5.7507	5.8666	5.9847	6.1051	6.3528	6.6101	6.8771	7.1542	7.4416
6	6.1520	6.3081	6.4684	6.6330	6.8019	6.9753	7.1533	7.3359	7.5233	7.7156	8.1152	8.5355	8.9775	9.4420	9.9299
7	7.2135	7.4343	7.6625	7.8983	8.1420	8.3938	8.6540	8.9228	9.2004	9.4872	10.0890	10.7305	11.4139	12.1415	12.9159
8	8.2857	8.5830	8.8923	9.2142	9.5491	9.8975	10.2598	10.6366	11.0285	11.4359	12.2997	13.2328	14.2401	15.3270	16.4991
9	9.3685	9.7546	10.1591	10.5828	11.0266	11.4913	11.9780	12.4876	13.0210	13.5795	14.7757	16.0853	17.5185	19.0859	20.7989
10	10.4622	10.9497	11.4639	12.0061	12.5779	13.1808	13.8164	14.4866	15.1929	15.9374	17.5487	19.3373	21.3215	23.5213	25.9587
11	11.5668	12.1687	12.8078	13.4864	14.2068	14.9716	15.7836	16.6455	17.5603	18.5312	20.6546	23.0445	25.7329	28.7551	32.1504
12	12.6825	13.4121	14.1920	15.0258	15.9171	16.8699	17.8885	18.9771	20.1407	21.3843	24.1331	27.2707	30.8502	34.9311	39.5805
13	13.8093	14.6803	15.6178	16.6268	17.7130	18.8821	20.1406	21.4953	22.9534	24.5227	28.0291	32.0887	36.7862	42.2187	48.4966
14	14.9474	15.9739	17.0863	18.2919	19.5986	21.0151	22.5505	24.2149	26.0192	27.9750	32.3926	37.5811	43.6720	50.8180	59.1959
15	16.0969	17.2934	18.5989	20.0236	21.5786	23.2760	25.1290	27.1521	29.3609	31.7725	37.2797	43.8424	51.6595	60.9653	72.0351
16	17.2579	18.6393	20.1569	21.8245	23.6575	25.6725	27.8881	30.3243	33.0034	35.9497	42.7533	50.9804	60.9250	72.9390	87.4421
17	18.4304	20.0121	21.7616	23.6975	25.8404	28.2129	30.8402	33.7502	36.9737	40.5447	48.8837	59.1176	71.6730	87.0680	105.9306
18	19.61	21.41	23.41	25.65	28.13	30.91	34.00	37.45	41.30	45.60	55.75	68.39	84.14	103.74	128.12
19	20.81	22.84	25.12	27.67	30.54	33.76	37.38	41.45	46.02	51.16	63.44	78.97	98.60	123.41	154.74
20	22.02	24.30	26.87	29.78	33.07	36.79	41.00	45.76	51.16	57.27	72.05	91.02	115.38	146.63	186.69
21	23.24	25.78	28.68	31.97	35.72	39.99	44.87	50.42	56.76	64.00	81.70	104.77	134.84	174.02	225.03
22	24.47	27.30	30.54	34.25	38.51	43.39	49.01	55.46	62.87	71.40	92.50	120.44	157.41	206.34	271.03
23	25.72	28.84	32.45	36.62	41.43	47.00	53.44	60.89	69.53	79.54	104.60	138.30	183.60	244.49	326.24
24	26.97	30.42	34.43	39.08	44.50	50.82	58.18	66.76	76.79	88.50	118.16	158.66	213.98	289.49	392.48
25	28.24	32.03	36.46	41.65	47.73	54.86	63.25	73.11	84.70	98.35	133.33	181.87	249.21	342.60	471.98
26	29.53	33.67	38.55	44.31	51.11	59.16	68.68	79.95	93.32	109.18	150.33	208.33	290.09	405.27	567.38
27	30.82	35.34	40.71	47.08	54.67	63.71	74.48	87.35	102.72	121.10	169.37	238.50	337.50	479.22	681.85
28	32.13	37.05	42.93	49.97	58.40	68.53	80.70	95.34	112.97	134.21	190.70	272.89	392.50	566.48	819.22
29	33.45	38.79	45.22	52.97	62.32	73.64	87.35	103.97	124.14	148.63	214.58	312.09	456.30	669.45	984.07
30	34.78	40.57	47.58	56.08	66.44	79.06	94.46	113.28	136.31	164.49	241.33	356.79	530.31	790.95	1181.88

Table A-4
Present-Value Interest Factors (PVIFA)—Ordinary Annuity

Period	1%	2%	3%	4%	5%	6%	7%	8%	9%	10%	12%	14%	16%	18%	20%
1	0.9901	0.9804	0.9709	0.9615	0.9524	0.9434	0.9346	0.9259	0.9174	0.9091	0.8929	0.8772	0.8621	0.8475	0.8333
2	1.9704	1.9416	1.9135	1.8861	1.8594	1.8334	1.8080	1.7833	1.7591	1.7355	1.6901	1.6467	1.6052	1.5656	1.5278
3	2.9410	2.8839	2.8286	2.7751	2.7232	2.6730	2.6243	2.5771	2.5313	2.4869	2.4018	2.3216	2.2459	2.1743	2.1065
4	3.9020	3.8077	3.7171	3.6299	3.5460	3.4651	3.3872	3.3121	3.2397	3.1699	3.0373	2.9137	2.7982	2.6901	2.5887
5	4.8534	4.7135	4.5797	4.4518	4.3295	4.2124	4.1002	3.9927	3.8897	3.7908	3.6048	3.4331	3.2743	3.1272	2.9906
6	5.7955	5.6014	5.4172	5.2421	5.0757	4.9173	4.7665	4.6229	4.4859	4.3553	4.1114	3.8887	3.6847	3.4976	3.3255
7	6.7282	6.4720	6.2303	6.0021	5.7864	5.5824	5.3893	5.2064	5.0330	4.8684	4.5638	4.2883	4.0386	3.8115	3.6046
8	7.6517	7.3255	7.0197	6.7327	6.4632	6.2098	5.9713	5.7466	5.5348	5.3349	4.9676	4.6389	4.3436	4.0776	3.8372
9	8.5660	8.1622	7.7861	7.4353	7.1078	6.8017	6.5152	6.2469	5.9952	5.7590	5.3282	4.9464	4.6065	4.3030	4.0310
10	9.4713	8.9826	8.5302	8.1109	7.7217	7.3601	7.0236	6.7101	6.4177	6.1446	5.6502	5.2161	4.8332	4.4941	4.1925
11	10.3676	9.7868	9.2526	8.7605	8.3064	7.8869	7.4987	7.1390	6.8052	6.4951	5.9377	5.4527	5.0286	4.6560	4.3271
12	11.2551	10.5753	9.9540	9.3851	8.8633	8.3838	7.9427	7.5361	7.1607	6.8137	6.1944	5.6603	5.1971	4.7932	4.4392
13	12.1337	11.3484	10.6350	9.9856	9.3936	8.8527	8.3577	7.9038	7.4869	7.1034	6.4235	5.8424	5.3423	4.9095	4.5327
14	13.0037	12.1062	11.2961	10.5631	9.8986	9.2950	8.7455	8.2442	7.7862	7.3667	6.6282	6.0021	5.4675	5.0081	4.6106
15	13.8651	12.8493	11.9379	11.1184	10.3797	9.7122	9.1079	8.5595	8.0607	7.6061	6.8109	6.1422	5.5755	5.0916	4.6755
16	14.7179	13.5777	12.5611	11.6523	10.8378	10.1059	9.4466	8.8514	8.3126	7.8237	6.9740	6.2651	5.6685	5.1624	4.7296
17	15.5623	14.2919	13.1661	12.1657	11.2741	10.4773	9.7632	9.1216	8.5436	8.0216	7.1196	6.3729	5.7487	5.2223	4.7746
18	16.3983	14.9920	13.7535	12.6593	11.6896	10.8276	10.0591	9.3719	8.7556	8.2014	7.2497	6.4674	5.8178	5.2732	4.8122
19	17.2260	15.6785	14.3238	13.1339	12.0853	11.1581	10.3356	9.6036	8.9501	8.3649	7.3658	6.5504	5.8775	5.3162	4.8435
20	18.0456	16.3514	14.8775	13.5903	12.4622	11.4699	10.5940	9.8181	9.1285	8.5136	7.4694	6.6231	5.9288	5.3527	4.8696
21	18.8570	17.0112	15.4150	14.0292	12.8212	11.7641	10.8355	10.0168	9.2922	8.6487	7.5620	6.6870	5.9731	5.3837	4.8913
22	19.6604	17.6580	15.9369	14.4511	13.1630	12.0416	11.0612	10.2007	9.4424	8.7715	7.6446	6.7429	6.0113	5.4099	4.9094
23	20.4558	18.2922	16.4436	14.8568	13.4886	12.3034	11.2722	10.3711	9.5802	8.8832	7.7184	6.7921	6.0442	5.4321	4.9245
24	21.2434	18.9139	16.9355	15.2470	13.7986	12.5504	11.4693	10.5288	9.7066	8.9847	7.7843	6.8351	6.0726	5.4509	4.9371
25	22.0232	19.5235	17.4131	15.6221	14.0939	12.7834	11.6536	10.6748	9.8226	9.0770	7.8431	6.8729	6.0971	5.4669	4.9476
26	22.7952	20.1210	17.8768	15.9828	14.3752	13.0032	11.8258	10.8100	9.9290	9.1609	7.8957	6.9061	6.1182	5.4804	4.9563
27	23.5596	20.7069	18.3270	16.3296	14.6430	13.2105	11.9867	10.9352	10.0266	9.2372	7.9426	6.9352	6.1364	5.4919	4.9636
28	24.3164	21.2813	18.7641	16.6631	14.8981	13.4062	12.1371	11.0511	10.1161	9.3066	7.9844	6.9607	6.1520	5.5016	4.9697
29	25.0658	21.8444	19.1885	16.9837	15.1411	13.5907	12.2777	11.1584	10.1983	9.3696	8.0218	6.9830	6.1656	5.5098	4.9747
30	25.8077	22.3965	19.6004	17.2920	15.3725	13.7648	12.4090	11.2578	10.2737	9.4269	8.0552	7.0027	6.1772	5.5168	4.9789

Rate

Table A-5
Present-Value Interest Factors (PVIFA)—Annuity Due

Period	1%	2%	3%	4%	5%	6%	7%	8%	9%	10%	12%	14%	16%	18%	20%
1	1.0000	1.0000	1.0000	1.0000	1.0000	1.0000	1.0000	1.0000	1.0000	1.0000	1.0000	1.0000	1.0000	1.0000	1.0000
2	1.9901	1.9804	1.9709	1.9615	1.9524	1.9434	1.9346	1.9259	1.9174	1.9091	1.8929	1.8772	1.8621	1.8475	1.8333
3	2.9704	2.9416	2.9135	2.8861	2.8594	2.8334	2.8080	2.7833	2.7591	2.7355	2.6901	2.6467	2.6052	2.5656	2.5278
4	3.9410	3.8839	3.8286	3.7751	3.7232	3.6730	3.6243	3.5771	3.5313	3.4869	3.4018	3.3216	3.2459	3.1743	3.1065
5	4.9020	4.8077	4.7171	4.6299	4.5460	4.4651	4.3872	4.3121	4.2397	4.1699	4.0373	3.9137	3.7982	3.6901	3.5887
6	5.8534	5.7135	5.5797	5.4518	5.3295	5.2124	5.1002	4.9927	4.8897	4.7908	4.6048	4.4331	4.2743	4.1272	3.9906
7	6.7955	6.6014	6.4172	6.2421	6.0757	5.9173	5.7665	5.6229	5.4859	5.3553	5.1114	4.8887	4.6847	4.4976	4.3255
8	7.7282	7.4720	7.2303	7.0021	6.7864	6.5824	6.3893	6.2064	6.0330	5.8684	5.5638	5.2883	5.0386	4.8115	4.6046
9	8.6517	8.3255	8.0197	7.7327	7.4632	7.2098	6.9713	6.7466	6.5348	6.3349	5.9676	5.6389	5.3436	5.0776	4.8372
10	9.5660	9.1622	8.7861	8.4353	8.1078	7.8017	7.5152	7.2469	6.9952	6.7590	6.3282	5.9464	5.6065	5.3030	5.0310
11	10.4713	9.9826	9.5302	9.1109	8.7217	8.3601	8.0236	7.7101	7.4177	7.1446	6.6502	6.2161	5.8332	5.4941	5.1925
12	11.3676	10.7868	10.2526	9.7605	9.3064	8.8869	8.4987	8.1390	7.8052	7.4951	6.9377	6.4527	6.0286	5.6560	5.3271
13	12.2551	11.5753	10.9540	10.3851	9.8633	9.3838	8.9427	8.5361	8.1607	7.8137	7.1944	6.6603	6.1971	5.7932	5.4392
14	13.1337	12.3484	11.6350	10.9856	10.3936	9.8527	9.3577	8.9038	8.4869	8.1034	7.4235	6.8424	6.3423	5.9095	5.5327
15	14.0037	13.1062	12.2961	11.5631	10.8986	10.2950	9.7455	9.2442	8.7862	8.3667	7.6282	7.0021	6.4675	6.0081	5.6106
16	14.8651	13.8493	12.9379	12.1184	11.3797	10.7122	10.1079	9.5595	9.0607	8.6061	7.8109	7.1422	6.5755	6.0916	5.6755
17	15.7179	14.5777	13.5611	12.6523	11.8378	11.1059	10.4466	9.8514	9.3126	8.8237	7.9740	7.2651	6.6685	6.1624	5.7296
18	16.5623	15.2919	14.1661	13.1657	12.2741	11.4773	10.7632	10.1216	9.5436	9.0216	8.1196	7.3729	6.7487	6.2223	5.7746
19	17.3983	15.9920	14.7535	13.6593	12.6896	11.8276	11.0591	10.3719	9.7556	9.2014	8.2497	7.4674	6.8178	6.2732	5.8122
20	18.2260	16.6785	15.3238	14.1339	13.0853	12.1581	11.3356	10.6036	9.9501	9.3649	8.3658	7.5504	6.8775	6.3162	5.8435
21	19.0456	17.3514	15.8775	14.5903	13.4622	12.4699	11.5940	10.8181	10.1285	9.5136	8.4694	7.6231	6.9288	6.3527	5.8696
22	19.8570	18.0112	16.4150	15.0292	13.8212	12.7641	11.8355	11.0168	10.2922	9.6487	8.5620	7.6870	6.9731	6.3837	5.8913
23	20.6604	18.6580	16.9369	15.4511	14.1630	13.0416	12.0612	11.2007	10.4424	9.7715	8.6446	7.7429	7.0113	6.4099	5.9094
24	21.4558	19.2922	17.4436	15.8568	14.4886	13.3034	12.2722	11.3711	10.5802	9.8832	8.7184	7.7921	7.0442	6.4321	5.9245
25	22.2434	19.9139	17.9355	16.2470	14.7986	13.5504	12.4693	11.5288	10.7066	9.9847	8.7843	7.8351	7.0726	6.4509	5.9371
26	23.0232	20.5235	18.4131	16.6221	15.0939	13.7834	12.6536	11.6748	10.8226	10.0770	8.8431	7.8729	7.0971	6.4669	5.9476
27	23.7952	21.1210	18.8768	16.9828	15.3752	14.0032	12.8258	11.8100	10.9290	10.1609	8.8957	7.9061	7.1182	6.4804	5.9563
28	24.5596	21.7069	19.3270	17.3296	15.6430	14.2105	12.9867	11.9352	11.0266	10.2372	8.9426	7.9352	7.1364	6.4919	5.9636
29	25.3164	22.2813	19.7641	17.6631	15.8981	14.4062	13.1371	12.0511	11.1161	10.3066	8.9844	7.9607	7.1520	6.5016	5.9697
30	26.0658	22.8444	20.1885	17.9837	16.1411	14.5907	13.2777	12.1584	11.1983	10.3696	9.0218	7.9830	7.1656	6.5098	5.9747

Table A-6
Future-Value Interest Factors (FVIFA)—Annuity Due

Period	1%	2%	3%	4%	5%	6%	7%	Rate 8%	9%	10%	12%	14%	16%	18%	20%
1	1.0100	1.0200	1.0300	1.0400	1.0500	1.0600	1.0700	1.0800	1.0900	1.1000	1.1200	1.1400	1.1600	1.1800	1.2000
2	2.0301	2.0604	2.0909	2.1216	2.1525	2.1836	2.2149	2.2464	2.2781	2.3100	2.3744	2.4396	2.5056	2.5724	2.6400
3	3.0604	3.1216	3.1836	3.2465	3.3101	3.3746	3.4399	3.5061	3.5731	3.6410	3.7793	3.9211	4.0665	4.2154	4.3680
4	4.1010	4.2040	4.3091	4.4163	4.5256	4.6371	4.7507	4.8666	4.9847	5.1051	5.3528	5.6101	5.8771	6.1542	6.4416
5	5.1520	5.3081	5.4684	5.6330	5.8019	5.9753	6.1533	6.3359	6.5233	6.7156	7.1152	7.5355	7.9775	8.4420	8.9299
6	6.2135	6.4343	6.6625	6.8983	7.1420	7.3938	7.6540	7.9228	8.2004	8.4872	9.0890	9.7305	10.4139	11.1415	11.9159
7	7.2857	7.5830	7.8923	8.2142	8.5491	8.8975	9.2598	9.6366	10.0285	10.4359	11.2997	12.2328	13.2401	14.3270	15.4991
8	8.3685	8.7546	9.1591	9.5828	10.0266	10.4913	10.9780	11.4876	12.0210	12.5795	13.7757	15.0853	16.5185	18.0859	19.7989
9	9.4622	9.9497	10.4639	11.0061	11.5779	12.1808	12.8164	13.4866	14.1929	14.9374	16.5487	18.3373	20.3215	22.5213	24.9587
10	10.5668	11.1687	11.8078	12.4864	13.2068	13.9716	14.7836	15.6455	16.5603	17.5312	19.6546	22.0445	24.7329	27.7551	31.1504
11	11.6825	12.4121	13.1920	14.0258	14.9171	15.8699	16.8885	17.9771	19.1407	20.3843	23.1331	26.2707	29.8502	33.9311	38.5805
12	12.8093	13.6803	14.6178	15.6268	16.7130	17.8821	19.1406	20.4953	21.9534	23.5227	27.0291	31.0887	35.7862	41.2187	47.4966
13	13.9474	14.9739	16.0863	17.2919	18.5986	20.0151	21.5505	23.2149	25.0192	26.9750	31.3926	36.5811	42.6720	49.8180	58.1959
14	15.0969	16.2934	17.5989	19.0236	20.5786	22.2760	24.1290	26.1521	28.3609	30.7725	36.2797	42.8424	50.6595	59.9653	71.0351
15	16.2579	17.6393	19.1569	20.8245	22.6575	24.6725	26.8881	29.3243	32.0034	34.9497	41.7533	49.9804	59.9250	71.9390	86.4421
16	17.4304	19.0121	20.7616	22.6975	24.8404	27.2129	29.8402	32.7502	35.9737	39.5447	47.8837	58.1176	70.6730	86.0680	104.9306
17	18.6147	20.4123	22.2144	24.6454	27.1324	29.9057	32.9990	36.4502	40.3013	44.5992	54.7497	67.3941	83.1407	102.7403	127.1167
18	19.81	21.84	24.12	26.67	29.54	32.76	36.38	40.45	45.02	50.16	62.44	77.97	97.60	122.41	153.74
19	21.02	23.30	25.87	28.78	32.07	35.79	40.00	44.76	50.16	56.27	71.05	90.02	114.38	145.63	185.69
20	22.24	24.78	27.68	30.97	34.72	38.99	43.87	49.42	55.76	63.00	80.70	103.77	133.84	173.02	224.03
21	23.47	26.30	29.54	33.25	37.51	42.39	48.01	54.46	61.87	70.40	91.50	119.44	156.41	205.34	270.03
22	24.72	27.84	31.45	35.62	40.43	46.00	52.44	59.89	68.53	78.54	103.60	137.30	182.60	243.49	325.24
23	25.97	29.42	33.43	38.08	43.50	49.82	57.18	65.76	75.79	87.50	117.16	157.66	212.98	288.49	391.48
24	27.24	31.03	35.46	40.65	46.73	53.86	62.25	72.11	83.70	97.35	132.33	180.87	248.21	341.60	470.98
25	28.53	32.67	37.55	43.31	50.11	58.16	67.68	78.95	92.32	108.18	149.33	207.33	289.09	404.27	566.38
26	29.82	34.34	39.71	46.08	53.67	62.71	73.48	86.35	101.72	120.10	168.37	237.50	336.50	478.22	680.85
27	31.13	36.05	41.93	48.97	57.40	67.53	79.70	94.34	111.97	133.21	189.70	271.89	391.50	565.48	818.22
28	32.45	37.79	44.22	51.97	61.32	72.64	86.35	102.97	123.14	147.63	213.58	311.09	455.30	668.45	983.07
29	33.78	39.57	46.58	55.08	65.44	78.06	93.46	112.28	135.31	163.49	240.33	355.79	529.31	789.95	1180.88
30	35.13	41.38	49.00	58.33	69.76	83.80	101.07	122.35	148.58	180.94	270.29	406.74	615.16	933.32	1418.26

Index

About the Authors

BENNIE H. NUNNALLY JR. is Associate Professor and Chairman of the Department of Finance and Business Law at the University of North Carolina at Charlotte. His articles have appeared in several journals, including *Financial Management, Southern Business Review,* and *The Journal of Consumer Affairs.*

D. ANTHONY PLATH is Assistant Professor in the Department of Finance and Business Law at the University of North Carolina at Charlotte. He has published articles in *The Journal of Retail Banking, The Mid-Atlantic Journal of Business,* and *The Journal of Consumer Affairs.*

HELENE W. JOHNS is Assistant Professor in the Department of Accounting at the University of North Carolina at Charlotte. She is also an attorney practicing in the tax area.